I0080035

# ReMatch

# ReMatch

*Love in Extended Adulthood*

## DR. DON HEBBARD

credo
house publishers

*ReMatch*
Copyright © 2025 by Dr. Don Hebbard
All rights reserved.

Published in the United States of America by Credo House Publishers,
a division of Credo Communications LLC, Grand Rapids, Michigan
credohousepublishers.com

Unless otherwise noted, Scripture quotations are from the Holy Bible,
New International Version®, NIV® Copyright ©1973, 1978, 1984, 2011
by Biblica, Inc.®. Used by permission. All rights reserved worldwide.

ISBN: 978-1-62586-303-4

Cover and interior design by Sharon VanLoozenoord
Editing by Donna Huisjen

*Printed in the United States of America*
First edition

To my lovely wife, Lisa,
who made the rematch journey worth the wait.


To Jared and Hailey,
who heard all my colorful dating stories.


To Dr. James Cail, Dr. Clif Davis, and Dr. Margaret Pinder,
my three "wise men and woman."

# CONTENTS

# THE REMATCH PROCESS

# CHAPTER 1

# IMPLODING THE LIFE STRUCTURE

Divorce Case number FD-2004-155 was heard in Judge Larry N. Brooks's court in Logan County, Oklahoma, on June 28, 2005, and was dispensed with in ten minutes. So ended my twenty-three-year marriage. Mine was one of 33,000 that ended in divorce nationwide that year.

When most marriages end, it represents the termination of a relationship with a spouse and the restructuring of relationships with children and extended family. When I filed for divorce, in the words of Dr. James Cail, my mentor and a professor of psychology, "You just imploded your entire life and career." The conclusion of the marriage was a conscious decision I made that would have long-lasting effects not only on my marriage but also on my career, religion, and status in the community. No area of my life would be untouched by this one decision.

I am a "marriage shrink," a Licensed Marriage and Family Therapist and Supervisor by profession. I had been practicing Marriage and Family Therapy since graduate school, conducting my first couple of sessions when I was twenty-three years old. I had opened counseling centers and graduate counseling programs in Irving, Dallas, and Atlanta and for the past ten years had led the Marriage and Family Institute at Oklahoma Christian University in Oklahoma City.

I traveled nationally, speaking on marriage and the family, and had written books and articles on relationships. I had developed a model of family life ministry that had been adopted by churches, and my book was a text used in graduate schools of theology. My university classes were filled with students eager to learn about healthy relationships and counseling students desiring to heal hurting lives. When church leaders struggled with infidelity or ethical violations, I was called in to consult and speak to hurting congregations.

In 2000, Governor Frank Keating launched the Oklahoma Marriage Initiative in an attempt to lower the divorce rate in Oklahoma. At the time Oklahoma led the nation in divorces. Cathy Keating served as the Chairperson of the Board for my Institute for Marriage and Family. I was invited to serve as the first Director of Marriage Education for the State of Oklahoma. Speaking on radio and television and at public seminars, I became the face of the Oklahoma Marriage Initiative. I was a standard bearer for the cause of healthy marriages.

When I filed for divorce it sent shock waves across my academic community, my religious community, and the statewide political community that had come to value my work. The results were immediate and decisive. I lost my tenure and position at the university and closed the institute I had worked ten years to build. My speaking engagements were canceled, my counseling clients dried up, churches stopped calling for help, and religious friends became distant or quietly disappeared. I couldn't find work, and the time clock was running as alimony and child support payments piled up. I would jokingly tell my friends, "There is nothing more worthless than a divorced marriage shrink in the Churches of Christ."

I had two children still at home in high school. My greatest loss was my daily contact with them. Being their father was the greatest joy I had ever known. We had just built a horse ranch to support the riding career of my daughter. I found myself going from living on thirteen acres and enjoying tractor, dogs, and horses to living in a small, one-bedroom apartment. To be clear, this was all the result of a decision I had made, and I was willing to embrace the consequences.

So began a twenty-year journey of dating, relationships, and mate selection in middle age. I had studied marriage as an academic field my entire professional life. I had counseled countless couples getting married for the first time or after a divorce or the death of a spouse. I'd read the books, attended the conferences, sat at the feet of many experts in the field. I thought, *How hard can this be? I'll date some, meet a nice woman, and eventually find love again in my life.* Without a doubt that was *the most insane thought* ever to pass through my mind! I had no idea of the complexity of dating in midlife and the brave new world of online dating that would challenge every principle of mate selection I'd been taught.

Thus, from 2005 to 2025 I became my own research case study of one on the subject of finding love during the mature years of adulthood. I made a commitment to do my own internal work and pursue every path of personal growth. I sought counseling through my divorce. I explored the family dynamics of my adopted family of origin. I looked at my attachment style, based upon my having been given up for adoption. I engaged in Jungian depth psychology and dream analysis, along with EMDR to heal trauma wounds. If there was a book, seminar, or therapist that would give me insight, I was willing to listen.

Along the way I engaged every method I could try to meet women and date. Match, eHarmony, Bumble, Silver Singles, It's Just Lunch—all became a common part of my everyday life. Online dating became a second job. I talked with countless clients about their experiences dating in midlife or later in elderhood. We discussed dating in later life in graduate classes with my adult students who were out there trying to meet someone. I compared what I was learning about this brave new world of dating later in life with what I had learned in graduate school about dating, attraction, and mate selection. It was clear that a *new era of how people fall in love* was emerging.

I kept copious notes and journals over the course of my two-decade personal research project and began assembling them into six identifiable stages of "rematch adjustment." This book will open the pages of my personal twenty-year journey as a marriage shrink seeking love later in life. I invite you to listen in on the conversations that mature men and women seeking love the second time around have shared with me.

I completed my doctorate in Adult and Continuing Education. In my class on Adult Development and Learning, Dr. Thomas Eaves shared with us the concept of the Life Structure. The life structure is like a tall building with four sides. In emerging adulthood, we build our first life structure. One side of that structure is our career choice and one side our relationships, such as with marriage partner and children. A third side is our values and beliefs, and the fourth is our relationship to our community. In early adulthood we make decisions about whom we will marry, if we will have children and how many we will have, what job we will take, and where we will live. We are building our first life structure that supports the development of our life.

By middle age some parts of that life structure will cease to function or not serve us well any longer. We change jobs or entire careers. We move to a different part of the country. Our values and beliefs change based on life experiences, and children grow up and begin to leave the nest. The life structure is not intended to be a static building but a flexible structure to allow for adaptability and change throughout the lifespan.

In my case the decision to divorce imploded the entire life structure: marriage and family, work, core beliefs, and community. All four sides came tumbling down that day standing in Judge Brooks's courtroom. My marriage was gone, my career was gone, my financial security was gone, and my church was gone. What was left? The foundation was left. My core sense of self. An optimistic view that a new future would be built.

This is a book about finding love in the second half of life. The basic human needs of love, intimacy, partnership, and meaning do not disappear as we age. They change and, I would argue, become even more meaningful and profound. But finding the love of your life at fifty, sixty, or beyond will look very different from falling in love in your twenties. And that is what this book is all about. Most of us will match, and, if that doesn't work, we will *ReMatch*. The ReMatching process is very different from love the first time around.

The ReMatch process has seven stages, with important work to be done at each stage. Skipping a stage does not eliminate the work; it will likely just delay it until the need emerges later on in a more powerful way. There is no shortcut to building a solid marriage, and the work begins internally with each person doing their own core work.

### Stage One: Ending before Beginning
Why it is important to "land the plane before taking off again"

### Stage Two: Doing the Core Work
Healing the core sense of self, preventing us from repeating past relationship mistakes

### Stage Three: A Strategy for Dating
How we are attracted to each other and a strategy for dating online

### Stage Four: ReMatch Red Flags
Three important red flags that can signal trouble in dating relationships

**Stage Five: Sexuality**
How to build a healthy sexual relationship and the dating styles used most often

**Stage Six: Decision Making**
Models of decision making related to relationship building

**Stage Seven: Entering a Family System**
How to enter and adjust to another's family system

I will be drawing upon three main sources in this book. First, we will look at models and principles from the field of marriage and family, looking especially at relationships from a lens of family systems theory. Second, I'll be drawing upon case experiences with clients and the work of talented colleagues who have counseled with couples in middle or later adulthood as they labor to build a good relationship. Finally, I'll draw upon my own experience, both as a clinician and as a person who walked into the brave new world of online dating that has transformed marriage over the past twenty years.

I hope you find this information helpful as you navigate your own journey of transformation and growth. First let's talk about the subject no one likes to confront—how endings shape our lives—and how we can shape those endings.

# CHAPTER 2

# THE CASE FOR REMATCH

## Wilmer and Catherine

Wilmer and Catherine were both raised on farms during the Great Depression and came of age during World War II. They met in Orlando, where Wilmer was a Captain in the Army Air Corp before the Air Force was a separate branch of the armed services, and Catherine was a telephone operator for Bell Telephone. They met at church, fell in love, and were married for fifty-three years. The structure of their lives fits into the characteristic three-stage model that was typical during the twentieth century.

The first stage was childhood and education, followed by decades of work and then retirement at age sixty-five. Retirement was a new addition to the life span, in contrast to previous generations, and Wilmer and Catherine looked forward to spending their "golden years" traveling and enjoying grandchildren, supported by a pension from the company to which he had devoted his life's work. Everyone assumed that this three-stage model of adulthood was normative . . . until the twenty-first century arrived.

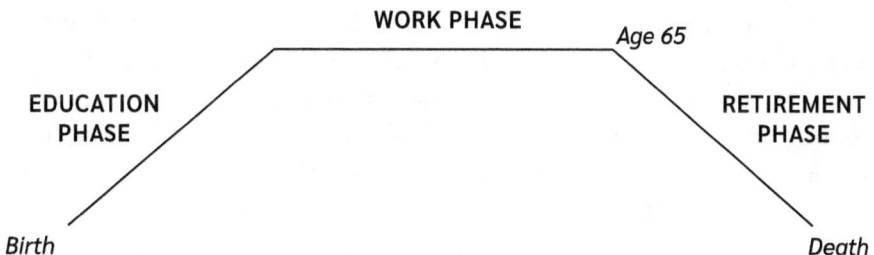

**WORK PHASE**

*Age 65*

**EDUCATION PHASE**

**RETIREMENT PHASE**

*Birth*

*Death*

## The One Hundred-Year Life

I was returning from a speaking engagement and perusing the bookstore in the airport when a title jumped off the shelf begging my attention. *The 100 Year Life—Living and Working in an Age of Longevity* by Lynda Gratton and Andrew Scott changed the way I looked at lifespan development and would have a huge impact on the way I looked at dating in middle adulthood.

Gratton and Scott make the important observation that "A child born in the West today has a more than 50 per cent chance of living to be over 105, while by contrast a child born over a century ago had a less than 1 per cent chance of living to that age. That means that if you are now 20 you have a 50 per cent chance of living to more than 100; if you are 40 you have an even chance of living to 95, and if you are 60, then a 50 per cent chance of making 90 or more."

In America improvements in health have marked a steady rise in the lifespan for the past two hundred years. Gratton and Scott continue, "For most of the last two hundred years there has been a steady increase in life expectancy. The best data currently available suggests that since 1840 there has been an increase in life expectancy of three months for every year. That's two to three years of life added for every decade. And perhaps more importantly, there is no sign that the trend is leveling off."

## Tackling the Killers

When Wilmer and Catherine were born, the major killers were infant mortality and diseases like smallpox and typhoid. From the 1920s on, reductions in child and infant mortality accounted for the improvements in life expectancy. Improved nutrition and expanded healthcare options helped people live longer.

The World War II generation's average life span was about sixty-two years. The chief killers were the diseases of middle age and beyond, especially cancer and cardiovascular disease. Improvements in the care of patients for these diseases has increased the average lifespan. Today medical science is tackling the diseases of old age, such as dementia and Alzheimer's, and, as Gratton and Scott note, we are already seeing a sharp rise in the lifespan as a result of progress in these areas. Simply put, today's adults can expect, with a healthy lifestyle, to lead a longer life than any generation before them.

## Two New Life Stages

You say, "This is all interesting science, Dr. Don, but what does it have to do with me dating as a mature adult?" Great question. We are now adding two new stages to the lifespan that did not exist a generation ago.

The first life stage is called *Pre-Commitment* and extends from the twenties into the early thirties. Past generations used the twenties to make key commitments and build their first life structures. They finished their education, met and married a partner, started a family, and selected a community to settle and build a family in. Today many of those decisions are being delayed into the thirties as young adults use the twenties to experiment with choices and delay making key commitments. This delay in marrying may be contributing to a decline in the divorce rate, as people marry at a later age.

The second new stage is key to our discussion of ReMatch. With adults living longer, a new stage of adulthood is emerging that we call *Extended Adulthood*. Wilmer and Catherine expected to retire at age sixty-five and live off their pension until they both passed. Today it is unreasonable to expect that a pension, if one is even available, will be able to financially support someone for thirty more years. Adults are making the decision to either continue working or enter into entirely new and exciting occupational choices in their sixties and seventies. My classes in counseling are regularly filled with adults coming back to graduate school to train to be therapists later in life.

The late fifties to the early eighties are now a stage of adulthood that is active, engaged, and filled with new transitions that did not exist a generation ago. That includes relationships and marriage. Marriages will end due to death or divorce, and people will seek out a new partner to share fulfillment with during this increasingly active stage of life. The improvements in medical care will keep adults physically active and, as we've seen in recent years, sexually active well into extended adulthood.

The future looks bright for adults past the ages of fifty, sixty, and seventy who want to date, find love, and enter a meaningful relationship or marriage. However, dating in extended adulthood looks very different from dating in our twenties and thirties. We all come with important life experiences, our baggage, that shape the way we view love and even the people we find ourselves attracted to. That is why the ReMatch process is so important. Adults at this stage say loudly and clearly, "I made that mistake once. I'm not doing that again."

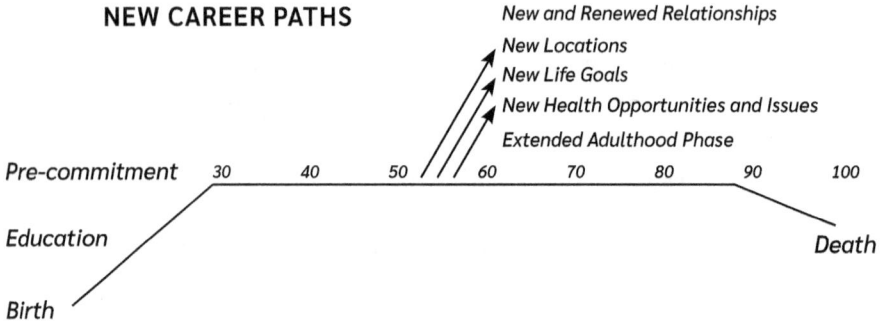

**NEW CAREER PATHS**

*New and Renewed Relationships*
*New Locations*
*New Life Goals*
*New Health Opportunities and Issues*
*Extended Adulthood Phase*

Pre-commitment    30      40      50    / / /  60      70      80      90      100

Education                                                                    Death

Birth

## Gary and Grace

Gary and Grace came to me for marriage therapy because at ages fifty-four and fifty-one there was no gas left in either of their tanks. They were in a parallel marriage and were making each other quietly miserable. They had done a great job of raising their two daughters, both of whom were now in college, and were capable business partners who agreed to manage the family affairs in a sensible way. But years of silent conflict had taken their toll.

Gary and Grace had both been raised in *Conflict-Avoidant* family systems. They lived by the unspoken motto "If you don't have something nice to say, don't say anything at all." That worked fine for social gatherings and polite conversations but was poison to a marriage trying to resolve daily difficulties. Problems piled up under the rug, and they had no communications skills to deal with years of pent-up resentments. And even less motivation to change.

Some years earlier Gary had found an escape in the arms of a lover and had carried on that affair to the point that he had found himself split between the woman to whom he was married and shared a family with and the woman he was in love with. Gary's "oughter and wanter were at war with each other." Grace had known about the affair for some time and had periodically made attempts to force him to end it. She was never successful, and her emotional reserves were depleted. She was ready for a new life.

Following their divorce, which came as a surprise to their circle of friends and family, Gary and Grace wanted to step into new relationships and faced important questions. Would they resolve the issues in their own lives before starting new relationships? Would they continue to bury conflict with a new partner? Would Gary resolve his conflict by triangulating with another lover instead of dealing with issues in his own life? What would be their *pocket list of non-negotiables* heading into dating in their fifties? Or would they fly blindly past this important transition and ignore the core work each of them needed to do before entering another relationship?

## Alec and Amber

Alec and Amber had been married for over thirty years and were business partners in Alec's architecture and engineering firm. Alec and his partners constructed the buildings, and Amber was the power behind the throne, running the business with precision and accuracy. They were professional, conventional with a buttoned-down look of success and tailored excellence. Alec was quiet, detail-oriented, and wore traditional conservative suits and Allen Edmonds oxfords. Amber dressed the part in business-professional clothing that telegraphed a serious professional woman of standing in the community. They presented as the ideal match. Then, without warning, Alec dropped dead of a heart attack on a construction site, leaving Amber a widow at age sixty-two. Amber soldiered bravely on, keeping the company profitable and walking through her journey of grief.

Sometime later Amber's friends at the country club were surprised to see her with a new male "friend" named Augustine. Augustine was nothing like Alec. He was gregarious, outgoing, and lit up a room with his presence when he walked in. And then there was the hair. All the hair. Everywhere from his head to his beard and chest he was the complete opposite of the balding, conservative Alec. Amber's friends and family were in shock!

Added to that were the changes in Amber. She had gone to counseling for her grief and to explore the next chapter of her life. She had traded in her business-professional look for a sexy and casual new wardrobe she loved and sported a new, stylish haircut, had hired a personal trainer, and was toned and muscular. There was even the new set of boobs that her girlfriends were gossiping about. She was dancing, laughing out loud, and for the first time since Alec's death seemed to have her game back—but this was a whole new game.

For Amber, the death of a spouse signaled a ReMatch process that would lead to a whole new kind of love. Amber and Alec had been in a *Symmetrical Relationship—birds of a feather flock together.* That had worked successfully for them, but Amber decided to do her core work following Alec's death. She got some help and learned some things about herself. When she started dating, she was open to a *Complementary Relationship—opposites attracting.* That change lit a spark in her that ignited love with Augustine in a whole new way. Her relationships with Alec and Augustine, while both good, were very different because Amber was at a different point in life and had worked through a ReMatch process.

The cases of Amber and Alec and Gary and Grace illustrate that, though marriages can end for a wide variety of reasons, the cessation of a marriage doesn't end a person's drive for intimacy and fulfillment. We were created to be in relationship, and the vast majority of people whose marriages end are going to "give it another shot."

The key question I've discovered in my work with clients is whether they will take the opportunity to use this transition following a death or divorce to stop and examine their own patterns. If not, we are at the mercy of those invisible patterns repeating in the future. ReMatch gives us the opportunity to make wise decisions and find meaningful love that does not repeat the patterns of the past.

## Basic Human Needs

In my first counseling course, Dr. Paul Faulkner lectured on basic human needs. He pointed out that there is a catalog of very basic human drives or needs that extend throughout our lives. People who are able to fulfill those needs live in a state of satisfaction, or what we would call happiness. Those who do not live in a state of dissatisfaction or unhappiness. These basic human needs start early and continue throughout our lifetimes.

The fulfillment of those needs is not based upon wealth, educational attainment, political affiliation, or address. Highly fulfilled individuals can be found in every economic stratum, from every walk of life, and in every age group.

Central to this is understanding that my needs are met both *in relationship* and *independently*. For most of us there is the drive to find fulfillment in relationship with a partner. We want a great lover and best friend to share our lives with. However, as Dr. Harville Hendricks notes in his book *Getting the Love You Want*, no one partner can meet my needs perfectly and completely. That's an unrealistic expectation. As an adult I learn to meet some of my own needs. The situation for mature adults isn't either/or but both/and.

What are those powerful basic human needs Dr. Faulkner spoke about?

### Love and Belonging

Attachment is the first need met, starting with the baby in its mother's womb and extending into elderhood. We long for a sense of belonging as another person's beloved. Belonging to a family gives one a sense of rootedness and identity. When someone has grown up without family cohesion, they may find that in the family of their partner.

### Significance

Significance is the sense that my life means something. That I make a difference in this world. That my life has caused others to be changed for the better. That I have lifted up my spouse, my children, and the communities I serve. Erik Erikson noted that the final stage of adult development holds the challenge of *integrity versus despair*. The older adult looks back on their life and either comes to terms with the decisions and contributions they have made or finds themselves regretting what they have done or not done. Extended adulthood gives adults second chances to make life-changing decisions and find meaning in the second half of life.

### Security

After my divorce I was talking to my biological mother, Jean, a self-proclaimed tough Yankee broad in Burlington, Vermont. Her advice to me on dating was simple: "Don, you're looking for someone in life that is a soft place to land." That was great advice. She was saying that life is going to kick us around and that we long for someone at the end of the day to come home to and share our struggles with. We long for a secure relationship that will help us carry the load. Many people in middle age will end marriages because their partner has never been capable of co-creating a secure relationship due to addictions, affairs, chronic lying, or personality disorders. The gradual wear and tear over the years eventually leads to an empty tank.

### Sexual Fulfillment

We are by nature sexual creatures. This is born into our DNA. People seek sexual fulfillment in marriage, and when it is great it is a powerful, lasting force that continues into extended adulthood. I recall one outspoken widow and grandmother being asked during the family's Thanksgiving dinner what she missed about her beloved husband, who had recently passed away.

"I just miss the sex! Your Papa was one great lover," she told the shocked grandkids. "Thanks, Grandma . . . ; er, could someone pass the stuffing, please?" People who have had a great sex life in their marriage are looking for a resumption of that fulfillment. A good many of my clients have never experienced that, and, understandably, that component of the relationship is high on their pocket list of non-negotiables.

### Goals, Purpose, and Meaning

People get married because they want to build a life together. Early in life that may look like buying a home, starting a family, and raising children. Later in life people still desire goals, purpose, and meaning, but this yearning may take on a different form. People may have spent years working hard, whether married or as a single parent, and with the family raised they now want to experience a life of their own. Many clients tell me that they are looking forward to their middle and later years as the best years of their lives and are searching for a "partner in crime" with whom to share the journey.

My daughter, Hailey, a police detective in Guthrie, Oklahoma, leads the force's Domestic Crime and Violence Unit. She talks about such scenarios as *trash-bag marriages*. There are those women who have so little that their life's belongings will fit into three trash bags in the trunk of the car. They may be likely to leave a bad marital situation because there is so little materially tying them to the marriage. Women in gated communities may stay longer because the interconnectedness—financially, legally, and materially—is much more complex. In both cases the women are searching to build goals, purpose, and meaning with a partner they can trust.

Basic human needs do not end with the passing of time. In fact, I would argue that those needs become more acute and profound as life experience speaks into them. When adults come out of marriages in which those needs have been ignored, they will often see their fulfillment as "non-negotiable" going into their next relationship.

## ReMatch Seven Stages

We are now ready to explore the seven stages of the ReMatch process. At each stage there will be important work to do in preparing for a healthy, satisfying relationship in extended adulthood.

Stage One, Ending Well (ending the divorce before beginning the dating), is the most important. It lays the foundation for everything that is to follow in the other six stages and is a point of critical decision making. Most of us hate endings. We dislike the pain and disequilibrium to the point that we want to rush through these transitional times. We want to get on with life as quickly as we possibly can. *Let's just put this behind us and forget it all happened. Then we can start to feel better.* But Ending Well is crucial to laying a foundation for a better relationship in the future. I learned in my own journey that, if we would just stop and embrace the pain of an ending, this would lead to insights and growth we could achieve in no other way. The gift of endings is priceless.

# ENDING BEFORE BEGINNING

# CHAPTER 3

# WHY MARRIAGES END

## It's Just Therapy or It's Just Lunch

My phone rang and it was Hillary, my It's Just Lunch dating consultant telling me breathlessly, "Good morning, Dr. Don. I am excited to inform you that we have another great match for you! May we set up a lunch for the two of you?"

Calls from Hillary were getting to be a regular occurrence. While that would seem to be good news for a guy dating in his fifties, it was becoming a mixed blessing. I was flattered by the attention It's Just Lunch was bestowing upon me; however, I was finding myself "doing therapy" more and more over these lunch dates. And I was not meeting any matches I would have wanted to pursue.

It's Just Lunch pitched itself as an elite dating service to busy professionals looking to meet like-minded matches but whose lives were simply too busy to cull through the masses of online profiles. Let the experts find the match for you! I filled out my forms, went through the interview process, described who I was and what I was looking for, paid the hefty fee, and was promised one date per month over the calendar year of membership. I thought, *Wow, those are going to be impressive dates!*

Soon my phone was ringing regularly with calls from Hillary, enthusing, "We have an exciting new match for you!" I would show up for a lunch date with a woman I'd never seen before—not even a preliminary photo. We would get acquainted and share some basic information about our lives. Then before too long she would turn the conversation to the story of her divorce and ask me for advice on getting started in the world of dating. She was clearly not ready to date and was processing through a wide range of emotions, looking for any port in the storm that might provide a listening ear. I'd pay for the lunch and stagger out two hours later feeling as if I'd just conducted a divorce recovery group session.

Because I was a therapist and easy to talk with, It's Just Lunch was feeding me all their recently divorced women who were still emotionally radioactive coming out of their divorces. I was the unofficial It's Just Lunch "orientation to dating guru" and found myself conducting free divorce therapy time and again with women who had no business dating yet. They were still in the process of working through the remnants of their marriage. I broke up with Hillary and It's Just Lunch after having learned some valuable lessons.

First, I could not turn over the hard work of finding good matches to someone else. No one but myself knows my heart and mind, and I would have to do the hard work of sorting through thousands of profiles myself. Second, many people will fly through a divorce and move quickly on to dating with no thought of what they had contributed to the failure of the marriage and of how that information might help them in the future. Third, the reasons their marriage has ended are vital for a person to understand in order to prevent replication of those patterns in the future or of focusing entirely on their ex-spouse, to the exclusion of doing their own core work.

Let's look at six common marital patterns that typically lead to divorce court. A seventh, extramarital affairs, we will save for a separate discussion because of its unique set of dynamics.

## Veggies and Dessert

Growing up in West Hartford, my mom would shop for groceries at the A & P. She'd wheel the cart into the canned vegetables aisle and proceed to pick up one can of every kind of vegetable known to man. There were carrots, beets, okra, and spinach. She would fix a different one every night of the month.

I liked three vegetables: peas, beans, and corn. Which meant that three nights of the month were great, . . . while the other twenty-seven were going to be rough. The toughest night of the month was mixed vegetables night. Mixed vegetables are the outcome when Dole takes all the veggies no one wants to eat, cuts them into tiny pieces, adds ten pounds of lima beans, crams them into a can, and then mixes all those awful juices together. Mixed vegetables night was the worst night of the month.

Mom was a good psychologist. She was also an excellent pie maker. Lemon meringue pies with sugary curlicues and homemade crusts were so good that we'd beg to just eat the crust like popcorn. On mixed vegetables night she'd always have a homemade pie sitting on the counter, and the message was clear: eat your mixed vegetables, and there is pie waiting for dessert.

I teach my graduate students in marriage and family therapy a powerful tool called Social Exchange Theory. We come into marriage with some powerful, positive things to trade with a partner. They come with some powerful, positive things to trade, too. We marry because we believe that we will be able to trade those things fairly and that those reinforcers will be more rewarding than with anyone else we could ever meet.

The "dessert" of a relationship will be complex and unique to that individual. It may include honesty, a shared view of the world, passion and sexual fulfillment, or simple things like the enjoyment of working out together. We trade those powerful reinforcers and build the fabric of a life together.

The veggies of a relationship are a part of it, too. We pay the bills regularly, clean the house, and handle the day-to-day frustrations of work and life together. We learn to lean on each other as a soft place to land.

In good marriages there is a healthy balance between veggies and dessert. No one is eating most of the veggies while the other is getting a big slice of the pie. The trading does not have to be even, but it does have to be fair.

Marriages implode because one partner ends up carrying the heavy load of responsibilities as the "adult" in the relationship. The other partner wants all the freedoms and payoffs of the relationship without any of the adult responsibilities. We call these *Over-functioning/Under-functioning Marriages*. One partner is eating too many mixed vegetables and the other too much pie.

The core work to be done in this scenario is for each of us in the relationship to ask whether we tend to over- or under-function. *Am I afraid to ask for what I want? Am I deaf to the requests my partner makes? Do I make changes so difficult on my partner that they just give up in frustration?*

People coming out of a Veggies and Dessert Marriage enter the dating scene with a sense of entitlement. *I put up with all of this*, is the mentality. *I gave so much and now it's my turn!* I encourage my clients emerging from this style of marriage to slow down, resist the urge to formulate their "must have list," and do some core work on themselves before hitting the dating scene. That way their list of non-negotiables will not be impossible for any human to meet.

## No Gas Left in the Tank

Cary's once bright smile and enthusiasm for life were gone. In its place were a blank stare and a hopeless heart. Cary's reserves had been depleted to the point that he was running on empty. Cary and Cathy had met in college and were seen as the campus's "ideal couple." They married after graduation and within a few years had bought a home and started a family, with Cary established in a successful career in sales. Life looked good and was going according to plan.

Then the first surprise hit. The local department store called, saying that Cathy had repeatedly run her credit card over the limit. Now they were demanding payment and shutting down the account. Shocked, Cary ran down to the store, paid off the account, and apologized profusely for the incident. Cathy was embarrassed, explained that the purchases had been for an emergency her mother was having, and promised this would never happen again.

A few years later Cary discovered a credit card account in Cathy's name he hadn't known existed. It too was maxed out, and the demand was coming for immediate payment. This time the balance was in the tens of thousands of dollars. The family savings account was wiped out in order to meet the payment deadline. Again, Cathy apologized with tears and a well-crafted story justifying her expenditures and blaming Cary's "bad temper" for her reluctance to come clean. She defended herself by stating that if he "just made more money" they wouldn't have to live from paycheck to paycheck.

So began a long and depressing game of marital hide and seek. Cathy would hide her uncontrolled spending and run up debt on credit cards or secret loans, only to be discovered and repeatedly bailed out by Cary. Cary worked overtime, went without personal purchases, budgeted, paid for marital therapy for the two of them, and grew increasing despondent. Nothing was working.

One day in my office he shared quietly that he'd had enough. He was done trying to fix a problem that wasn't fixable. He'd run out of gas with

Cathy's behavior and empty promises to the point that the emotions he'd felt for the woman he'd fallen in love with in college had been replaced by resentment, confusion, and sadness. To be in the same room with her was painful. Cary filed for divorce and moved into the world of single-ness. He wondered if he would ever trust anyone again.

In my work with couples over forty years, I've come to recognize that there are many reasons spouses run out of gas. The root of the problem may be lying, cheating, emotional coldness, verbal aggression, addictions, or personality disorders. In Cary's case it was uncontrolled spending—an issue I have over the years had very little success in changing.

When the gas dial on the dashboard goes from full tank to empty, the red warning light comes on. We are running on fumes. In this case Cathy had ignored the warning lights repeatedly, to the point that Cary had found himself totally depleted in the relationship. Before Cary starts dating again, he'll need to start a ReMatch process to get some gas back in the tank and explore his own part in the dynamic between himself and Cathy. This recovery will take some time.

## Conflict-Habituated Marriages

I'd flown into Tucson to meet a match for the first time. When dating on-line you can set your geographical limits to any distance, and this woman was looking nationwide. We had chatted online and by phone for a while, and she had invited me out to meet in person.

I'd been at her home for a short time when her sister arrived. She blew in like a thunderstorm, full of bluster and talking ninety miles an hour. She was there to check out the "new guy from Texas" and to offer her much coveted (in her mind, at least) stamp of approval.

She spent a few minutes asking about my work, family, and children and, upon learning that I taught marriage and family therapy in Dallas, launched into a long rant about her no-good husband back home. "He's a jerk. I can't get his lazy ass off the couch. All he does is sit around and watch sports, and I do all the work around the house. It's been this way for years; in fact, when we were first married, he cheated on me, and I've never forgiven him for it. Men are such bastards—no offense meant, but they really are, you know!"

When she finally took a breath and the smoke cleared, I took a sip of coffee and asked her, "Wow, you don't sound very happy. Why do you stay with him? Do you think hanging on to all those old resentments is making today better or worse for you?"

At first, she looked stunned, then puzzled, and finally blew off my questions and went back to her complaining. I wasn't invited back to Tucson, thankfully, and I'm certain I failed the all-important "sister interview."

The Conflict-Habituated Marriage is a form of marriage I learned about early on in graduate school. The couple stays together to fight, and the fighting becomes a part of their daily routine. They have been arguing for so long and over so many issues that they've forgotten what the original "sins" in the marriage were—covered over each time in a new round of fighting.

These couples become experts at scorekeeping and retelling the stories of past offenses, revealing the sense of pride and victimization that gives their lives purpose. As Elton John sang, "Levon wears his war wounds like a crown." Try to suggest that they might take some personal responsibility for their situation, and you'll be shut down and dismissed as a traitor.

Marriage relationships, when functioning properly, are about positive bonding, which includes affection, goodwill, empathy, and understanding. Conflict-habituated couples have reversed that process and bonded over the pain. I will discuss the powerful impact of attachment styles in Chapter 11.

If a spouse does come out of a relationship like this—and many choose not to—they will have to learn how to attach to another person in a positive way. They will have to learn healthy attachment that is not characterized by negativity, scorekeeping, and resentment. If these folks will do their core work in a ReMatch process, they can come to experience a relationship in a whole new way.

## Parallel Lives and Metal Fatigue

I have a beautifully renovated 1950s era home off the north runway of Love Field in Dallas. I hear those 737 jets talking off and landing night and day and love the sounds of those engines revving up to take off, reminding me of my father, who worked for Pratt-Whitney Aircraft.

On the west side of Love Field, Southwest Airlines has its maintenance hangers. On a set schedule mechanics will pull a plane off the line and do routine maintenance. I'm told that they place special stress gauges on the skin of the plane to see if there are hairline fissures referred to as metal fatigue. Put a plane under continued pressure, and eventually it will develop problems around its weakest points.

Relationships are the same way. Put them under enough stress and eventually they will break down, suffering from what I call relationship metal fatigue. If the pair is a conflict-engaging couple, one or the other will file for divorce. If they are a conflict-avoidant couple, the two will tend to go on in parallel ways and stay together in name only.

One common factor that ends marriages in extended adulthood is the long-term wear of parallel lives. Many adults hit their fifties and sixties and decide there is just not enough connectivity to keep them together. The emotional, psychological, and sexual bonds that kept the marriage going have slowly eroded away. The couple has long since moved, almost imperceptibly, into parallel lives. Eventually those parallel lives lead them apart.

In developmental terms, it is during our fifties that our perspective on time shifts. Early in life we look at the future as a harbor filled with enormous amounts of available time. *I have decades to live.* As we grow older, however, our perspective on time changes. We start asking, *How much time do I have left?* When that shift occurs, some adults will look at their parallel marriage and decide, *I'm not doing this anymore.* They want to find the love of their life.

I've experienced that people coming out of parallel marriages are often in a hurry to date, find a partner, and start enjoying everything they've been missing. They sense that the "timeclock is running" and are not in the least interested in a ReMatch process that would help them gain some insight into how they ended up in a parallel relationship to begin with. Sadly, they often end up repeating the same pattern by unconsciously attracting the same kind of partner. The dynamics do not change because they have not changed.

## The Sand in My Shoe Phenomenon

If I am walking down the street and get a grain of sand in my shoe, I will not be able to tell it is there. Even if I pick up a few more grains of sand, I won't be able to feel them because they are so small. However, if I spend the next week, month, or year dropping sand into my shoe, eventually I'll want to take it off and dump out the sand. So it is in marriages, when too often by middle adulthood potential problems have become actual ones.

If these irritations are not dealt with effectively, one partner may want to dump the relationship.

There are many examples of otherwise mature marriages that suffer from the Sand in My Shoe phenomenon. For example, spouses who cannot manage their money, habitually run up excessive credit card debt, or needlessly gamble away funds are eventually very difficult to stay married to. Middle age is a time when addictions begin to take their toll on the fabric of the relationship. Partners grow tired of the effects of alcoholism, drug usage, prescription drug addiction, or out-of-control sexual behavior and desire some degree of normalcy in their lives.

Personality disorders, which we will discuss in more detail later in the book, wreak havoc on marriages, leaving partners and children exhausted, confused, and resentful. Partners who are authoritarian, rigid, and controlling have taken what I term the "Touch Bargainer" approach. Over the years this bullying style of conflict resolution wears out the family, and spouses declare, "Enough! I'm done with this." Closely associated with this scenario are partners who have poor social skills and lack social radar. Everywhere they go they leave dead bodies in their wake because of the things they say and do. They, too, are dumping sand into the shoes of the marriage.

In extended adulthood, a long-term affair may go public and bring the marriage to an end. Sometimes there has been only the shell of a marriage long before the affair is discovered. In other situations, people may be members of highly toxic churches, and the long-term effects of involvement in these noxious congregations causes a spouse to reject their partner's religion and the crazy belief systems being imposed on them. Simply because there is a sign in front labeling the location a church does not mean there is anything spiritual going on inside. Spouses get tired of the effects of spiritual abuse hammered on them with a "thus sayeth the Lord" sense of superiority.

The sand-in-my-shoe dynamic can be complicated by extended family conflicts. Unresolved issues with in-laws or parents can lead to an eventual blowup as problems long covered over find their way out. Hurt feelings and resentments from arguments decades old may bring about the demise of a marriage. People have had enough, pull off their shoe, and dump out the sand.

Extended adulthood is marked by a shift in one's perspective not only on time but also on energy. What spouses were willing to put up with in their twenties they may refuse to deal with in their fifties and sixties. There is also a shift in energy expenditure. In early adulthood a partner may be willing to be a heroic agent of change to "save the person I love" and "love them into being the person they are capable of being."

With age, though, one begins to realize that the work of becoming a functioning "adult" emotionally, psychologically, and spiritually is a responsibility each person must embrace for themselves. No one else can work out on my behalf and get me into shape; I must do the heavy lifting. Extended adulthood is a time when people wake up to realize that there are a lot of fourteen-year-old kids masquerading in sixty-year-old bodies. Chronology does not equate to maturity.

## The Love of My Life

I had driven from Dallas to Lubbock to meet Kate, a match I thought might hold some promise. Like me, she worked in higher education, lifted weights religiously, and enjoyed classic rock music. We had been communicating for a while, and I accepted her invitation to spend the weekend at her home in the panhandle and meet in person.

Dinner at a Mexican restaurant gave us a chance to get acquainted and share some stories in person. We had a promising connection, and the evening seemed to go well. The next day we met her parents for lunch at a local burger dive so they could check out this new guy from Dallas. I found them to be down to earth and easy to chat with. Kate's daughter stopped by and seemed more than a little excited to meet me, expressing that she hoped I'd be back—and winked at her mom as she left.

That evening as we were watching a movie at Kate's house, however, she grew quiet—more reserved and seemingly somehow darker. When I asked if she was all right, she pressed the mute button on the remote, turned to me, and confessed, "No, I guess I'm really not. My husband died two years ago. He was such a great guy. He was a college president, very smart and great with people. I thought that, since you were in university work and we liked so many of the same things, I might be ready to date— but I'm not. I'm not over him. My daughter signed me up for this dating site and wrote my profile. She said it was time for me to get out there. But I'm not sure I'll ever be over him. He was the love of my life."

Kate was experiencing something I have encountered many times, both in dating and in my counseling—the long-term effects of grief. I have noticed that people dating fall somewhere along a continuum between those who feel they've already experienced the love of their life, like Kate, and those who have processed their grief and are ready to move into the next relationship.

My adoptive mother and father were married for fifty-three years. When my father passed away in 1998 my mom lay down on her couch for five years and grieved—with the aid of the Home Shopping Network! She lived for another twenty-four years but never considered being with another man after my dad had died. My birth mother also shared with me that my birth father had been the love of her life, declaring that no other man could take his place. Both women fit into the first category of "one and done" when it come to love.

Mike and Mandy were married for only seven years, but the intensity of those years would last a lifetime. Mandy, at a tragically young age, contracted cancer, leaving her incapable of doing the simplest things to manage her life. Mike changed his work schedule and spent day and night caring for Mandy. He watched the woman he loved dying before his eyes and was powerless to do anything to stop it. Her death left a hole in him that could not be filled. Years later, though he had tried dating occasionally, he had not managed to process the impact of his grief. No one knew what the future would hold for him.

Dating in extended adulthood brings important questions to the forefront of the conversation about love. What is my relationship history, and what is the relationship history of the person I am dating? What are the effects of "sand in my shoe" behaviors? How have each of us dealt with grief from our past relationships? Has the grief been processed, or is it still present and pervasive? These are relevant questions in extended adulthood that don't typically enter the conversation during our twenties and thirties.

## CHAPTER 4

# THE AFFAIR SYNDROME

## Eric is Split

Eric came alone to counseling for his marriage because he was emotionally split. He was in love with two women simultaneously. He had been married to Erin for twenty-three years, and the couple was well known in the community and had a beautiful family with three girls now in high school and college. Eric had met Erin in graduate school and had been swept away by her energy and drive. She had set her sights on Eric as her perfect match, and all of his family had said she was an ideal catch. Eric, who was more emotionally reserved that Erin, found her passion intoxicating but, looking back, now feels that she was the person he felt he "ought to marry but never was really in love with." He had hoped that spark would ignite over time.

Amy was a student in one of the accounting classes Eric taught in his part-time job at the community college. She was ten years younger, and they began having coffee after class, immediately hitting it off. His connection with her was in his words almost instantaneous, as he felt caught up in a chemistry he had never experienced before. A short time later they started having sex, and the chemistry was off the charts. That was seven years ago. He had tried to shut down the affair several times, but like a wildfire it kept reigniting.

Eric was now fifty-one and found himself split over his feelings for the two women. Erin represented the life and family he had built, and he adored his three girls. If he were to leave his family it would destroy both them and his reputation in the community. His entire family would support her and assume he had lost his mind. On the other hand, Amy fed his passion and energy and nurtured his lighter side. She had listened to his promises that he would leave Erin and was tired of waiting. She wanted a family with Eric and could feel her biological clock ticking. Eric had simultaneously nurtured two very different but powerful love reward systems, and now his choices were coming back to haunt him.

I have worked with clients through a wide range of affairs and have found the dynamics of affairs in extended adulthood to be especially important. The aftermath of affairs can leave scars on partners that are carried into future relationships. This chapter will focus on the kinds of affairs that occur in mature marriages, the affair syndrome, and the effects of affairs on partners as they start to date again.

## Types of Affairs

Early in my career I was seeing many couples dealing with extramarital affairs. I sought out training from a specialist in the field, Dr. Emily Brown, author of *Patterns of Infidelity and Their Treatment*. Training under her, I learned that there are different kinds of affairs and that each one impacts the relationship in a different way:

### The Empty Nest Affair

This scenario involves a couple in middle age with one partner split between his or her feelings of love for the spouse and also for the lover. The couple may have married initially because each felt that this was the right person for them to be married to, though lacking chemistry and passion for their partner. An affair starts and is carried on for a long time, slowly splitting their affection and drive to keep the marriage together. Spouses start leading parallel lives, and eventually the lover pressures the spouse for a permanent commitment.

This kind of affair is very serious and capable of ending the marriage. The spouse having the affair is emotionally split between what I call "their oughter and their wanter." They ought to stay married and honor their commitment to their spouse but simultaneously want to leave and pursue the lover, with whom they perceive they will find greater happiness. When they do leave, the remaining spouse is emotionally bloodied and broken, unsure they will be able to trust anyone again. This is the kind of affair Eric was having, and it is common in middle age.

### The Conflict-Avoidant Affair

Keith and Kara are courteous and pleasant people. They never argue, never fight, and when their feelings are hurt, they stay quiet for a while and then silently move on. Problems get shoved under the rug year by year, and the big issues in the marriage are rarely dealt with. Both lack the emotional strength and communication skills to walk into difficult conversations, and both grew up in religious families who felt that any display of anger was "wrong and sinful" and that good Christians follow the rule "If you don't have something nice to say, don't say anything at all."

With their backlog of unresolved hostilities, it is not surprising to learn that Kara is vulnerable to advances from a coworker who is interested when she shows up to work upset by something Keith has said. What starts out as a friendship soon spirals into an emotional—and then a sexual—affair. Keith and Kara are vulnerable because they bury conflict and don't know how to resolve their differences. If they divorce and reenter the dating scene without going through a Rematch process, they will likely carry that same conflict-avoidant style into their next relationships. The past may repeat itself as conflict is once again buried and everyone acts cordial.

### The Intimacy-Avoidant Affair

I had a hard time controlling the sessions with Mike and Mandy. They were yelling, cursing, and screaming at each other and at me. Every time I'd interrupt them; they'd catch their breath and go at it again. I felt like the line judge in an NFL game pulling offensive and defensive linemen off one another after a play.

Mike and Mandy's conflict was like a Wild West gunfight on main street. Accusations and old stories were flying like bullets, and you either shot back or ducked for cover. Unlike the situation with Keith and Kara, this couple's conflict was out in the open and central to their marriage. What Mike and Mandy struggled with was not conflict but intimacy. This couple lacked a healthy attachment style. They didn't know how to be close, so they fought with each other, allowing conflict to replace closeness.

When Mike had an affair, it was discovered early and became the source of a new round of hostility. In fact, he made sure Mandy found out just to intensify the hurt. Mandy countered some months later with an affair of her own, and World War III was on. The affairs, while serious, were not the real issue. The core issue for each partner was how to experience true intimacy and allow a spouse to be close emotionally. If Mike and

Mandy divorce and do not each do their own core work, they will likely carry this attachment style and avoidance of intimacy into their dating life. They will "entertain" potential matches with long stories of how they have been wronged and look for the "perfect match" that can make up for all the horrible things done to them.

### The Out the Door Affair

Sarah and Steve came for one session together, and then I never saw Steve again. It seemed to me as if he had delivered Sarah up to me for safekeeping. They had been married for twenty-five years and had raised one son who now lived close by. During our first session Steve was polite and distant. He cooly explained that they had grown apart over the years and now lived parallel lives. There had not been any connection between him and Sarah for a long time. Recently he'd begun seeing a woman with whom he'd graduated from college and later reconnected on Facebook.

Sarah, devastated, alternated during that initial session between crying and lashing out at Steve. She did not understand how some other woman could just "come in and steal away" her husband after all those years. When I pressed them both for more details on the history of their marriage and how they dealt with the issues of intimacy, conflict, and attachment, they glossed over years of discord with nonspecific histories.

Sarah and Steve's marriage was over. The affair, though painful, was not serious. It was likely that, after the divorce, Steve would move on to another lover, and so would Sarah. The affair functioned simply as a stimulus to end the marriage, a vehicle to get them to the point at which one person would file and end a painful, unfulfilling relationship. Sarah could then tell her friends that "this woman stole my husband away."

What was missing in this case was the will to walk into the narrative of their story and look at the factors that had led to their moving apart. One of the keys to success in any Rematch process is the willingness to attain insight. To ask the hard questions: What did I do to contribute to this problem? What patterns am I carrying forward into the next relationship? Unless I am armed with this information, I am destined to make the same mistakes I made in the past.

### Compulsive Sexual Behavior

Judy opened Jordan's business laptop to obtain some receipts for taxes, only to discover a hidden email account with emails from dozens of women going back five years. Painfully reading through this catalog of hidden lovers, she was devastated to learn that the man she had thought she was married to had been carrying on a secret sexual life.

Tom and Teresa's sex life and affectionate relationship had been a rollercoaster careening from hot and heavy to nonexistent, and Tom had stayed in a continual state of confusion. Most nights Teresa would slip into their king-size bed and curl up on the edge in the fetal position to avoid all contact with him. Occasionally she would attack him multiple times with a sexual aggressiveness and orgasm. He never knew which woman he was married to.

Then there was the public Teresa, who was flirtatious and sought the attention of all the men in the room. There was always one special guy who seemed to be buying her gifts and hanging around way too much—and there was always an overarching feeling that something was going on behind Tom's back, though Teresa was an expert at keeping things hidden.

The cases of Jordan and Teresa illustrate the impact of out-of-control sexual behavior and sexual trauma on relationships. In Jordan's case, he was trying to heal an inner core wound, probably encountered early in life, with multiple partners. Instead of alcohol or drugs, Jordan's drug of choice was sex. One partner led to another, and another . . .

Teresa was the victim of childhood sexual abuse that had dramatically affected the development of her sense of self and sexual identity. She had learned early on to relate to men sexually as a means of gaining value and attention. In Teresa's case we see something Dr. Heather MacIntosh refers to as "bifurcation" or splitting of one's sex life. Teresa carried on a somewhat normal sexual relationship with Tom—although her sexual behavior was unpredictable and confusing to her husband. She also bifurcated or carried on a secret sexual life hidden from her spouse with multiple partners throughout the marriage.

After their split but before dating once again, Jordan and Teresa would each be well advised to do the difficult work of healing those old inner wounds and establishing a healthy sense of self. Tom and Judy would each need to address their own issues that might center around codependency and the need to find a "fixer-upper project" to be in a relationship with in order to validate their sense of self. Without doing that core work they would tend to repeat past patterns and attract the same sorts of partner to themselves.

Affairs don't just happen. The process is not like a Hollywood movie where two people get on an elevator, immediately experience overwhelming chemistry, and are screwing each other's brains out by the time they hit the thirtieth floor. Dr. James Cail calls this ramp-up process "the Affair Syndrome."

## The Affair Syndrome

Dr. James Cail, my friend, mentor, and colleague at Oklahoma Christian University, is a pioneer in the field of marriage therapy. Early in his career he observed the patterns of people involved in extramarital affairs and proposed the Affair Syndrome as a way to explain the stages people move through as an affair develops. The Affair Syndrome will leave lasting effects on a partner reentering the dating world.

### Stage One: Proximity

Dr. Cail notes that people typically have affairs with other people they are regularly in contact with on a day-to-day basis. Proximity is the first determinant of who a person will be involved with in an extramarital affair. Coaches have affairs with players, teachers with students, doctors with nurses, and ministers with church members. However, the internet has changed the impact of proximity. If an individual wants to meet someone and have an affair, they can construct a fake identity and meet someone from another town.

### Stage Two: Mutual Awareness of Attraction

We all carry a "template of attraction." This template is a set of physical, emotional, and psychological characteristics we find attractive. We are romantically drawn to a particular kind of person. When we decide to date and find a mate the radar is on, and we attend to those men or women we find attractive. People swipe through profiles on their phone, immediately eliminating 99 percent of the possible matches; however, when we see one and the radar turns on, we know it immediately.

When we marry or are in a committed relationship, we turn that radar down. It never fully shuts down, but we apply cruise control on its engine, and when it does go off, we don't attend to it. Some men and women choose not to control their attraction radar, so they are constantly sending out messages to people they find attractive. When two people are aware of their mutual attraction but hold it in check and maintain a respectful friendship, they are using healthy boundaries.

### Stage Three: Seductive Message Is Sent

When I was in the sixth grade I had my first crush on a girl in class. I sent Suzy the typical note at that time. "I like you do you like me; yes or no—check one." As adults we do the same thing, only in more complex and seductive ways. The two people have seen each other. Their radar has gone off, and they are aware of the reciprocal attraction. Now it is time to send a tentative message to the other person that says, "I find you attractive."

One woman was standing in the church foyer visiting for the first time. The minister made his message very clear as he walked up to her and proclaimed her to be the loveliest woman he'd ever seen. The message was clear: "I find you attractive. Do you share my sentiment?"

Normally the seductive message is more sublime. The holding of a look a little longer than usual, the brushing of the arm or hand as one walks buy, or the standing in close proximity to the other person, where they can be noticed—any of these may be messages broadcasting, "I'm here, and I notice you." For some men and women, it's the excitement of chase that becomes an addiction, the idea of something being forbidden that becomes intoxicating.

If the message is sent, received, and reciprocated, the relationship has started, and we are off to the races. The two people are each telling themselves that they are becoming good friends, but the core attraction is driving them to spend more time together.

### Stage Four: Increased Interaction

The two individuals will begin spending more time together. They will arrange to accidentally meet at the coffee bar at the same time every morning. They will be at the gym for the same workout class. At church they will make a point of meeting and exchanging looks before class to check in with each other.

These casual encounters will become a regular pattern the two people look forward to. One of the definitions of love is "an anticipation of being in the presence of one's beloved." They are looking forward to seeing the other person and being in their presence.

In time they will exchange phone numbers, and the phone may become an important link to the other person as they text throughout the day.

### Stage Five: Downplaying the Marriage

Conversations between the two people become more personal and intimate. They are attracted to each other, receive reinforcement that the attraction is mutual, and have both begun investing time and energy into building the relationship. Eventually they begin sharing information about their "disappointment" with their marriage. His wife simply doesn't understand him, and the woman, recently divorced, discusses her failed marriage and her ability to find a "good guy on Match.com."

### Stage Six: Illusion of Invisibility

At this point in the relationship an emotional affair is in full bloom. They are meeting each other on a regular basis and have arranged their schedules so they can spend time together. They are making excuses and lying to their spouses at home about their activities. There are no boundaries now concerning the content of their conversations; they speak as lovers speak to one another.

An interesting phenomenon occurs in Stage Six. Coworkers and friends begin to notice the chemistry that is occurring between the two of them. He looks at her from up on stage, and she begins to glow from the inside out. They stare at each other from across the room. She laughs a little too long at his jokes and holds his forearm, keeping him close in the foyer. People see the attraction clearly for what it is—a budding romance turning into an affair.

The couple is oblivious to the messages they are broadcasting, each assuming that their new "best friend" relationship is well hidden from pesky outsiders. Dr. Cail calls this "the illusion of invisibility." When an affair is blossoming into a full sexual relationship, the two people involved will assume that no one around them notices their behavior. Nothing could be further from the truth.

### Stage Seven: Taking the Position "We Are Just Good Friends"

Eventually the question is put to one of the partners: "What's up with you and Katy? You are spending a lot of time together." Or one or the other spouse complains about the time being spent in each other's presence or the inappropriate comments or gifts that are being exchanged. Their radar regarding the affair has gone off.

The couple moves to a defensive position, realizing that the illusion of invisibility has been shattered. "We are just good friends" is the position they take—with an air of disbelief and a signal that offense has been taken. Neither can believe that people would question their behavior or motives. "I've been spending time with her because she's a coworker who's been through a terrible time in her life. You're crazy. You are so insecure. Once again, you have issues with trust!"

The "new couple" now has a pattern of spending time together. They have regular conversations in person, by phone, and through ongoing texts. They may each have a separate iPhone to hide the affair from their spouses. Gifts are being exchanged as they map their new partner's likes and dislikes. This is dating behavior, the only difference being that it is taking place while one or both are married to someone else.

If it has not turned into a fully active sexual relationship, which by this point it likely has, it soon will. They are fully engaged in an emotional affair, and the commitments they made to fidelity in the marriage have been left far behind in the rearview mirror.

## Signs of an Extramarital Affair

- Looking forward to seeing someone, anticipation of being in the presence of the other person
- Mapping their likes and dislikes, habits and tastes
- An urge to buy the other person gifts
- Sudden desire to lose weight, going to the gym, getting in shape
- Change in personal appearance or style of dress
- Frequently mentioning the name to friends
- Disappearance of money
- Unexplained disappearance of time
- Contact on social media sites
- Unusual texts, messaging, or calls that must be hidden or taken privately

## Issues to Resolve Following an Affair

In my experience there is no more painful event to harm a marriage than an extramarital affair. The damage it does is multi-layered, and the effects naturally carry forward into the future. Before a client reenters the dating scene, we'll take a look at a number of important areas to determine whether they are healthy enough to date.

### Capacity to Trust Again

Dr. Cail states, "Trust is the ashes from the logs of mutually shared experiences." When a couple gets together, they start doing things to show the other person they care about them. Listening attentively, learning their likes and dislikes, remembering special days, and sharing hopes for the future become the fabric of the relationship. I do what I say I will do, and that throws a log onto the fire of the relationship. When she does what she says she will do, that tosses another log onto the fire. Over the years couples burn lots of logs together. The byproduct of burning those logs is trust.

I can't merely say to someone, "Just trust me," because trust is built upon time and consistent actions. I do what I say I will do. When an affair occurs it's as if I take a vacuum hose to the fireplace and empty out all that trust in one swift movement. It's all gone. And it cannot be replaced quickly. It's going to take time and effort to rebuild the marriage. There is Marriage Book One, the affair, and then Marriage Book Two. That's why many of my clients end the relationship. They cannot or will not do the hard work of rebuilding trust with time and consistent actions.

When my clients move quickly from a marriage that ends due to an affair into the dating scene, they may carry with them the tendency to distrust their partner. They inflict upon the new dating partner the unresolved issues of trust from the former marriage. One key to a Rematch process is repairing my trust capacity with time and inner healing.

### Staggered Disclosure

Marty was at the airport getting on a plane when she ran into Julie, a sorority sister from college who had heard about Marty's divorce from Michael a year earlier. "I thought about calling you several times because I ran into Michael quite by accident at a concert with a woman he introduced as Michelle, and she was hanging all over him." Quite stunned, Marty does not know what to say. She has never heard of Michelle, as Marty told her the affair was with woman he had met at the gym named Carolyn. Marty has just been side-swiped by something I call *Staggered Disclosure*.

My clients who are recovering from an affair in their marriage build what I call "the narrative": their understanding of the events that occurred around the affair and the ending of the marriage. This is an important part of the healing process; the problem is, however, that the narrative can be built too soon. People in a hurry to move on and date again often find themselves, like Marty, standing in public when a friend unknowingly downloads a new chapter to the narrative that had previously been hidden. Remember, a hallmark of affairs is secrecy. People are invested in hiding the truth and underreporting details.

Staggered disclosure hits, and my clients are sent back to square one in the divorce recovery process. Issues of distrust, lying, and manipulation fuel anger and resentment once again. I regularly alert my clients to the possibilities of staggered disclosure and encourage them to take time after the divorce to allow previously unknown information to surface. Otherwise, the new boyfriend or girlfriend gets thrown into the unhealthy role of being surrogate therapist for a wounded dating partner still stuck in an emotional divorce.

### Hypervigilance

A close cousin to lack of trust is hypervigilance. My dog Dutch, an Australian Shepherd, would sit for hours scanning the pasture as our horses grazed. He was hypervigilant for any signs of wolves or threats to the horses and had a trigger reflex to attack. That was great for a herding dog, but it's an awful way for well-adjusted adults to live their lives.

Adults are not designed to be in a constant state of stress alarm. Extramarital affairs install triggers within the partner, who often is in an ongoing state of watchfulness. They check emails, follow the partner, look at Facebook accounts, and snoop around bank accounts looking for signs of cheating and lying. Sadly, this can become a lifestyle—their relationship normal. If there has been an affair before, they are waiting for the next shoe to fall.

The Rematch process allows people time to wind down from the effects of hypervigilance. I don't have to be constantly watching everything my partner is doing. People are capable of telling me the truth about where they are going and what they are doing. I don't have to imitate Dutch, sitting in the pasture of my relationship waiting for the next threat of attack from wolves. Relationships are intended to enrich my life, not stress me out.

### Sexual Dissatisfaction and Doubt

Some people come out of affairs complaining that they have never been sexually satisfied in the relationship and that their partner has devoted all their sexual attention to the lover. They have never known a healthy sexual relationship with that person and are deeply resentful. Others report that the sex stayed active, engaged, and passionate, even though their spouse was carrying on an affair the entire time. Their level of shock and confusion is magnified by their partner's ability to carry on a complex double life.

Often associated with this dissatisfaction is a quiet, understated set of questions about one's own performance as a sexual partner. Was I not good enough in bed? Did he want different things than I was able to give him? Did she stop being attracted to me because of how I looked or performed in bed? These doubts can carry into future relationships unless we take some time to explore our own sexual identity as a part of the healing process.

### Pornographic Memories

When an affair is revealed, oftentimes the first base my clients run to is "Tell me all the sexual details. I want to know everything." Questions are voiced about where sex took place, what positions were used, what size he was, how large her breasts were, whether they had oral sex, . . . and the list goes on. My clients can fill their minds with so much pornographic memory that they self-traumatize and make their own recovery more difficult.

While I completely understand the desire to know sexual details—and in some cases, such as those involving sexually transmitted infections, they are essential to know—I encourage my clients to press carefully for details. Do you truly want to carry that image in your head for the rest of your life? I trained with Dr. Richard Stuart, one of the pioneers in couples' therapy and the author of *Helping Couples Change*. He noted that there is something in couples' communication he calls the Norm of Measured Honesty. Simply stated, there are some things in a relationship that would be better left unsaid. It helps me recover faster if there are some things I don't know or don't have described to me. When it comes to recovering from an affair, treading carefully into the sexual detail applies the Norm of Measured Honesty in an important way.

Extramarital affairs are significant and unique events, each of which comes with its own package of long-term effects. It takes time and intentionality to heal from them. When people embrace a Rematch process that gives them space to rebuild their capacity to trust, explore their own sexuality, and process painful memories, they will be better prepared to hit the dating scene and find love in the second half of life.

# DOING THE CORE WORK

# CHAPTER 5

# A "GOOD DIVORCE"

I was talking to my son following his first session with a therapist I had recommended to him following a breakup with his girlfriend. "I think we're going to work well together," he observed. "She told me I treat women in my life very well. I told her, 'I learned how to treat a woman watching how my dad treated my mom going through their divorce.'" I sat in stunned silence on the phone. This was one of the most meaningful compliments I had ever received.

At the conclusion of my own therapy following the divorce, my therapist looked at me and commented, "Your family does divorce very well. In fact, you may have done divorce better than you did marriage." I believe he was right. Divorce is by definition a painful process. It is the restructuring of the entire family system and is loaded with difficult emotions and changes. However, if approached with a mindset of "Work from a place of respect and adulthood," it can be navigated with as little damage as possible to everyone involved.

## A Working Definition

Divorce is the social, emotional, and legal process through which former spouses come to regard themselves and to be regarded by others as single. It is a restructuring of the entire family system that Whitaker and Keith define as "a psychological amputation." In my course in conflict management, we define divorce as a conflict management tool to be employed when all other approaches have broken down. Experts who track crime rates note that, as the divorce rate has increased, the murder rate among family members has decreased.

## Two Phases of Divorce

Divorce typically occurs in two phases: the decision-making phase and the restructuring phase. The decision-making phase begins with consideration of divorce and ends with physical separation. This phase is a time during which marital difficulties increase, and talk of divorce tends to escalate the decision to follow through with the marriage dissolution. Once the word "divorce" hits the table, it tends to take on a life of its own; it becomes "normalized" as a possible option to manage the couple's conflict.

The decision-making phase includes several indicators that the couple will move forward with the divorce. These include a willingness to accept responsibility for the decision to divorce; apathy toward the marriage; and the increase in divorce talk, indicating that there remains no commitment to the marriage. Often one partner is ahead of the other in the decision-making timeline. That partner is ready to call the attorney even while the other partner is still in shock.

Couples may bounce back and forth in the decision-making phase for months or even years. I've seen spouses move out, determined to end the marriage, and a few weeks later move back in and announce that the couple is experiencing a second honeymoon. This lasts for a few short weeks before they separate once again. Typically, the ending of a marriage does not come with one swift blow; instead, the puppy tail gets cut off in several slices.

The restructuring phase is a longer period that begins with physical separation and ends with the person settled into a relatively stable and autonomous lifestyle. The restructuring phase includes five important sub-phases we will look at in detail. Navigating these transitions will not only be key to one's divorce adjustment but will also set the stage for a healthy Rematch readiness. Too often I see clients rush through the restructuring phase, only to have those issues reappear once they are dating again—the issues do not go away but just wait to reappear with future relationship partners.

## Bundt Cake Divorce

When my students ask me how to work with a client going through a divorce, I liken the process to baking a bundt cake. My mother would take vanilla and chocolate cake mixes and combine them in a bowl before pouring the combined batter into a round mold. When it was baked, she would slice into it, and every slice would have a different black and white pattern.

Counseling clients who are going through the restructuring phase of a divorce is like slicing into that bundt cake. Every day involves a different crisis and a different set of adjustments. You never know what to expect. There are five important sub-phases to the restructuring process, so there are literally five divorces happening at once. The bundt cake contains all five ingredients, and any one slice can show more of one "phase" than another. The "five divorces" are the legal divorce, the emotional divorce, the financial divorce, the social divorce, and the parental divorce. One of the signs that a person is ready to date is that they have navigated each of these five divorces.

### The Emotional Divorce

Divorce is, almost without exception, the most emotionally difficult experience any adult with endure, with the exception of the loss of a child. It is loaded with high-powered emotions that can spring up unexpectedly. Divorce is a "de-courting process." When we start dating, we begin building a vast array of highly specialized emotional connections to our spouse. Over time those emotional bonds are strengthened and become more complex and rewarding. Divorce rips apart those connections, signaling that they are dead. Someone going through a divorce has the same emotional needs as any other person, but they no longer have access to the same means of fulfillment.

The emotional process may include the following adjustments:

- Loss and grief
- Guilt and failure
- Acceptance of the divorce
- Management of day-to-day activities
- Implementing small decisions
- Developing new social relationships

- Accepting and managing change
- Understanding why the marriage failed
- Accepting responsibility for one's own contribution
- Developing autonomy
- Establishing long-term goals

People experience the emotional divorce in different ways. There are those who are in shock and disbelief when their partner walks in and announces that they are done with the marriage. There are others who see the train running down the tracks and are not surprised when the discussion of divorce hits the table—they had anticipated this discussion already long ago. Then there are spouses who experience divorce as the laying down of a heavy burden. Having carried the weight of the marriage for many years, functioning as the only adult in the relationship, they experience divorce as a release from years of pain and disappointment.

Divorce presents a wide range of feelings to be resolved:

- Vulnerability
- Helplessness
- Loneliness
- Fear
- Guilt
- Failure
- Anger
- Humiliation
- Fear of sexual inadequacy

For some people divorce will be the first time they have ever lived as a single adult, and it wil take time to learn to function in that role.

### The Social Divorce

Who will attend the kids' parent-teacher conferences? Who is going to stay at our church, and who will be transferring their membership? What if I run into him at the gym? I don't know what I'll do if he brings that woman to our child's soccer game! He's working in my dad's company—what do we do with that?

Divorce is a restructuring of the entire social network of a family. Extended families, schools, churches, memberships in the community, couple friends, and a host of other examples all have to be restructured and renegotiated.

Key tasks in the social divorce phase include:

- Rearranging personal habits from married to single
- Informing all family members on both sides
- Adjustment to new relationships with extended family
- Entering the new world of the formerly married
- Adjusting to new social groups, such as church, school, gym
- Building a new network of friends
- Adjusting to friends and family who have abandoned one or both spouses during the divorce
- Creating boundaries around those who use the divorce as a context in which to be abusive

A word of caution: the dissolution of a marriage is a time when people are emotionally vulnerable. There are those individuals who will use that vulnerability to hurt the person going through a divorce. This can be done with vicious words, unkind actions, or stories shared that are intended to exact retribution for perceived wrongdoing. In the Old Testament King David was fleeing Jerusalem because his own son Absalom had organized a revolt and was attempting to take the capital. The devastated king was running for his life, and some citizens of Jerusalem used that moment to meet David in the streets and jeer at him over his actions as king. They waited for his moment of susceptibility to exact revenge.

I was attending my high school reunion just a month following my divorce. I was a keynote speaker, and everyone there knew my situation. Late that night as I was sitting with a group of high school friends, a woman I had barely known in high school used that as an opportunity to criticize me and my ex-wife. I was stunned, and the table fell silent—embarrassed by her lack of class. I learned early on that single-again individuals enter a world where they constitute their own first line of defense, having to protect their own boundaries from outsiders who demonstrate personality disorders, lack of empathy, or a low emotional IQ. Sometimes, as in the case of David, those enemies are members of our own families.

### The Financial Divorce

Divorce is a restructuring of the financial life of the family, and normally no one comes out ahead. The former couple is moving from supporting one household to maintaining two, and there are never enough dollars to go around. Economic issues make this even harder on a woman if she has opted out of pursuing her career to raise a family or to work part time. Now she is bloodied and tired from an exhausting divorce process and her attempts to repackage herself to enter the workforce.

The financial divorce is a time when family secrets come out of the closet. An offshore bank account that was hidden becomes known. A hidden credit card debt that was run up to the limit is now a part of the divorce negotiations. Expenses a spouse paid for hotels, trips, and gifts during an affair are exposed, to the shock of the other spouse. Forensic accountants may be hired to expose the secret business dealings of lying partners. The more money involved, the dirtier it all becomes.

Key areas to address financially include:

- Living arrangements
- Childcare
- Job skills and training
- Family budgeting
- Use of community resources and services
- Use of family resources and services
- Credit
- Health insurance

### The Parental Divorce

Carol didn't see her son, Chris, very often anymore. Occasionally he would come back to Dallas for Thanksgiving or Christmas, but otherwise he stayed in San Diego, where he had moved right after graduating from high school. He'd had several offers to go to college close to home, but as soon as he was able to leave the house he did so. He was tired of being the "messenger boy" in his parents' messy divorce.

Carl and Carol had divorced when Chris was in elementary school. The divorce was nasty as Carl, a high-profile attorney, had engaged in an affair with a paralegal fifteen years younger. So had started a marital civil war that had continued throughout Chris's upbringing. Carol, wounded and vengeful following the affair, made it her life's mission to ruin Carl's life. She became obsessed with every move her ex-husband made and used Chris as her little "secret agent man" to spy on his dad and the paralegal lover now living in her mansion.

Chris, a sensitive kid already, bounced between his mother's fits of rage and his dad's miserable denials. It was no wonder that when Chris walked across the stage at graduation, he also graduated from his family of origin. Carol was hurt, confused, and once again blamed Carl for everything. When Carol began dating again, men were put off with the never-ending stories of her ex and how she had been wronged. It seemed to her dates that she had never fully divorced. They were right.

Key actions to help children through divorce:

- Resist the urge to triangulate them in the conflict.
- Resist the urge to use them as messengers and collectors of information.
- Move to a "business and professional" tone of respect with the ex-spouse.
- Remove in the child any feelings of self-blame suggesting that they may have somehow caused this.
- Discuss the child's feelings that they can fix the situation.
- Get them their own therapist and keep the person available throughout the high school years on call.
- Do *not* use the teenagers as Mom or Dad's "date coach"—let kids be kids.
- Resist the temptation to move them into adult responsibilities too early—let them have a childhood.
- Work with exes to maintain as much continuity in schedule, living arrangements, schools, and church as possible.
- Do *not* use the child as surrogate therapist; they are not emotionally equipped to handle this.

### The Legal Divorce

Andy couldn't get his divorce moving. Every time he called his attorney the receptionist had a new set of excuses: "We have been in court all week." "The other attorney has not responded to our requests for information." "Ms. Johnson is out for the month on maternity leave." And the list went on and on. By accident one day he mentioned his frustrations to his soon-to-be ex, who assured him that they had complied with every request from the absent attorney, Ms. Johnson, and were anxious to get the divorce over and done with. Andy had been poorly represented by a divorce attorney who was milking billable hours. He quickly replaced her, and the divorce moved forward with no further issues.

Amy was involved in a nasty divorce with a vengeful ex-spouse who had both hidden and frozen assets that made her life miserable from a financial standpoint. She hurriedly found a job selling clothing at a local department store and removed her kids from the private school her ex now refused to pay for. He had enrolled his new girlfriend's kids in the pricey private school and was now paying their tuition instead.

On the day of the final divorce hearing, Amy was returning home to an empty apartment. She had no furniture and didn't even own a bed to sleep in. Her divorce had cost her everything. Upon hearing of her situation, her attorney stopped at a furniture store on the way home from court and bought her a bed and mattress so that her client would not be sleeping on the floor any longer. The attorney understood that representing the law equates to representing people, and, unlike Andy's attorney, she fulfilled her mission.

Divorce is by definition an adversarial process. My experience both with clients and personally is that whatever conflict exists going into the divorce will only be heightened by the legal process. The ability of couples to communicate and problem solve is gone, leaving it up to the state to resolve conflict. That process will ordinarily not be pleasant and will only deepen the wounds.

In my practice I always kept on hand the names of several attorneys who specialized in divorce and approached it from a caring legal perspective. I knew that, when I referred a client to them, they would care for both the person and the case. My clients would not come out of that experience carrying scars from working with their own attorney.

## Dr. Don's Eight Keys to a Good Divorce

### Key One: Work toward maintaining a business and professional tone with your ex.

We don't have to like them. We don't have to agree with them. We don't have to share the same perspective with them. What we can do is speak to them as we would someone with whom we are conducting an important business transaction. Simple respect goes a long way toward building a "good" divorce.

### Key Two: Select an attorney who values equally the client relationship and the case.

Interview several attorneys before selecting one. Ask for referrals from friends or your therapist. Go into the interview with your questions written down, and take a friend along to offer support and help you remember details from the meeting. Listen to your gut when selecting an attorney, and don't be afraid of letting one go if necessary.

### Key Three: Kid continuity is important.

Try to maintain as much continuity in the children's lives as possible. Keeping them in familiar schools to maintain friendships, keeping the family home if possible, and maintaining their schedule in some realm of normalcy will help them feel that a foundation remains beneath them. Consider getting the children their own therapist to speak with privately over the years as they grow up. The effects of the divorce will resurface in different ways during the adolescent years.

### Key Four: The Mary and Joseph Rule.

I was given a lot of crazy advice when I was going through my divorce. One ridiculous request came from a university official at the college I was being released from due to my divorce. He recommended that I meet with all the faculty in my college and explain to them why I was filing for a divorce. Thanks . . . I don't think so.

Being a person of faith, I recalled Matthew 1:19, referring to the discovery that Mary was pregnant prior to her marriage to Joseph: "Because Joseph her husband was faithful to the law and did not want to expose her to public disgrace. he had in mind to divorce her quietly." I used that as my guideline. When it came to our social and professional network, I went silent. I didn't discuss the divorce except with one close friend and with my therapist. Twenty years later I recognize that this had been one of the smartest choices I made.

A word about the religious community, because I have worked with churches for most of my career as a consultant and therapist. Churches and church leaders are among the world's worst at gossip and slander.

The reason many of my clients left organized religion during or after a divorce is that too many good church members simply do not know how to keep conversations confidential. They would do well to take Joseph's advice in Matthew 1:19.

### Key Five: Get and keep a good therapist throughout the divorce process.

A good therapist can be an essential part of the healing process through a divorce. If divorce is like a bundt cake, with new struggles appearing every day, it helps to have a safe place to download the stress. I train licensed marriage and family therapists and have found that people are often confused as to who counsels and what kind of counseling they offer. Marriage and family therapists specialize in understanding the family as a system of interrelated parts. They are able to speak to the needs of the individual going through a divorce and its impact on the children, teens, and former spouses involved. They come armed with a theory of change that is designed to help people navigating divorce.

### Key Six: Don't treat divorce adjustment with quick dating.

This is the most common trap I see divorced people falling into. A well-meaning friend convinces them that the quickest way to deal with their emotional pain is to "get back out there and have some fun." Seriously? You just got out of a ten-year marriage, ending with emotional turmoil, and you think you're dating material? Do you have a clear idea of what you're looking for in a new partner? Or are you ready to go wild and have some sexual fun after all those years of misery? That sounds like a sure recipe for happiness and contentment, right?

So, my clients put up a profile on Match.com, run out there and start dating again, and drop out of therapy because they don't want to face their therapist and explain why they are acting like an impatient teenager. And we wonder why this doesn't work. Two years and three failed relationships later, they end up back in my office, saying, "You know . . . I think the problem here may be me because I keep picking out the same guy!"

### Key Seven: Process the emotions—don't get stuck in them.

Growing up, we had a family tradition of hamburgers every Saturday night. This was my favorite night of the week, and I can still smell the burgers frying in my mother's cast iron skillet in the kitchen. I thought she served the best burgers in Dallas. After dinner my mom would run water in that skillet and let it sit on the countertop overnight. There was burned beef and grease in the bottom of the skillet that wouldn't come off with only an application of elbow grease. Overnight it would soak, and by Sunday morning the burn would have floated to the top.

Painful emotions are like that. We can't command them to process. It takes time and healing for them to float to the surface to be dealt with. A caring therapist can create an environment of safety and offer insight to help a person deal with the many competing emotions that rise to the surface in a divorce. Interestingly, I've discovered that our emotions in themselves are benevolent, emerging only when they are ready to be healed. Allowing time and space for us to heal emotionally is an aspect of the self-care we all deserve. As a therapist friend told me, "You need to care for Don as well as you have cared for everyone else in your life."

### Key Eight: You'll be surprised by the people who stand by you . . . and by those who abandon you.

The sun was setting over the lake as Joee, Kubby, and I loaded Tim's wheelchair into the powerful ski boat to spend the evening on the water. This was a reunion of football buddies I had never dreamed would happen. I had moved to Dallas in 1968, going into the sixth grade, and would spend the next six years in class and on the football field every fall afternoon with these three guys. Kubby played fullback, Joee was a receiver, Tim was an offensive tackle, and I played center. When we graduated in 1975, we all went our separate ways, occasionally reconnecting at high school reunions.

In the middle of my divorce, I got a call from Tim—the spokesman of our group. "Heeb!" he shouted into the phone. "You got to meet us at Kubby's place. We're taking you out on the lake. We heard what's going down. We're here for you."

Tim was battling MS and confined to a wheelchair, but he was ready to suit up and play another half game of football if given the chance. Kubby brought old pictures of us playing ball against St. Marks, Cistercian, and Ft. Worth Country Day. Joee was still the master storyteller and had us laughing at stories we'd long ago forgotten. As it got dark Tim said to me, "Heeb, you were always there for us. We're here for you now." That was the kindest thing anyone said to or did for me during the course of my divorce.

I had been warned that many of my friends and colleagues would pull away, but I must confess that I was surprised when this actually occurred. The religious community was quiet, and conservative family members sent articles condemning divorce but never reached out to talk. People I had thought would reach out went silent and slipped away.

What surprised and pleased me, however, were the people who appeared in my life to replace them: therapists and colleagues who understood and offered support; academic friends who were going through similar circumstances in their own marriages; and friends I never would have imagined would reach out, like Tim, Joee, and Kubby offering support after years of separation.

Divorce is certainly at the top of the list of painful processes we would not wish on anyone else. It is also one of the processes that must be walked through completely. Despite all its pain, disappointment, confusion, and uncertainty, if it is embraced as a learning experience, we do the work and emerge from it hopefully wiser, kinder, and with a greater understanding of ourselves. That self-awareness is the next step in the Rematch process.

# CHAPTER 6

# MY MAN PICKER IS BROKEN

## Picking the Same Guy

Julie showed up for our first appointment twenty minutes early, carrying a notebook and pen and obviously anxious to get down to business. She was fifty-five, educated, and running a family business, she had inherited from her highly successful father, a legend in the trucking industry. During our conversation Julie informed me that she had been married twice and had been divorced now for five years.

She had been dating online and through more traditional meetings at the gym or through friends. She had just been through a rather difficult breakup and announced, "I really thought he was the one until I learned that a lot of the things he had been telling me were just not true. That has happened repeatedly to me. I seem to attract serial liars, or at least men who put up a false front. I don't know if it's me or if there are just no good men out there, but Don, I suspect my man picker is broken."

Julie was expressing a sentiment I've heard many times from my clients and students in class. People reach extended adulthood and look back on the relationships they've been in. Many times, if there has been a series of failed relationships, they start to notice a pattern emerging. They are repeating the same relationship over and over, just with a different partner. The one common denominator in all the false starts is *them*. My clients, like Julie, experience this as a sobering realization and come to therapy armed with a mindset to end the pattern and get some insight into their own motivations.

Why do intelligent, successful, well-intentioned, and mature adults keep picking the same type of person over and over again even when that person treats them poorly? The presence of that pattern may be a signal that there is something deeper and more profound going on in their life. There may be an internal core wound that is trying to be healed by repeatedly running to unfulfilling relationships and replaying the same scenarios. Extended adulthood becomes a key time when doing one's core work moves to center stage to end such patterns.

## This Coat Doesn't Fit Me Anymore

I was in session with Dr. Clif Davis, who was doing some work with me on my adoption and attachment issues. We were exploring the idea that I might repeatedly be picking women who were "fixer-upper projects" based on the attachment wounds I had experienced during my first year of life in foster care. Clif stood up and took off his coat. He then put one arm into a sleeve the way it normally would fit and tried to force the other arm into the other sleeve elbow first. It became stuck halfway in and looked ridiculous.

"Do I look like I'm comfortable? Does this look like it fits me at all? Of course not! I was meant to wear a sports jacket with both arms comfortably down the sleeves, right? But what if this is the only way you've ever worn a jacket? What if this is all you know? What if having my elbow crammed down a sleeve is my normal? Then I'm going to think this is the way my life is supposed to be. A jacket is supposed to fit this way."

Clif continued, "If I take off this jacket and go shopping for a new one, I'll choose a jacket and proceed to shove my elbow into the sleeve. That's my normal. And if a nice salesperson comes along and eases my arm correctly into the sleeve, I'll wear it that way for a time, but before too long I'll get rid of that jacket because it's comfortable. I'll go back to the old jacket, the one in which I can comfortably shove my elbow into the armhole and then complain that there are no good sports coats out there . . . and that my tailor sucks."

Clif was graphically illustrating to me the fact that my adoption had left a core wound in the development of my sense of self. There was within me an internal core void that I was trying to fill with some rather self-defeating behaviors. I had trouble seeing them because I was inside looking out. I could identify the aftereffects once the relationship was over, but without insight into who I was—my internal sense of self—I would repeat the same pattern over and over again.

## Fix This Family

I was born Peter Nicholas Economou in Burlington, Vermont, in 1957, relinquished for adoption, and placed in foster care for the first year of my life. I was adopted into the Hebbard family in Hartford, Connecticut, and my name was changed to Don William Hebbard. Back in 1958 it was assumed that the personality was a blank slate and that there was no genetic or nature component to a child's development. I was in a great home and presumably receiving excellent nurture, so my life would be good!

Adopted children carry a core attachment wound. Their birth mother has given them up, and the people who were supposed to love them have instead left them. I was not a "good baby," and therefore I was abandoned at the moment in life when a child is most vulnerable—the moment of birth. All of the finest medical care, institutional programs, and adoptive parental love will not replace the severed bond between biological mother and child.

I had a core fear of abandonment. Like many other adoptive kids, I morphed into the kind of child I thought my adoptive parents wanted and, in many ways, submerged the development of my own sense of self. My Greek culture was dismissed as irrelevant, and my natural personality was expected to meld into that of my adoptive family in terms of values, religion, and cohesion with the extended family.

My adoptive mother, a highly volatile woman, could be both adoring and aggressive with the flip of a switch. In my early years I was afraid of her, but as I grew older, I became the only one in the family to stand up to her and challenge her when she attacked people verbally in public or private. She was a bully, and I was expected to fix her, challenge her, and clean up the mess.

To be clear, no one had told me to function in this way; I was not given instructions or a script to follow, but as my adoptive father avoided conflict altogether, and my sister, who was also adopted, ran away from home. I was left with the role of dealing with this explosive woman and doing damage control. So, the coat I put on was that of family hero and fixer.

As Clif and I worked together I began to see that my "template of attraction" drew me to many women who not only had certain physical attributes but also needed a "knight in shining armor" to come in and rescue them from all their problems. I was attracted to the damsel in distress or the girl with the hard luck story I could love back into wholeness. This was a recipe for disaster, but I kept attracting "fixer-upper projects" online like a magnet. It was as if our two magnetic poles would invariably find a connection.

What we know today is that I was simply replaying in my love relationships the patterns I had learned in my family growing up. I had learned to suppress my own needs and take care of everyone else's out of fear of abandonment. I picked partners who would betray me because I had originally been betrayed by my birth parents who had failed to care for me. I picked fixer-upper projects as romantic partners also because this was replaying the dynamics I had unconsciously experienced in my adoptive family with my unpredictable mother.

Clif took off his coat, sat down in his chair, looked me in the eye, and declared, "This is not the ending. This is a new beginning. When you take responsibility to give yourself the things you didn't get growing up, you heal that core wound. Once you do that it's almost like magic. You'll no longer appeal to those fixer-upper projects because you won't be attracting off each other's woundedness. You'll attract a whole different kind of woman." He was right.

## Dr. Cozzolino and Joaquin

Dr. Louis Cozzolino in his excellent book *The Neuroscience of Human Relationships* tells the fascinating case of Joaquin that illustrates the impact of core wounds. In his words,

> Joaquin came to therapy feeling anxious and exhausted. He was 35 years old, with a successful import business that kept him very busy. He talked to me as if he were leading a meeting of shareholders—visionary and expansive, he gave me an intensive sales pitch. He had had a series of relationships that invariably started strong but then faded when he became restless or dissatisfied. Despite his bravado and apparent mastery of business, Joaquin was quite fearful. He feared falling into poverty, having to return home a failure, and

was very afraid of taking risks. He hoarded his money, kept his home orderly and neat, and had difficulty dealing with strong emotions, both his own and other people's. He labeled all of his past girlfriends as "hysterical" because they expressed feelings that were "out of control."

As we got to know each other, I reflected to Joaquin the paradox between his big personality and his fearfulness. "Who, me?" was his first response, but over time he discovered, with amazement, that he was fearful. Not only was he afraid in a number of business situations, but despite his social sophistication, he had anxiety about interacting with other people. "How did this happen to me?" Joaquin boomed. "That is a good question!" I responded. I suggested that an answer may come from his early life and encouraged him to tell me what he remembered about his childhood.

Joaquin recalled a good childhood; his family had emigrated from Eastern Europe before he was born and he had grown up with his parents, grandparents, and a number of aunts and uncles. No one in his family talked much about their experiences before coming to America, but they lived a comfortable life and he remembers always being surrounded by family and friends. There was no deprivation, trauma, or abandonment that he could recall, and, despite occasional arguments between members of his family, relationships were maintained and disagreements eventually resolved. "What am I so afraid of?" Joaquin wondered. I suggested to him that his fears may not be based in his own experiences but be something he may have learned from his family. "But they've never talked about anything frightening," he replied. "Well," I answered, "maybe you should spend some time with them and get them to talk about what their lives were like before you were born."

At our next session, Joaquin burst through the door carrying a pile of notes. He sat down at the edge of his chair and leaned toward me, eager to share his discoveries. "You're not going to believe this," he said. Joaquin had found out that there had been political oppression, brutal secret police and torture in his family's past. His mother's younger brother had been shot and killed while they were walking down the street one quiet afternoon and her father had been ripped out of his bed in the night never to be seen again. For years, the family had tried to find him without success. They knew that if they stayed in the country, they would eventually all be killed, so they made a family decision to escape and seek refuge elsewhere.

Selling everything they owned, they were smuggled out of their country and made their way to the United States, where relatives helped to set them up in business. Joaquin was born a year later. For all his life, Joaquin's family kept an unspoken agreement not to share their suffering with him. They wanted to protect him from their pain, and, perhaps, renew their own lives through his innocence. Although at first family members were hesitant to talk with him about their history, once they started talking the stories began to roll out in a stream of gestures, shouts and tears. Their discussion went late into the night, ending with exhausted hugs and everyone lying awaked in their beds, replaying the words and images they had exhumed after so many years.

In the months to come, Joaquin and I gradually made connections between his family's history and his own life. While these stories had never been shared in words while he was growing up, he had learned about his family's history through gestures, eye contact and facial expressions. He recalled how his mother held him close when they walked down the street and the frightened look in her eyes when he strayed too far from her side. His family spent as little money as possible and hoarded what they had as if always preparing to take flight. They avoided making new friends and lived as an island unto themselves, immunizing themselves from the risk of betrayal. Although Joaquin never understood any of these actions in the context in which they occurred, he experienced the emotions within the context of his life. As he looked into his mother's eyes to determine whether the world was safe or dangerous, her expression told him to be afraid—despite the fact they were at an amusement park or on their way to school.

## Examples of Core Wounds

At this point you may be saying, "That's all fine and good, but I was not adopted and my family did not immigrate to America after being tortured in some foreign country. What does all this have to do with dating?"

That's a fair question. Not everyone who enters extended adulthood is going to carry core wounds that will affect with whom and how they fall in love. However, many of my clients hit middle age and recognize that life has kicked them around some. They carry scars from the wars of life and former relationships, and the old "pull myself up by my bootstraps" mentality just isn't working any longer.

Some of the issues that emerge from a wounded core sense of self may include

- Trauma—physical, emotional, psychological, or spiritual
- Abuse
- Neglect
- Exposure to psychopathology
- Exposure to addictions
- Excessive control mechanisms
- Exposure to criticism and judgmentalism
- Profound loss of a key person
- Exposure to a boundary violator
- Betrayal by a spouse
- Exposure to a toxic family, institution, or work environment
- Exposure to a sexual predator or sexual misconduct
- Religious abuse or religious toxicity

## Failed Attempts to Fill the Hole

People use a wide range of self-defeating patterns to fill that internal hole formed by a core wound. Julie, my client, was moving from one disappointing dating relationship to another. She was picking out the same guy each time, though just in a different suit. Joaquin was dismissing his matches as being "too emotional" and "pushing him for a commitment" so he could run to his work as soon as the relationship turned serious. There are many approaches people use to unconsciously fill an internal void, including:

### Achievement

"The more mountains I climb and the greater the accolades I receive, the more chance I have to feel significant."

### Rebellion

"I'll fight against any institution, any rule, or any authority put into my life to prove that I cannot be controlled—therefore exerting my own sense of power."

### Self-Sabotage

About the time a person achieves their goal, finds a good partner to date, or eliminates a long-standing problem, they do something to blow up the relationship and have to start all over from scratch.

### Addictions

Many use drugs, sex, alcohol, or gambling as a way to fill that void within that is too painful for them to face.

### Power/Control

Many of my bossy/bullying clients who are specialists at telling everyone else in the world what to do are themselves some of the most insecure people I know. Their need to control originates from a core sense of being out of control or of never having felt seen in their family growing up.

### Self-Sacrifice

"Maybe if I give you enough, at some point you'll come back and give me the things I need to make me whole." Reciprocity is good in a relationship, but sacrificing oneself at the altar of another is not!

### Overinvestment

Overinvestment in one's children, sports, politics, church, or hobby may be a sign that we are finding our identity in someone else or something else. Our true sense of identity can only be found internally by being true to who we are and what we believe.

### Rugged Independence

Some wounded individuals take a "me against the world" attitude: "I don't need anyone or anything. I can manage my own life alone without any help, and the rest of you are all weak because you need each other to lean on."

### Clingy Dependence

The opposite of the rugged, independent style is the clingy, dependent dater who abandons their own identity, tastes, friends, and interests with every new love that comes along. Their security is tied to being accepted by someone—by anyone who will have them.

## A Two Gets a Ten

I tell my interns that there are some clues when I tripwire a core wound with a client. An issue that should evoke a rather calm or mild response brings forth a high-powered reaction. The response may be anger or sadness. The client may get very quiet and begin to cry. In other words, a number two stimulus evokes a number ten response. This is a clue that there is more buried inside that needs to be explored.

As I visited with Julie, I asked her what it was like taking over the business from her successful, powerful father. She had come from a sales background, and I asked her about her adjustment to having to learn the financial side of the house. Julie, who was normally quite talkative, became guarded and quickly changed the subject. I filed that away and a few sessions later asked about it again.

When we broached the topic of the finances that second time, Julie confessed to having been surprised one day when she was reviewing the books. There was an ongoing entry for the Mesa Account. When she investigated, she found that there were no venders, customers, or even employees by that name. When she pressed the CFO, a longtime employee, she learned that Mesa was the resort to which her father had taken his mistress for years when he had been alive and running the company.

Julie had been raised by a serial philanderer and, on further discussion, admitted to having met the woman at company functions. Her mother had been aware of this affair and others but had chosen to look the other way. Julie was unconsciously playing out the dynamics of her relationship wounds with her dad in her own adult romances. She was comfortable putting on a coat with one sleeve in the presence of men who were dishonest with her.

### Clues of a Possible Core Wound

- The issue is strongly denied and reactions are out of proportion.
- The issue is probably of long-term duration.
- The issue is probably pervasive—it has a powerful silent impact.
- The issue is significantly defended.
- The issue may never have been talked about or explored.

Julie decided not to recycle and repeat the past. She took some time to explore herself, her family of origin, and especially her relationship with her father. She began to offer herself some of the honesty and authenticity she had never received from her family growing up. In time the wound healed, and as she reentered the dating world, she discovered that she was no longer attracting the same sorts of men. It was as if the magnetic poles between the north and south had been shut down permanently. In the next chapter we will explore the path many people take that denies the wound and moves forward without a healing process.

# CHAPTER 7

# I'LL KEEP MY SWAMP

I met Claire online, and we hit it off immediately and began dating. She was a nurse in the recovery room of a local hospital that allowed her, in her words, "to interact with fewer people. I prefer them asleep." She was athletic, petite, and reserved and declared herself to be attracted to "hunky Harley Davidson guys I can ride on the back of their bikes with on the weekends." I was not sure why she had reached out to me, a lean marathon runner and drummer, but I was definitely interested in her, and she obviously was in me.

Claire was quiet about her past. She was quiet about many things, such as how many times she'd been married, where she had lived, and what her upbringing had been like. My polite questions, not intended to pry, were met with rather vague, rehearsed answers that seemed to hide a past she'd rather leave behind. I respected that and gave her the space she wanted.

Claire let me know in no uncertain terms that her top priority in life was to support the ministry of the televangelist and healing ministry of the church of which she was a member. She had moved to this part of the country to be close to his church and believed everything he said to be "gospel truth." I respected her boundaries and faith and even attended with her several times, though she resented attending my church with me, complaining that it detracted from her attendance at her own church.

Claire had a strong need for affection and loved to hold hands and sit together while watching a movie at home. She had a strong sex drive and found herself drawn to a healthy sex life in a committed relationship, although she would afterward experience a sense of guilt and remorse, feeling that the sexual intimacy had violated her religious beliefs. Her behavior could range from being cool and aloof to being very compliant and rule-following and then all the way to highly seductive, all within a short period of time. Every day was a new day with Claire, and as I came to know her better, I was never sure which woman I was going to encounter.

She suffered from a wide range of physical ailments that seemed to appear out of nowhere. She would be sick in bed with a migraine or complain of phantom body aches or rashes and experience periods of itching during which she felt compelled to wash everything in the house. Test after test revealed little, and her doctors were perplexed. She would turn to her pastor and attend a healing service, confident that it would resolve her physical ailments. It never did.

We had been out shopping for Christmas decorations one Saturday and were sitting around drinking coffee afterward when the conversation turned to our Christmases growing up. She began sharing more of her life story. Her memories of growing up in a home with a father who had sexually abused her as a young girl came flowing out. This was followed up by stories of abuse, and even rape, at the hands of husbands and boyfriends. The memories flowed out of her as the walls momentarily came down. I listened and tried to be as supportive as I could. I understood that I was hearing a history that was not often, if ever, told.

Sometime later, after she had missed work for a long time due to another round of migraines and unexplained body aches, I asked her if she had ever talked with a therapist about the things she had been through in her life. "I don't need to talk to a therapist; my pastor says all I need to do is have faith and pray."

I suggested, "Perhaps faith without works is dead. Maybe there are some things you could do to help in addition to prayer. I know some folks who work on issues like the ones you've faced. Let me know if you ever want to talk to one of them."

Weeks went by, during which Claire was characteristically quiet and reserved. Her health was getting no better. One day she ventured, "Could you make an appointment for me with the person you recommended? I'd like you to go with me." A short time later I found myself in the waiting room of a female psychotherapist who specialized in trauma work. She was experienced, soft spoken, and kind, and I thought she and Claire would really connect.

The session ended, and I drove Claire home. She didn't have much to say but looked tired. When I asked later if she were going to make a follow-up appointment, she said no. I began seeing less of her, and the phone calls and texts became few and far between. A few weeks later she informed me that she was breaking off our relationship. I wasn't the kind of guy she was looking for in a relationship, and she coolly ended it, once again retreating back inside her shell. I never saw her again.

## Tough Girl, Good Girl, Seductive Girl

Claire, like many women and men who are victims of sexual abuse, finds the results of that abuse to be affecting her adult romantic relationships. A person who has experienced abuse has learned early on that the very individual who is supposed to protect you, a parent or other adult, becomes the abuser. The impact of this recognition on the development of the sense of self is deep and profound, and in my experience most men and women in this situation would, like Claire, rather soldier on and keep it all dammed up inside than risk opening up that wound and following a path of healing.

McClarin noted in her work on female survivors of sexual abuse that they sometimes develop one of three different personalities to mask the pain. The "Tough Girl" person is cool, aloof, and capable of taking care of herself. She doesn't need anyone or anything. If she is in a relationship, she is either going to be in charge or will at least let her partner know that she is not that emotionally attached. When she wants attention, you had better show up, and when she wants to be left alone, you'd be wise to steer clear. She has a real disdain for men who are "needy" and seem to want too much of her time and effort. *Why can't everyone be more self-sufficient like I am?* she asks herself in disgust.

Claire was partially a "Tough Girl." She worked in a hospital but in a setting where her patients were asleep much of the time and could make few demands on her. When I met her daughters, they shared stories of their mom coming home from work, walking into her bedroom, shutting the door, and staying there all evening. Her own daughters were not sure she liked them, but any attempt to broach the subject in conversation with Claire was met with a shocked look and a quick dismissal.

The "Good Girl" manages her core wound of abuse by trying to be compliant, rule-keeping, and respectable. She is going to do what she is told, accept authority, and not question what she's told to do. Once again, there was a piece of Claire's personality that fit this mold very well. She had substituted her abusive father with a televangelist-healing pastor who promised her a quick fix to all her problems if she would just pray hard enough and keep sending him large portions of her income.

The "Seductive Girl" manages her sexual trauma by telegraphing her sexuality and turning into a party girl sending seductive signals to every guy in the room. Claire could not understand why the neighborhood men flirted with her when she jogged in skin-tight running gear showing off her curvy body. The only argument Claire and I had was over her continual contact with an ex-boyfriend at the gym. When I asked if she had ever told him we were dating, she looked at me with a shocked expression and asked, "Why would I need to tell him that?" Many sexual abuse survivors are either unaware of the sexuality they exude or just don't care. In either case this behavior makes forming a sustainable relationship with them very difficult.

Claire had formed a protective barrier over her wound that was a combination of the Tough Girl, Good Girl, and Seductive Girl approaches. The constant shifting in her personality from one to another, while confusing to me, was a perfect defense mechanism for her to avoid the pain of dealing with her internal core wound. In the end it was easier for her to blame others and walk away than to do the hard work of her own healing.

When I began working on my own core healing, I recognized that it would take time, patience, and the use of some important tools to help me along the way. I've had the honor of walking along this journey with a wide range of clients who have chosen to embrace a path of healing and come out changed from the inside out. Let's explore the path of healing and some of the tools you might find helpful on your journey.

## Nine Steps of Core Healing

As I mentioned earlier, my core wound started when I was given up for adoption at birth and placed in foster care for my first year of life. The normal bonds of security and attachment were not present, and the wounds went back to preverbal stages of my life. Those wounds, I realize now, were about as deep as one can experience. My role in my adoptive family was that of hero and fixer, trying to manage rather unsuccessfully a highly volatile adoptive mother and to seek approval through high levels of achievement. Those deeply ingrained patterns walked out in my template of attraction.

Now that I was dating in middle age, I seemed to be attracting fixer-upper projects, women who wanted a "come close and get away" relationship, and I found myself codependently over-sacrificing in love relationships. I was picking matches who would abandon the relationship, just as I had experienced in my childhood. The pattern had worn me out, and I was committed to working on myself to heal this inner wound. This would require a long journey of self-discovery that would include nine steps.

### Step One: Insight

I am a classic rock drummer. I learned to play in the 1960s, back when you dropped a vinyl record on the turntable and held your ear to the speaker to try to pick out the drum part on a recording. We didn't have any way of seeing the drummer but could only listen to the music. I loved the live version of Bob Seger's song "Hollywood Nights." The hi-hat and snare groove was amazing and drove the song to an amazing climax. However, I never could quite match the groove. It was too hard—I didn't have the chops. Then I saw him in concert with the Silver Bullet Band, and he was using two drummers on the song. I had been trying to do with one drum set what he was getting out of two drummers. I needed this new insight to make sense of the problem I was having in playing the song.

Insight is powerful when it comes to change. We have to see it first before we can change it. By middle age many of us have replayed many times the pattern our core wound has produced. Most of us have had conversations with people who care about us trying to point out an issue we might want to take a look at. Many of my clients, like Claire in talking about her past, have well-rehearsed scripts to avoid the painful discussions they don't want to get into. Extended adulthood is a time when men and women finally say, "I've ridden this ride long enough. I think it's time to do something different."

Insight is like waking up out of a dream. When I'm driving down the highway I can get lost in my thoughts, only to be startled back to reality as a large truck goes screaming past me in the left-hand lane. I was in a trance and hadn't seen him coming. Insight is like installing a rearview mirror and lane alert alarms on our car. With these aids I can see the truck miles before it reaches me, and I get an alert on my dashboard if I start to move into its path. Insight is that powerful moment when people become aware of what they've been doing repeatedly to detonate their own lives and realize that they can choose to do something different.

### Step Two: Will

My major professor in my marriage and family master's program was a famous pioneer in the field, Dr. Paul Faulkner. We asked him in class one day, "Dr. Faulkner, what is the most important key to a person changing?" Without a moment's hesitation he replied, "It's the will. They make up their mind they are going to do something different, and they do it." Dr. Faulkner was right.

My colleague at Restoration Counseling in Ft. Worth, Dr. Lee Long, introduced me to a new term he called "pre-therapy." Pre-therapy happens when folks come in and sniff around therapy but don't really sit down and eat the meal. They come in for a few sessions, listen to what the therapist has to say without really engaging, and then drop out a few sessions later. Then they tell all their friends they went to Restoration for counseling and report, "That psychology stuff just doesn't work for me." No, . . . you didn't do the work.

Contrast that to the person who decides, "I'm not doing this anymore." They've made up their mind that, whatever it takes, they will not allow the future to be a repeat of the past. They show up in my office with notebook and pen in hand, armed with a list of questions they want to ask and a determined look in their eye. "I've been through this, and it's not happening to me again," they declare. "I don't know what it is I'm doing, but whatever it is, I'm going to stop. Is that clear, Dr. Don?" Yeah, I got you. What they don't know is that the biggest battle has already been won. They have elicited the power of the will.

### Step Three: A Team of Wise Men and Women

I was fortunate over a period of years to be surrounded by a team of professionals who offered me outstanding psychotherapy and support. I sought both individual therapy and group therapy to work on my issues of attachment and codependency. I learned as much as I could about adoption and attachment and even found my birth family. I worked with family systems therapists to explore my role in my adoptive family growing up and looked at the impacts of sexual abuse and borderline personality disorder on a family system. I had been impacted by a complex dynamic, and there was a lot to unpack.

I was blessed to work with a team of wise men and women whom I allowed to speak into my life at various stages in the process. Dr. Clif Davis, a pioneering psychologist in Dallas, had known me since my college days, and I went to him for divorce adjustment therapy and to help me begin to think about the assumptions I had about my relationships with women. Clif was profoundly helpful in providing some of those initial "aha!" moments that got the ball rolling.

I met Dr. James Cail as a college student when I as nineteen, and he has become a lifelong friend and mentor and even a father figure. No one else has impacted my thinking or career more than James Cail. He has had a fifty-yard-line seat at every major event of my life, and my regular phone calls with him became a staple in my new dating life. James would shoot straight with me and call me out on my stuff when I needed it.

Dr. Margaret Pinder, a colleague and close friend at Amberton University, where I teach, is past president of the Texas Association of Marriage and Family Therapy. I encounter people who declare Dr. Pinder to be the finest classroom professor they ever had in college. Margaret became my designated "date coach," and I recommend that everyone involved in dating have a member of the opposite sex in that role.

Dr. Maureen Lumley, a Jungian analysist and marriage and family therapist in Dallas, did the deep, careful work of walking me into the wounds of my childhood. Her skills at depth psychology are unmatched, and she blended healthy doses of support with gentle confrontation to help me heal from my past. She wisely recommended EMDR (eye movement desensitization reprocessing) as a way to heal my preverbal trauma.

My team was large and multidisciplinary and extended their help to me over a period of years. I'm not advocating that for everyone, but my case was complex and started early in life. Nor did the healing occur in one continuous flow. My issues came to the fore when they were ready to be worked on. If you want to pursue healing a core wound, it will in my experience require some outside help to do so. It is very difficult to gain the perspective to identify the patterns we are in while we are enacting them. Having a trained set of outside eyes allows the process to go more quickly and be more effective.

### Step Four: A Plan

Any good builder who is going to construct a house starts out with a blueprint that shows him how to frame it up. As with a musician playing a piece of music, the sheet music and the charts show us how to transition from verse to chorus. When we address a core wound, there needs to be a treatment plan.

When I sit down with my clients for the first time, I share with them a little about how therapy goes, and then I ask them to share their story with me. "What brought you here today, and what are you concerned about?" Then I shut up and listen. At some point they will finish, and I'll have all this new information laid out in front of me. Then I'll ask a simple question: "If your life were a car and I were a mechanic at your repair shop, what would you tell me needed to be fixed first?"

I'm in the preliminary steps of trying to build a treatment plan with them that will address the key areas they are struggling with. They will specify some issues for me to put on the list, and I may add some things I've heard them talk about. Together we come to an agreement on where we want our sessions to go. Then we talk a little bit about the time factor. Whether this will take six weeks or six months depends on the issues to be confronted. In my case dealing with issues of attachment, I was going to need to reparent myself, which would take some time to accomplish.

### Step Five: Resources

Looking back on my own healing journey, I used a wide range of resources, from therapy sessions and reading assignments to EMDR and trips to meet biological family members with whom I had arranged a reunion. Not everyone will require or use all of the tools I did, but we are fortunate today to have a vast array of healing tools and techniques at our disposal. These include

- Individual therapy
- Group therapy
- Homework
- Reading books and articles
- Podcasts
- Journaling
- Attending seminars
- Retreats
- Body work
- Relationships with others on a similar journey of healing
- Time-outs from commitments and dating

- Genograms
- New problem-solving strategies
- Communications, conflict resolution, and assertiveness training
- Contracting with key individuals
- New activity scheduling

### Step Six: *Risking New Thinking*

One of the great lessons I learned in therapy was, "I don't have to believe everything I think." Dr. Frank Dattilio, in his book *Cognitive Behavioral Therapy with Couples and Families*, introduces the concept of the English word *schema* (Greek *scheen*), meaning "to have" or "to shape." Webster defines the term as "an organized way of perceiving and responding to a complex situation." Aaron Beck wrote, "Schemas are central to a person's thoughts and perceptions and have an integral influence on emotions and behavior. In essence, schemas are a template for an individual's life experiences as well as how he or she processes information." The schemas I learned as a child in my family system played a powerful role in shaping who I am today and how I approach love relationships.

I had two "mother schemas" as a child. My biological mother schema was one of abandonment and betrayal. I had been given up at birth, and the unconscious messaging in that schema was that I hadn't been a good enough baby to be kept, along with the expectation that people who love me will leave me. That schema was a profoundly disempowering force that was completely invisible to me prior to my therapy.

The second "mother schema" was that of the unstable adoptive mother. As a child I would find myself in a department store, and if the clerk did or said something my mother didn't like she would relish the opportunity to publicly humiliate the poor lady and cause a scene in the store. Restaurant or shopping center visits and school events were preloaded with the threat that she might go off and lose her temper. As a young boy I was terrified of these rants, and as I grew older, I would apologize and try to smooth things over. Then, as I gained my own personal strength as a teenager, I became the one in the family to confront her and tell her to back off. My complex schema of love was wrapped in messages of abandonment, betrayal, and the accountability to fix a loved one, all while achieving highly in order to make the family proud. This was a recipe for exhaustion.

As I began dating again in middle age, I discovered that I was attracted to and attracting women who were a blend of these two familiar mother schemas. I was shopping with my daughter at a department store in Oklahoma City, and the sales woman and I began to chat as my daughter was trying on outfits. I asked for her phone number, and a few nights later we went out for dinner.

Over the weeks I learned that she had moved to town to recover from a bad relationship in Atlanta. She had very little money and was crashing on a girlfriend's couch. She didn't even own a bed. My codependent schema of "hero and fixer" kicked into high gear, and I had a mattress and frame delivered to her friend's house. A short time later I learned that she was back in Atlanta with the old boyfriend and that my bed had gone with her. My old pattern of fixer, rescuer, and hero was working just fine.

I would like to say that the playing out of that schema ended with the bed purchase. It did not. I continued to play the hero-fixer role until one day in therapy Dr. Lumley gently laid out the pattern on the table and asked me to take a look at what I was doing in relationships. I had been focused on what the woman was doing.

The good news was that, once we had identified my pattern, I began to see it playing out. I was out of the fog. I had a rearview mirror and could see that monstrous eighteen-wheeler hurtling toward me. It took time to change. Sometimes I would be in the middle of a date and recognize the fixer-hero dynamic at play. But my response time grew quicker, and the more I healed the less attraction there was between me and store clerks who needed bedroom furniture.

### Step Seven: Choosing New Behaviors

It was one of those weeks. I was in group therapy complaining about life. My counseling students were lazy and didn't want to do the work. Three of my clients had been no shows that week without explanation. My adoptive mother made another fake trip to the ER to get checked into the hospital so she could get some more good drugs. And my dog Dutch bit the repair guy in the leg. *The last one was completely understandable: the guy was a jerk!*

Mike, a rough-around-the-edges truck driver and veteran of the group, was known to shoot straight with us. He looked at me and offered some of the best therapeutic advice I've heard: "Don, man, you need to leave it the f—— alone."

Mike understood right where I was living. He recognized that core wound. Give me a problem, I was going to find a solution. Point out a mountain, I was going to climb it. Present me with an under-functioning student, client, or even companion, and I could inspire them into adulthood and responsibility. My automatic hero / fix it schema jumped into play so quickly and naturally that I was not even aware I was on autopilot.

Mike continued, "Hey, man, what if you just took a day and did nothing? I mean, when the alarm bell goes off what would happen if you just took twenty-four hours to decide whether you were going to do anything? Would the world end?" *Well, yes! I'm supposed to be Superman leaping tall buildings, right?*

I remembered something Dr. Dan Mitchell, my clinical supervisor in marriage and family therapy, had taught me when I was starting out in counseling. He called it "administrative neglect." Dan said, "There are times when a friend or family member will call, and they are all worked up about something. If we engage then, we will be tied up for hours. If we leave it alone the storm may pass, and they'll figure it out on their own."

A part of my core healing began as I started using some new phrases. "Let me think about that" became my automatic response to requests for time, effort, and commitment—and became my new best friend. It wasn't a flat *no*. It was a safe place for me to retreat from the conversation in order to listen to my gut telling me if this was something I was interested in pursuing. The rewiring of old schemas was leading to some small but significant new actions. Back in group, Mike's comment was, "Yeah, that's what I told you to do!"

### Step Eight: Risking New Emotions

Deep down, Claire knew she was running away from her past instead of dealing with it. In her heart she knew her daughters were right. She had not been emotionally available to them. Her Tough Girl style had done damage to the people she loved and who were trying to love her. However, there was a core fear surrounding that wound: *What would happen if I ever let the manhole cover off all those emotions? What if I do go back and unlock the secrets behind all that past pain? Will I be able to manage the flood of feelings that come out?* Most people don't want to risk it. It's easier to power on in the current unproductive patterns and pray that the preacher will come up with a new sermon to exorcise the pain without my having to do any of the authentic work myself.

I understood that fear very well. As I spoke with Dr. Lumley about the attachment therapy we were going to do together, I shared with her that the manhole cover had been screwed down pretty tightly. I wasn't sure what to expect if I were to start messing around with the memories of my past. She assured me that my emotions were benevolent, that they would come up only when I was ready to deal with them. Not only that, but I might experience them as a positive force in my healing process. I was skeptical at first, but the farther we went in my core work the more powerful and productive those emotions became. I came to the point of connection with my full emotional life, not just the parts tied to anger, resentment, and fatigue.

Dr. Sue Johnson in her book *The Process of Emotionally Focused Couples Therapy* notes that there are six primary emotions:

- Anger
- Hurt and sadness
- Surprise and excitement
- Disgust and shame
- Fear, freeze, and fight-or-flight responses
- Joy

My work became to move out of my head and into my emotions. I am an academic. My "go to" response in analysis, and I can think and reason my way out of almost anything. I can find a model, construct a paradigm, and explain away my problems. But my journey of healing led me to ownership of all of my emotions—including excitement, fear, and hurt—representing the full narrative of the life I had lived. Much to my surprise, I discovered that my emotional life was as rewarding as, and much more playful than, my rational life.

### Step Nine: Small Steps

My father-in-law was a Colonel in the Air Force in the Strategic Air Command and a navigator on B-52s during Viet Nam and the Cold War. He would spend long hours telling me stories of nuclear missions designed to bomb Russia flying over the polar cap. They would take off from a base in the heartland and climb to altitude, and then the radio operator would receive orders with the coordinates for the bombing run deep into Russia. It would be a military installation, an industrial complex, or a nuclear arms facility. If they survived the mission, he would plot a landing site somewhere in a friendly Mediterranean country.

They had no onboard computers at that time. No punching in the co-ordinates and the computer spitting out the navigational path with auto-pilot doing the rest. He had maps, a pencil, and a slide rule. The rest was up to him and his highly skilled navigational abilities. He asked me once, "Don, do you know what the hardest thing was about my job?" I had no idea. "It was one degree."

I looked at him, totally confused. "It was one degree. You see, if I were off one degree in my calculations going over Omaha in the US, I would be off six hundred miles by the time we got to Minsk." One small deviation from course could have made a huge difference in the final destination.

That one conversation changed the way I went about doing therapy and the way I pursued change. I stopped going for the big-ticket changes with my clients and started instead looking for the small, incremental changes. The ones that could be accomplished simply and consistently over an extended period of time. Those small corrections would eventually move someone through a larger change and would build their confidence and commitment to the process. If Claire had been willing to go back for just that second session of therapy, she might have started the change process rolling that could have altered the course of her life. For any of us, once we see ourselves making that first small step, the next one becomes easier. We build our own momentum.

I discovered, both in myself and with my clients, that minor steps hold the key to life-changing success. I could start with changing the way I thought, the way I felt, or the way I was acting. Any of those starting places would work because, once I had changed one of the three, the other two would follow closely behind. It became clear to me that we as humans are not wired up to be or to stay wounded. We are wired to heal

In Stage Three, to follow, we will make a plan to date in extended adulthood, in the process looking at some key questions. What are the big questions that need to be answered during dating? Why am I attracted to the people I'm attracted to? How do I successfully date online if I've never done it before or have had a bad experience in the past? What do the dating experts advise about dating at this time of life? These are some of the questions we will help you address as you develop a dating strategy.

# A STRATEGY FOR DATING

# CHAPTER 8

# THE REVOLUTION IN DATING

Maria and I met online, and after texting and talking we felt there was a connection and that it would be worth meeting. She suggested a public park with a lake for a first meeting. I thought this somewhat odd because the park, though in a North Dallas suburb, was in an isolated location. Most people on first dates opt to meet in a public place where lots of people offer some degree of security. Maria assured me this more remote location would please her, so I agreed to the date a few days later.

We met at the park, and she suggested we take the walking path around the small lake. She led the way at a brisk pace, with me trying to keep up and carry on my side of the conversation. For some reason she seemed to be in a hurry. I also noticed that she kept scanning the lake and parking lot as though looking for someone to arrive. I thought that perhaps I hadn't made a good first impression and that she was anxious to get this date over with, so I was surprised when she stated that it had been great meeting me and suggested that we meet again, "perhaps for dinner, where we can visit longer." We agreed to dinner a few nights later.

We met at a well-known steak house, and Maria had already selected a booth at the back of the dining room facing the front door. Being the father of cops, I've learned to sit facing the door. The dinner was going quite well. She shared that she had grown up in Mexico but had moved to the United States when her husband's business had "expanded and we needed a presence here in America." Once again, she seemed distracted.

She rarely maintained eye contact and continually scanned the room—again, as if looking for someone else to arrive. She was obviously nervous, but I attributed this to second date jitters.

During dessert and coffee two well-dressed Hispanic men entered the foyer of the restaurant and scanned the room. She stiffened and went silent, watching them as they left. I couldn't contain my curiosity any longer and asked, "Is everything all right?" At this point she shared her story.

"Look, I'm recently divorced. I've gone online to start dating and try to start my life over again. The problem is my ex-husband. He's in a federal penitentiary for drug smuggling. We were part of a large drug family, and he still considers himself married to me—he doesn't recognize the divorce. He thinks I'm still his wife."

Suddenly all the anxious looks made sense. The meeting in an isolated place had been her plan for protection. The selection of the booth from which to watch the door and her fear when she spotted two Latin businessmen all made sense. Maria was embarking on a new chapter of her life and carrying some enormous baggage she could never have anticipated when she was twenty years old.

While Maria's case is not the norm, it does illustrate that adults in middle age come with a very different set of dynamics and questions about dating than in their younger years. They are not concerned with buying a first home, how many children they want to have, or the other typical questions young couples bring to a first marriage. The questions tend to be deeper and more profound. What kind of character does this person have? Do we share a similar worldview, given our life experiences? How can I know if the person online is really who they're presenting themselves to be? What if there are "big issues," like bankruptcy, addictions, or personality disorders? Do they lead a healthy lifestyle, or am I signing up to be a nurse's aide?

Researchers now tell us that since 2005, over a third of marriages in the US happened after meeting online (Cacioppo, Cacioppo, Gonzago, Ogburn and Vander Weele, 2013, Proceedings of the National Academy of Sciences). In this section we will look at some of the best advice dating coaches give to mature adults looking for love. We will explore a plan for dating with a special emphasis on the current revolution based on online dating. Online dating, more than any other one factor in two thousand years, has changed the nature of mate selection. We will look at some models that explain why we are drawn to the people we find attractive and why that sometimes works but at other times gets us into trouble. First, in this chapter we will explore the nine big questions people ask as they begin to date in extended adulthood.

## Question One: Is This a Person of Character?

"Indebted, addicted, or incarcerated!" That was the synopsis of the dating pool of men over the age of fifty-one marriage therapist described in a joking way. He was saying that you'd better get to know someone really well in order to tell what kind of character they possess before getting into a serious relationship with them.

Character is about who I am as a person. What are my values and beliefs? How do those values and beliefs walk out in the things I say and do? When my values and beliefs are congruent with what I say and do, my would-be partner can build trust in me and in the relationship.

It is easy to mask character for a while, and this is one of the great dangers in moving too quickly in a relationship. People talk a good game and can present a convincing image. They can come on strong and appear to be a prize catch. Potential matches wonder, *How did this guy get away?*

But let some time go by. Slow down the process. I tell my couples in premarital counseling that they'll want to get to know someone for four seasons before getting serious. That allows them to see the person in a wide variety of circumstances. The true character of an individual will come out. For clients in extended adulthood I lengthen the timetable, advising them to date for two years. The reason is simple: I've seen too many second or third marriages end quickly because couples were in a rush and one person was sold a bill of goods on the basic character of their new partner. Some clues to watch for:

- How do they treat service personnel and wait staff at a restaurant?
- Do you find them telling small lies and then explaining them away?
- Do the things they say align with the things they do?
- What does their employment history say about them?
- How do their children speak of them, and what is their relationship like?

## Question Two: Do They Like Men [Women]?

I was getting ready to date for the first time following my divorce and was talking to my mentor and close friend Dr. James Cail. His first piece of advice really shocked me: "You need to find a woman who likes men . . . and likes the kind of man you are." I was taken back. "Do you mean to suggest that there are men and women out there dating who really don't like the opposite sex?" "Absolutely!" was Dr. Cail's assertion.

I have spent my life counseling, and the majority of my clients have been women because they are more likely to seek out a marriage and family therapist. I like women. I like the way they think. I have always found it easy to connect with women and find their lives to be interesting and complex. I enjoy the differences between the two sexes and have seen that dimension add real value and adventure to a loving relationship. Men and women bring very different but equally important gifts to marriage.

Online dating promotes the "Get into my box" phenomenon. Too many men and women want their date to fit into their little box of acceptable reality so they can check off all the items on their "must-have" list. "I'm looking for the perfect match who meets all of my criteria; otherwise, I'm not interested," they telegraph. Rather than getting to know a match holistically and being curious about the things that make them uniquely themselves, social media has created an environment of date shoppers who throw people back into the pond when they do not fit their little box of reality.

I've discovered that sometimes the "man haters" and "women haters" create such impossible lists of characteristics as must-haves in a potential partner that no one would be able to meet their expectations. They then use the repeated failure of dates to underscore their belief that "there really aren't any good guys [or women] out there." Perhaps, as I suggested in Section Two, the answer lies closer to home.

## Question Three: Do We Share a Similar Worldview?

Katie was a "satellite date." We met online and enjoyed communicating. She had a quick sense of humor and a cutting edge to her sarcasm. We would meet for dinner, go out a few times, and then not connect for a while, after which we would reconnect, share some laughs, and go out again. We enjoyed each other's company, but the relationship never seemed to gain traction. The problem wasn't chemistry (she was very attractive) or intelligence (she had a highly developed sense of humor). What, then, caused the lack of traction?

The problem was the police. Katie was a staunch advocate of "defunding" the police and was fairly aggressive in pushing her arguments to anyone who would listen. I, on the other hand, am the father of three police officers—my son, my daughter, and my son-in-law all serve. I am a cop dad and take very seriously my role of supporting them, so for me to buy a date dinner at a nice restaurant and then be lectured on how my three children are a societal evil quickly became "a bridge too far." I would not bring Katie around my three children because this would have been offensive to them . . . and despite her intelligence she couldn't grasp this. We didn't share the same basic worldview. And that was fine.

I was dating before the acrimony in politics of the last few years had become so acute. Now profiles that include statements of one's political affiliation or warnings for those who belong to a particular political party wave red flags indicating "need not apply." Politics has become a flashpoint and defining variable in mate selection.

A number of years ago I counseled a marvelous couple who had learned to bridge their political differences for the good of the marriage. He was a highly successful lobbyist for one political party, and she was the chairperson of the opposite party for that state. They viewed the world from different lenses politically but left those wars at the front door. Their marriage was remarkably healthy and built on a solid foundation of love and respect. We need more of that high level maturity in dating today.

Besides occupation and politics, religion can be an area in which one's worldview is tested. We will talk in greater detail about the role of religion and spirituality in the discussion of decision making. For now, it is helpful to recognize that religious differences can fall into one of two categories. The first category is content. What do I believe spiritually, and how does that line up with what you believe? I dated a lovely Jewish woman who took me to temple and introduced me to her faith. Her family was warm and welcoming. For me as a Christian it was a great experience to have my faith journey expanded through meeting her.

The second category of religion is intensity. How often and to what extent do I practice my faith? Two people may be of the same denomination, but one attends church every week and the other only sporadically or on major religious holidays. Their differences are not of content but of intensity. This scenario presents a different set of challenges.

By the time people reach extended adulthood they have formulated a worldview that is a part of the life structure we discussed in the first chapter. The key at this point in life is the relative adaptability of that worldview. Am I open to accommodating the worldview of a partner and let that speak into my life's experience? If so, the next phase of life may hold some exciting new adventures.

## Question Four: Are They Honest?

One of the biggest complaints I hear from my clients and students about online dating is how dishonest people can be. The profiles are often misleading. The pictures, rather than current, are ten years old, so that the person who shows up for the first coffee date looks nothing like the one in the profile. Someone who is engaging online can barely string two sentences together in person. The list goes on and on.

I lead a fairly public life. With a website, YouTube Channel, and published books under my name it's easy for someone to fact check me. Matches would often show up for a first date armed with far more knowledge of me than I had of them. But not everyone leads that kind of open or public life. Some take pains to hide their past and be vague about their history. Indirect answers to clear questions may be a sign of dishonesty.

Online dating opens the door for people who are married to carry on extramarital affairs via fake profiles. Dan's company has him based in his hometown, but he travels to two other major cities monthly to make sales calls. To avoid marital problems at home, Dan created a dating profile in each of those cities and regularly dated other women when he was on the road. When his wife happened onto his work laptop and discovered the scheme, they ended up in my office trying to salvage a marriage that was ending due to issues of dishonesty.

People who are candid and authentic will be able in time to share:

- A full narrative of their marital situation, divorce, or the death of their spouse
- Their employment history
- A narrative of their life growing up and their relationship to their parents
- Their relationship with all their children
- Their health status and any medical concerns

## Question 5: Do They Lead a Healthy Lifestyle?

Connie had been single for ten years following an acrimonious divorce. She obtained her real estate license and built a thriving real estate firm, cashing in on the influx of people moving to the Dallas-Ft. Worth area. Her life was stable, and she decided to date again. Connie was contacted by Charlie, who lived on the East Coast, and while she was not thrilled with the idea of a long-distance relationship, Charlie pursued her with enthusiasm, and she finally decided "Why not?" A year later, following numerous trips by both of them, Connie and Charlie were married. Charlie, retired from having owned his own manufacturing firm, moved to Dallas to allow Connie to continue running her real estate company.

One day Charlie disappeared. He was on his way to Albertson's to buy some groceries and then couldn't find his way home. Three hours later Charlie called Connie from a suburb miles away from their home to report that he was lost. Connie was frantic and soon arrived to lead him home. This strange event for a sixty-six-year-old man was repeated a month later as once again Charlie became lost while driving alone. Within a few months Charlie was forgetting keys and memories of things he had just done and becoming more irritable with Connie.

When they came to me for counseling, I recommended that a battery of tests be run, and it was confirmed Charlie was suffering from dementia. At this point Charlie confessed to having been diagnosed a year before meeting Connie and having been well aware of his diagnosis when he had gone online to date. Charlie's children and brother back East had quietly "co-conspired" to keep the family secret away from Connie. They were more than happy to see him pack up and leave and "let his new wife take care of things."

Connie spent the next two years caring for Charlie, setting him up in long-term care and arranging for the financing. She was fortunate that he had the finances from his manufacturing business to afford excellent care. When she was finished arranging his future, Connie filed for divorce. She told me that she was done with dating forever and returned to resurrect her company that had suffered during her years of caring for Charlie.

When we are young there can be medical issues that are a concern, but they move front and center during the second half of life. The car has more mileage on it, and we have to take it in for more maintenance.

Extended adulthood is a time when the way a person has cared for themselves during the first half of life either pays big dividends or comes back to haunt them.

What is my match's attitude toward medical care? Do they see the doctor regularly? Are they disciplined about taking medications? Do they maintain a healthy diet and exercise regularly? These questions move center stage as we get older. Many clients tell me, "I don't want to sign up to be someone's nurse. I want someone as devoted to being healthy as I am." They are afraid of the same fate that Connie experienced.

One of my red flags in dating had to do with matches who had sworn off doctors and medical treatment and had devised their own treatment protocols for their ailments. They would spend hours Googling the latest treatments for their form of cancer and pursuing their own unique treatments. I respected their decision to do so but didn't want them on my Medical Power of Attorney. I suspect that they assumed a therapist would understand their mentality, but I did not under any circumstance want to trust my own long-term health care to the internet expertise of someone who had barely passed Biology 101 in college but was now a self-appointed expert on pancreatic cancer. Some pertinent questions in this regard:

- Do we share a similar approach to diet?
- Does my match work out and stay in shape?
- Do we share a similar outlook on medical care, prescription medication, etc.?
- What has been their medical history, and have I shared mine?
- Do they have a long-term care policy that covers dementia and Alzheimer's disease?
- Are they healthy enough to travel and pursue the interests I have in the coming years?

## Question Six: Do They Really Want to Date?

*What a strange question!* you say. A person wouldn't be on a dating website if they didn't want to date! Right? Wrong, Olivia—there are plenty of matches out there who have no intention of showing up for an actual date. If they do it will be weeks or months down the road, and you will likely be disappointed and let many other good matches slip by while waiting on them to get into the game.

Online dating has created a safe haven for folks with an insecure attachment style. They are fearful of a real, in person relationship, so they create a relationship online that remains safely at a distance. They can send emails and texts, flirt, exchange pictures, sext, and carry on a virtual relationship without ever meeting. They will continually have "justifiable reasons" why they cannot make that first meeting. If they do ever agree to meet in person, there will be something they find in the new match that triggers their fight-or-flight response, and they will end the communication. The match is left angry, resentful, and confused, kicking themselves over the other matches they let slip by while working on this "relationship" that was really an illusion.

This case illustrates two key principles of dating in extended adulthood that we will explore in more detail in the Survival Guide chapter. First, effective daters keep on fishing. They keep the lines of communication open between themselves and multiple matches. They don't lock in too quickly. They enjoy the process of dating and meeting new people.

The second principle is that it is wise to avoid getting emotionally married too quickly. The goal at this point is to date, not to get married. The people I observe who are successful at online dating enjoy the journey of dating around, and they keep on fishing. You may be surprised who you are attracted to as you leave yourself open to meeting more matches.

One woman described her dating approach as being like a funnel. At the wide end of the funnel were the men she would consider dating or with whom she had exchanged a message. In the middle were men she was actively communicating with but had not yet met. Nothing had happened yet to exclude them from a meeting at some point. Then, at the narrow end of the funnel, there were the guys she had been out with. Her approach to dating was to continuously move possible matches into and out of the funnel based on her realization that there are many reasons someone might fall away from being a potential match—for example, no chemistry, they ghost on you, or they meet someone they are interested in and end the communication.

Online dating is meant to be an introduction, nothing more. If it is to work, I recommend that people get offline quickly and meet in person. It is only in face-to-face dating that we discover who a person really is, if there is a connection, and whether we feel that wonderful chemistry people are looking for in a partner. Some questions to ask yourself:

- Are we moving from emails and texting to plans for meeting in person?
- Do I have a strategy or plan for meeting more than one match rather than putting "all my eggs into one basket"?
- Can I see my immediate goal as dating rather than getting married too quickly?
- Do I tend to lock in emotionally and "get married too fast"?

## Question Seven: Can I Live with Their Baggage?

We were moving from Atlanta, where I'd opened the Genesis Center for Christian Counseling, to my first academic appointment in Oklahoma City, and the movers were packing us up. The veteran dish packer was a rough old chain smoker who had packed fine China and dishes for years. He was in the garage smoking a cigarette during a break when he looked at me and commented, "Doc, you've got more dishes than some restaurants I've packed up!" My generous in-laws had stocked us with a kitchen full of pottery, and now it was his job to pack it up for the move. I came with a lot of "baggage."

Adults in their fifties come with a fuller life narrative than adults in their twenties. We have lived more life. We have raised children. We've held different jobs and lived in towns and cities across the country. We have experienced the bumps and bruises of doing life. We come with a certain amount of baggage, and that is to be expected.

The point is that people who reach the second half of life tend to come with more than their fair share of baggage. My chain-smoking packer was trying to say that to me. His real message was something like, "Doc, you come with more than your fair share of dishes, and this is a lot of work." I should in the first place have shown the estimator my kitchen load of dishes when he came out to do the estimate for the move.

The same principle applies to dating in extended adulthood. If there is an area in life in which I have "a lot of dishes," I at some point need to share that with my potential partner. I am, as I've mentioned, a classic rock drummer, and I come with three massive double-bass drum sets and a garage full of sound equipment. I make a lot of noise! . . . and at some point, early on I need to explain to my date that my home looks like a music store . . . and then let her decide her response.

One of the best first dates I had was with an attorney who met me for drinks at an upscale hotel in Ft. Worth. While there was no chemistry between us, we enjoyed meeting and had a lively conversation because she worked in family law. The thing that impressed me about her was that she was upfront about her children. She had five kids ranging in age from elementary school through high school. She put it right out there, and I appreciated that, while I do *not* consider children "baggage," she was being open about her life situation. "Life with me would be very busy," she offered, "but I have help and strategies to manage it all. We would not be just parents, though—I'm looking for someone to build a marriage with."

Some of the most remarkable people I've met dating at this stage of life have complex and challenging life narratives. It's not so much the absence of baggage as it is the way in which they have managed their "stuff" that I find impressive. What we must guard against is the tendency to get hooked into relationships in which we're tempted to take on someone else's baggage and rescue them or fix their situation. In my own experience, I have found it all too easy to move from one such exhausting relationship to another.

Writing to the church at Galatia, the apostle Paul in the Bible makes two seemingly contradictory statements in the same paragraph: "Carry each other's burdens" (Galatians 6:2) and "Each one should carry their own load" (v. 5). Which one is it, Paul? Am I expected to bear my brother's burden or to carry my own load?

Paul was referring to ancient customs when traveling. Each man on a journey carried his own day pack slung over his shoulder, and every traveler was responsible to carry his own load. However, if I were moving goods to the next town, and the load became too heavy, it was fine for me to ask for help from a fellow traveler.

Healthy boundaries in dating require that I do my own work and take responsibility for those things that are mine to deal with. The attorney I dated was fully committed to being a wife and raising her five children. She was not looking to offload those responsibilities onto someone else. Healthy boundaries also allow us to ask for help when we are overwhelmed and cannot manage the challenges life presents to us. In the attorney's case, she would want a partner who would enjoy children in general, and her children in particular, and be willing to roll up his sleeves and get involved building a family life with her.

My chain-smoking mover would remind us that we each come with a restaurant load of dishes in some area of our life.

## Question Eight: Will They Reciprocate in a Relationship?

I tell my couples that a healthy relationship is like volleying in a tennis match. We are hitting the ball back and forth, both contributing to the game. Some couples feel as if one person is serving and acing the other continually. Other relationships feel as though one partner is on the court, ready to play, and is coaxing the other partner onto the court. These are questions of reciprocity, and they are very important to the success of a relationship.

Reciprocity refers to my investment of time, energy, goodwill, interest, and all the other key ingredients that make a relationship meaningful. I'm bringing the important reinforcements we talked about earlier in this book to make the relationship successful. And my partner is doing the same for me. The trading does not have to be equal—fifty-fifty—but it does have to be equitable. We both feel that we are investing fairly in the relationship.

Lisa and I dated long distance. She lives in Houston, and I'm in Dallas. During one nine-month period I had a weekly speaking engagement, and she drove up every week to hear me speak. This was a significant commitment of time, money, and energy! When that gig ended, I reciprocated by hitting the road for the next year and regularly driving to Houston. Good relationships keep the dessert flowing in both directions.

In extended adulthood a match should let you know pretty early on if they are interested in you and are willing to expend the time and energy to date. Simply put, some people are just too lazy to date or be married. It takes work to get to know someone, effort to get into shape, buy new clothes, plan dates in a different city, or even drive across town to meet someone new at Starbucks.

One of the key signs of relational success, especially online, is that your efforts are met equally and enthusiastically by the match. Emails are answered in a timely fashion and phone calls and texts returned. Questions are not ignored but responded to. Dates make suggestions about a good restaurant in their locale if you are dating long distance. People get a rush of excitement when they meet a new potential match and that energy is reciprocated.

Dating is the time when two people are likely the most motivated to please each other. If I am already feeling as if I'm having to drag this person onto the tennis court to play ball, this may be a sign of things to come. Again, some people are just too unmotivated and selfish to invest in a relationship. They are the center of their own universe, and your "demands" may prove to be just too much for them. Watching what matches do, not just what they say, is a good rule of thumb. Relevant questions:

- Are we both contributing equally to this relationship?
- Does this person seem as excited about the idea of falling in love with me as I am about them?
- Am I always the one initiating, or does my partner plan things and offer ideas?
- Do we both offer relationship enthusiasm and energy?

## Question Nine: Are You My Best Friend, Lover, and Partner in Crime?

Over my years of being single again, I have read tens of thousands of online profiles from women from all across the country. In doing so I have encountered a consistent verbiage among many women—and I suspect men as well. Profiles will often state, "I am looking for my best friend and lover" or "I'm looking for a partner in crime" with whom to live the best part of my life. These clauses are common enough to warrant some attention because they illustrate three of the important dynamics of love: friendship, passion, and life energy. Let's explore each one briefly.

"I'm looking for my best friend," the profile states. What he's saying is that he's looking for someone he can trust to talk to at the end of the day. She's looking for someone she can run an idea or problem by when she's not sure what to do. He's looking for a safe place to land in a challenging world. She'd like to have someone besides her older sister two states away to list as an emergency contact. We all long for that one individual who is "our person in this life."

"I'm looking for my best friend *and lover*," the profile goes on. We desire that special chemistry that sets our life on fire. As one writer expressed it, "Love is friendship that's caught fire." My father and mother were married for fifty-three years. In the evenings Dad would walk through the door and proclaim, "Dad's home." My mother would drop whatever she was doing and meet him at the front door, and they would kiss as if they hadn't seen each other in a year. They were each other's best friend and lover.

"I'm looking for a partner in crime," the profile playfully expresses. The second half of life is a time when people decide to do the fun things they've never tried before. "Let's travel and see the world." "Let's try golfing together." "Let's get tickets to the symphony this season or go on a road trip to see a part of the country we've never seen before." The partner in crime criterion speaks to the life energy people bring to a relationship. I find that the more closely aligned is the shared vision of what adventure looks like, the easier it will be for the two to match up. This is one area, I've discovered, in which the truism that opposites attract does not work well.

# CHAPTER 9

# WHY ARE WE ATTRACTED?

An official looking email arrived in my online dating account with a diplomatic address from a country in the Middle East. I was intrigued and opened it immediately. Attached was a formal letter of introduction from two gentlemen who described themselves as Director of Staff and Chief of Security for the princess Pricilla of that country. They asked my indulgence as they explained her situation.

The princess and her now late husband had been commissioned by her father to serve in America as diplomats and representatives of the crown. The family some years earlier had moved to the United States and settled in the Washington, DC, area, eventually moving to Virginia. As time passed America had become a second home to her and her family. The husband had passed away a few years earlier, and the princess, now comfortable in the States, had decided to continue her diplomatic responsibilities for her father.

As time passed Princess Pricilla longed to be married once again, but it would have been impractical for her to return to her homeland and pursue normal dating protocols in that country. She was also limited in scope by her station in life. She simply wasn't going to get a gym membership at LifeTime Fitness and meet a nice guy on the elliptical machine.

The princess had done her research and decided to pursue online dating in America. However, security did not permit her to post a profile or actively search online—the exposure would have been too great. So, she contracted with an online dating service to allow her Director of

Staff and Chief of Security to be her "online date scouts." Armed with her description of what she was looking for in a second husband, these two were transformed into online matchmakers—no doubt not exactly what they had signed up to do when they'd applied for their jobs in security and operations management.

The email was courteous, informative, and straight to the point. Would I be willing to look over her private, diplomatically approved profile and let them know if I would consider opening up communication first with her agents—the two men—and then eventually with her? Obviously, this would be a formal, well-scripted courtship, heavily controlled by protocols and cultural norms far beyond my experience.

Attached to the email was a file with a collection of Princess Pricilla's official royal pictures that I assumed were used for publicity purposes. There was the princess in the throne room. There she was in her royal attire, wearing some of the most impressive jewelry I'd ever seen. Here was a picture of her bestowing an honor on a military figure. I felt as though I would be walking into an episode of *The Crown*, and the sensation was quite remarkable.

The email forced me once again to examine what I call my "template of attraction." What are those aspects I find to be most attractive and compelling in a match? We all have a radar of attraction, and when it goes off, we are aware that someone has come into our presence whom we find attractive. If we are dating, this sensation is responsible for the powerful experience daters call "the instant click." That experience can occur whether we are sixteen or sixty.

I mulled over the email for several days and considered all the possibilities. I was certainly intrigued by her life's story and experiences. Here was a complex woman of obvious substance with compelling life experience. I was drawn to our cultural connection, reflecting that her Middle Eastern background, paired with mine as a Greek, would make for interesting conversations.

Two factors, however, caused me to decline the invitation. First, I was not interested in a romance with many other people to manage—social directors, security chiefs, secretaries, and diplomats. I know myself well and value my privacy. Second, there was simply no physical attraction. I would open the pictures daily to see whether something, *anything*, sparked my interest. It never did. Strip away the royal dress and jewelry, and this was a woman I'd never look at twice on the street. That would not be fair, either to her or to me. I had discovered that when I ignored my template of attraction and tried to force physical attraction to a match, it never worked.

This case brings up the timeless question, *Why am I attracted to the people I'm attracted to and not to others?* This topic is one of my students' favorites in my class on marriage and family, and one that the textbooks offer a number of interesting theories to explain. While there is no definitive answer, there are a number of models and theories that shed light on the process of falling in love. This chapter will briefly present a few of them in an attempt to arm you with the tools you'll need to understand your own template of attraction.

## Template of Attraction

Cary was married for seven years to Cathy, who was a school teacher, petite at five feet one inch in height, dark haired, and with an athletic figure and an outgoing personality. Her extroversion complimented Cary's quieter and more introverted nature. Following their divorce, Cary started dating Christine. Christine was also petite at five feet tall, also with dark hair, and working as a school counselor at the high school. They met online, and Christine reached out to Cary, initiating the first contact and later suggesting that they meet.

I would observe that Cary has a highly predictable template of attraction. He is drawn to petite, dark haired, educated and outgoing women who complement his personality. Cary's template may remain constant, though other people have more variability in their template. Cary could also have been drawn to a quiet blonde who did not work in education and preferred reading a good book rather than working out with him at the gym.

I suggest that our template of attraction is composed of a complex set of qualities and characteristics that began their development in childhood and progress on thorough adulthood. There are certain physical features, personality characteristics, nuances of humor, and even cultural qualities and voice characteristics that we find attractive. Others turn us off. Someone will say, "I find his voice so soothing I could listen to him all day long," while another will observe, "I couldn't take listening to that voice for five minutes." They are speaking about their templates of attraction.

The template of attraction may remain stable over time, as in Cary's case. I ask my clients in a ReMatch process to do an exercise: go back and list the boyfriends or girlfriends, lovers, and spouses you've had over the course of your lifetime. Then see if there are any common characteristics across your partners, either in personality, looks, interests, or even the problems they bring to a relationship. Some clients find that they have a predictable template of attraction, while others notice that their template is highly varied. There is no right or wrong. The key is to be aware of what constitutes your template of attraction and look for those characteristics when you date.

Both online dating and traditional dating in extended adulthood gave me the opportunity to explore my template of attraction and expand it if I chose to do so. Perhaps Cary would learn some things about himself if he were to date a woman who was less extroverted and less open to initiating. He might discover in the second half of life that he enjoyed taking the lead and being a little more outgoing. Dating and expanding his template to allow him to consider a different kind of woman might give him new insight into parts of himself that have been hidden away. I personally followed a rule of accepting dates with a wide range of matches, even those just outside my normal template of attraction, just to see what my reaction would be and what I could learn about myself.

However, I also learned to be faithful to my template of attraction. There were delightful matches who really wanted to date but with whom I simply found no connection. This happened with a very interesting woman who taught music. We had a great connection in that she taught piano and I played drums. Our first date was spent discussing classic rock and her career in music. It was an interesting evening, but it never led to dating. Shortly, we will look at one model of attraction suggested by Harville Hendricks that explains how our template can have its roots in our early experiences.

## A Behavioral Model of Attraction

When I'm teaching my students in my marriage and family class, I begin with a basic model of attraction that goes a long way toward explaining the process of why we are attracted to the people we want to date and eventually marry. There is an easy-to-understand behavioral model of attraction that outlines four progressive stages, as follows:

### Stage One: Sampling and Estimation

A wink comes in on the dating site from a new match. An email arrives. Someone swipes your profile and you are notified that you have a new match. These are the first steps in online sampling and estimation. A potential match finds you attractive.

Sampling and estimation refer to the first step when my attraction radar goes off. Someone walks into the room, and we are immediately aware of their look, presence, or energy. Our attraction radar is normally "on" and running in the background. Chances are that we find the vast majority of people neither attractive nor unattractive. We are simply neutral. Occasionally our attraction radar goes off and we are aware that someone at work, in the gym, or on our iPhone screen is attractive to us. If we are married or in a relationship, we simply ignore that message, refer to our boundary, and move on. If we are interested in dating we answer the message, swipe right, or strike up a conversation.

Sampling and estimation are the stage at which my advice to "keep on fishing" is very appropriate. Getting locked into a new match too quickly can lead to disappointment as people online move on to communicate with another match with no explanation or response to a message. Ghosting is a common experience.

### Stage Two: Bargaining

Stage Two is Bargaining, during which we begin to exchange important information and expend time to see if there is more to this attraction than simply the radar going off. Social exchange theory suggests that we come into relationships with powerful goods "to trade." Carl's quiet confidence gave his match Christine a sense of grounding and security she found very attractive. Christine's outgoing personality helped Carl keep social and family connections strong, which was something he didn't naturally attend to on his own. As they dated, they learned that the blending or trading of those characteristics worked well for them.

As we date, we exchange important information about ourselves, our lives, our personalities, and our habits. Our dates are doing the same thing. We discuss where we grew up, what our jobs are like, where we live, and what hobbies we enjoy. As we mutually share, we are engaging in an elaborate process of social exchange that we call bargaining. "Here's something about me; tell me something about you." We are trading information, opinions, and experiences. This is extremely important in extended adulthood as our life's narrative is richer and more expansive than it was in our younger years.

Bargaining is also a time when we observe our date. How are they dressed? What kinds of entrees do they order from the menu? How do they treat the service staff? Are they on time or habitually running late? What kinds of things make them laugh? These questions and hundreds of others are being unconsciously processed as a couple goes out on their first date or two.

Generally, the bargaining moves from more surface level sharing ("Have you been in this area a long time?") to deeper level questions ("How long have you been dating, and how's it going?"). In some cases, the more we share the more we discover that we like this person and want to continue the bargaining process. So, two people decide to keep seeing each other.

In most cases the bargaining ends when one or both persons feels that they've encountered information, experiences, or habits that fail to align with their "Pocket List of Non-Negotiables." These are the qualities or issues I just would not live with. Or the template of attraction is not activated. There just isn't any chemistry there. So, the dating ends and they return to "keep on fishing."

Bargaining in extended adulthood can be an elongated process. People bring longer histories to share, and matches have complex family systems to integrate into the new couple relationship. People are dating long distance and must figure out work and living arrangements. There are a wide range of bargaining issues to be navigated in the second half of life, and it is appropriate to take one's time. In the princess's search for her next husband, bargaining would involve a partner who would enjoy a public diplomatic life and a scripted schedule that incorporated a large staff.

Bargaining also takes on a different air when comparing traditional dating and online dating. When I meet someone in person, I am already taking in information about them by listening to them and observing the way they interact with me and other people. I have already begun to build my set of impressions. I may already know that they have some powerful attractors that will be highly rewarding to me. This takes place, for instance, when someone has lost a spouse and afterward dates a close friend who has also lost a spouse or is divorced. They already know that person and have enjoyed the interaction, so the bargaining stage has already in some sense been engaged.

Bargaining online is delayed to some extent until we actually meet. When I was Academic Vice President at Amberton University, I hired faculty. I discovered that there were some professors who were highly engaging and personable as online instructors, but put them in a live classroom and they fell flat. They had a dynamic online presence but a reserved personality in real life. The same thing can happen with online dating. A match may seem to be highly engaging online, but we meet for coffee and find that they can barely carry on a conversation. The real bargaining does not start until people meet in person.

Bargaining is also a time when we begin to build our mental map of our lover and best friend. Dr. John Gottman calls this our "Love Map." After having been married for a few years, Jon and Jessica can order for each other off a menu and sometimes will finish the other person's sentences when asked a question by a stranger. They know each other well because they each have a highly detailed "love map" of the other person. This is good stuff that builds a strong level of commitment and satisfaction in the relationship. The process of building the love map begins in stage two and continues across the length of the relationship.

### Stage Three: Commitment

Once two people have made a connection, discovered that there's chemistry there, and spent time dating and exploring the dynamics of their relationship, they reach a point when they say to themselves, "This is my best deal." They are ready to make a commitment to the long-term viability of the relationship. They are, in essence, saying, "Of all the people I could be married to or in a committed relationship with, you are the one I choose."

Social media sites regularly list a person's relationship status as "married" or "in a committed relationship" or other such terms. This is the stage that formalizes the exclusivity of the couple. We are going to focus our attention, energy, and love on our one partner, and that will shut down exploring other potential partners. I always encourage my clients to be open with their partner that they are off dating sites and have discontinued communication with other matches. Be aware that some dating sites will repost one's picture for a brief time in an effort to get them to subscribe once again. Others continue to send matches after the membership has expired. Years after ending my It's Just Lunch membership their salespeople were continuing to call, trying to get me to resubscribe to their service.

Stage Three is also a time when a potential partner may shy away from making a firm commitment. They may be commitment avoidant. Others may inexplicably end the relationship or begin doing things to sabotage it in order to avoid making a commitment. We will explore attachment styles later in this chapter. But for those who have done the work well in Stages One and Two, moving into the commitment stage brings a sense of relief. We can focus in on deepening the love and enjoyment of the person we are excited about spending our lives with.

### Stage Four: Institutionalization

Every society has a process that moves two single individuals in the culture to being recognized as a married couple. In our culture there is a vast business industry tied to the engagement, wedding, and honeymoon. Couples file for a marriage license, pick out engagement rings, plan a wedding, and send out invitations. The mere cost of the wedding is often staggering, to say nothing of the time and energy that go into its production. This is the institutional process, designed to say to one another, the two families, and society as a whole that the couple is now married. The institutionalization process has a legal; social; and, for many people, a religious component to it. Marriage is viewed by such people as a covenant, not just a social contract.

In extended adulthood the question is often asked, "Will you marry again, or are you just looking for a committed relationship?" Some dating sites ask you to indicate whether you're looking for a marriage partner, a committed relationship, a travel partner, or casual dating. Men and women in the second half of life may look at marriage with a very different set of lenses. Some will say they are firm believers in the institution of marriage and want that level of commitment. They may hold strong religious views that sway them away from considering living long-term in a committed relationship. As Frank Pittman, a noted marriage and family therapist, observed, "Marriage is like a submarine. For it to work you've got to get all the way into it."

Other adults will approach this question more pragmatically. They may declare, "I almost lost everything financially during my divorce. I'm never going to leave myself that exposed again." Others will note the power differential they experienced in their marriage and want to maintain a level of independence that helps them feel more secure. One woman told me, "My name will always be on the lease agreement. I'm never being put out on the street again by a man." History and former marriages play a huge role in informing the decision making.

Clearly, the question of whether a couple chooses to get married, live in a long-term committed relationship, or a combination of the two is an important decision and one that will require considerable discussion. I will note that a significant number of clients have started the process in the "never marry again" category but shifted to the "Let's get married" category when they met a partner who fulfilled many of the desires they had for a spouse. Sometimes the answer is not conceptual but experiential— Who is this person standing in front of me?

The four stages of Sampling and Estimation, Bargaining, Commitment, and Institutionalization form a handy guide to let someone know where they are in the relationship process. But there are other aspects to attraction. For instance, why are some people attracted to people very similar to themselves and others to their personality opposites? Which one of these patterns works best in a marriage? These are questions of Complementary Relationships and Symmetrical Relationships, and we will explore that attraction pattern next.

## Birds of a Feather

My students often ask, "Which works better in a marriage, likes attracting or opposites attracting?" I answer, "That depends." Relationships of likes attracting or "birds of a feather flocking together" are called Symmetrical Relationships. The partners enjoy the same things and approach life, decision-making, and communications in a similar manner. These couples connect quickly and easily when dating and will remark, "We are so much alike."

The strength in the Symmetrical Relationship is that the agreement they share involves not only how they see life but how they will go about doing life together. If they both believe that being on time means being ten minutes early, they won't argue about running late. The downside to a Symmetrical Relationship is the question of who is responsible for doing the things neither one is particularly good at or inclined to tackle. If being on time is a struggle for both of them, then someone has to step up on the morning they are to catch a flight to make sure they make it to the plane on time.

The "opposites attracting" relationship is interesting and dynamic because, while the couple may share a core set of values, outlooks, and interests, there will be other areas in which they differ significantly. During their dating they may find these differences to be pleasing and even exciting; some will reflect, "It feels like you complement me so well."

I was working with a church pastor and his wife. He was highly extroverted and energized by the company of people. After a service ended, he would spend an hour in the foyer talking with his parishioners, all of whom he knew by name. His wife was a delightful and intelligent woman who preferred to socialize one on one. After church she would retire to a parlor, where she served coffee and visited with people in more private conversations. The two were opposite in the way they dealt with people—extrovert and introvert—yet they were able to negotiate these differences by playing off each other's strengths. So, the attraction of birds of a feather versus opposites attracting is really a "that depends" question. Both can be extremely rewarding and healthy, and both come with their own unique set of challenges.

A part of the success of opposites attracting couples is their ability to do what I call "installing a good clutch." I learned to drive in a two-step process. First, I learned to drive a stick shift and then adapted to an automatic transmission. Learning to drive with a stick was far more difficult because my left foot had to learn to operate the clutch: press in the clutch, disengage the stick from the gear it's in, and select a new one before slowly reengaging the clutch. I remember popping the clutch too fast and immediately killing the engine. I would try to engage the stick into the next gear without enough clutch and be rewarded with a wonderful grinding sound. Before I could switch gears, I had to engage the clutch.

Couples in Complimentary Relationships who differ on some major issues would do well to engage a clutch in those discussions: slow down, take a breath, try to see things from the other's perspective, and take some time to think about it. "Let me mull over that and get back to you," may be a wise response in heated discussions between two people in an opposite attracting marriage. Couples in therapy will often come into a session confessing that they didn't engage their clutch and ended up grinding the gears. Understanding some of our innate differences is valuable toward the goal of accepting our spouses for who they are. The work of Carl Jung and his personality theory shed light on these key differences.

## Just Your Type

Dr. Carl Jung proposed an optimistic view of personality centered around four questions. First, "What energizes me?" A person who gets his or her battery charged by being with people is called an extrovert. A person who gets their battery charged by being alone in the private world of their thoughts and ideas, on the other hand, is called an introvert. Introverts and extroverts marry all the time, and as I discussed with regard to the pastor and his wife, many learn to negotiate their different approaches to recharging their batteries. At the end of class my introverted students are worn out from the evening lecture, while my extroverted students are standing in line to tell me a story. There is no right or wrong—they are just different.

The second question Jung proposed was, "How do I take in information?" Some personalities take in information through their five senses: taste, touch, sight, smell, and hearing. These individuals are very aware of the environment and tend to be good athletes and musicians because they are comfortable in their own bodies.

My son and daughter, as I've mentioned, are police officers. After eating lunch with them I can't help but notice that they are able to recall the guests in the restaurant—what they were wearing and any unique behavior that caught their attention. They are high sensers, intuitive folks who look at the big picture. They take in information from a sixth sense or gut feeling. In therapy I've often asked a question with no logical reason other than a gut feeling that something important might surface.

The third question Jung proposed was, "How do I make decisions?" Thinkers make decisions with their heads and feelers with their hearts. Neither approach is superior; the two individuals will just approach the decision from a different vantage point.

My father was a thinker. When he was suffering from cancer and nearing the end of treatment, he called me into his study and pulled out a sheet of paper. "The doctor says I can do more treatments and maybe live another nine months, or I can stop now and soon enter hospice care. I've made lists of reasons on this piece of paper that I should live or die, and I'd like to talk it over with you. I've already decided that it's time to die, and I'd like you to do my funeral."

Dad, the thinker, was processing this life-ending decision in the way that made sense to him. I as a feeler was doing everything I could to hold back my tears. Thinkers and feelers can have wonderful relationships as long as they bear in mind that they are coming at life from very different perspectives.

One key difference between thinkers and feelers has to do with what I call "the way they come into the room." Feelers enter the room and spontaneously appreciate: "Wow, I really like the way you've redecorated the house." Thinkers enter the room and spontaneously critique. My wife's close friend entered my house for the first time, and the first thing she did was walk to a picture hanging crooked and straighten it out. She is a thinker and was helping me out! My advice to the thinkers is to add some appreciation with their critique and to the feelers to not be afraid to say what they really are thinking.

The fourth question Jung proposed was, "How do I organize my world?" This speaks to the Judging vs. Perceiving scale on the Meyers-Briggs Type Indicator. Judging individuals prefer an ordered and structured lifestyle. They love lists, timelines, and procedures. Going on vacation? They will have it all planned out and organized ahead of time! Perceivers prefer a more open lifestyle. They will delay decisions to get more information and may be the last ones to arrive. My perceiver students will wait until the night before the due date to write their papers because they need that last minute burst of adrenaline. The Perceiver going on vacation may ask several times, "What time does our flight leave?" The Judger/Perceiver relationship functions from two different experiences of time, and I've found that this difference has to be negotiated.

There are many aspects to Jung's theory and the Meyers-Briggs Type Indicator. I use an excellent book, *Just Your Type* by Paul and Barbara Barron-Tieger, to help couples explore the similarities in and differences between their personalities. The MBTI, based on Jung's theory, types people into one of sixteen different personalities, such as ENFP or INTJ, and *Just Your Type* devotes a chapter to what happens when each type marries another type. A good homework assignment for extended adulthood would be to read over the explanations of the sixteen personality types and note which ones you could see yourself in a relationship with and which would leave you feeling cold and frustrated.

## An Attachment View of Love

Dr. Sue Johnson and the school of Emotionally Focused Couples Therapy believes that secure attachment is at the core of building a healthy relationship. Attachment Theory, or what EFT calls "Bonding Science," has proven that the way in which we experience early life attachment in the home has great significance for the way we bond as adults. That makes sense. I learn to attach as a baby with my mother or caregiver—my first learning experience with love. Out of this come both secure and insecure attachment styles that are played out in our adult love relationships. Let's explore each one briefly:

### Secure Attachment

Dr. Johnson notes in *The Practice of Emotionally Focused Couples Therapy* that "People with secure attachment styles find it easy to get close and are comfortable depending on others. They do not worry about being abandoned or someone getting too close. They have a full and cohesive narrative about their childhood. The partners demonstrate acceptance and availability, offer comfort, support, nurturance, and express love and desire."

Emotionally Focused Couples Therapy notes that secure partners can:

- Retain emotional balance and are less flooded by anger or anxiety when disconnected or threatened and less reactive and defensive.
- Tune into emotions and formulate coherent direct messages regarding needs.
- Remain flexible and open, tuning response to contact and reflecting on experience and interaction.
- Trustingly take in comfort and care.
- Give the benefit of the doubt and resist fixed negative appraisals of the other.
- Maintain a positive view of self.
- Turn toward others and respond with empathy and caring.
- Deal with ambiguous responses with less catastrophizing and numbing.
- Turn back to the world and explore—learn and adapt to new situations

There are three other styles of attachment that affect the way we bond in love relationships in adulthood.

### Preoccupied/Anxious Attachment

At first Katie was flattered by all of Karl's attention, but now she was feeling overwhelmed and pressured. After their first date he wanted to see her again right away. Texts, phone calls, and flowers flowed in, and she was blown away by all the attention. Now, however, if he couldn't reach her immediately or she didn't respond to his texts, he would become anxious and upset. Once when she was on a girls' weekend with sorority sisters, he bombarded her with messages all weekend, to the point that she could not enjoy herself. Katie was secure in her attachment style—she could be comfortable either together or apart—but Karl's insecure attachment style was cause for concern.

Dr. Johnson describes persons with preoccupied/anxious attachment in this way:

- Display anxious, clinging behaviors
- Inconsistent care and support from caregivers
- Feel unlovable and want to merge completely
- Worry that their needs will never be met
- Give in order to get and then feel resentful
- Have little tolerance for being alone
- Have difficulty receiving love and care
- Need to address fear of abandonment and repair past injuries
- Need to increase their capacity to recognize and receive love and care when it is present

### Dismissive/Avoidant Attachment

Mike and Mary had been dating for several months and with their hectic schedules had very little time alone. They booked a vacation at an all-inclusive resort in the islands, packed their bags, and headed south for four days of couple's time. When they arrived, Mandy booked three half-day spa treatments alone and then arranged for solo training in the gym with one of the local trainers. Mike was left to fend for himself. When they went to the pool, she found the company of two men with whom she engaged in animated conversation about her new business venture and shared drinks. Mike swam laps alone.

She was too tired for sex after her workouts and spa time, and when Mike mentioned at dinner that they seemed to be "somewhat parallel on this vacation, which I thought was couple time," Mandy was shocked and accused him of "having anger issues and being highly narcissistic." When they returned home Mary broke off the relationship, stating that Mike was "too controlling and demanding, with serious anger issues" and then lamenting, "Aren't there any normal men out there?"

The dismissive/avoidant style of attachment we see in Mary is described by Dr. Johnson as having the following characteristics:

- Caregivers not emotionally present, and emotional needs not attended to
- Have high levels of self-sufficient, independent behaviors
- Feel uncomfortable getting close
- Find it difficult to trust
- Dismiss others as being too needy and overfocus on self; may placate, dissociate, or disconnect
- Devote time to nonrelational activities—work, sports, TV, computer
- Think of others as weak and irrational
- Expect abandonment and rejection in relationships
- Childhood narrative that may be factual but superficial, with no real sense of experience
- Childhood with no one to go to for comfort

### Disorganized/Fearful Avoidant Attachment

Carol's ex-boyfriends were always confused by the mixed messages from her. At times she seemed to want an intense, close relationship, while at other times she would say or do things to push them away. The signals were always changing in this rollercoaster of a "Come Close—Get Away" dating dynamic. Finally exhausted, her boyfriends would end the relationship for good, and both partners would emerge tired, confused, and hurt. Carol had been brought up in a home where the caregivers were scary, harmful, abusive, or addicted. Carol had no safe place to go, so she bounced from intimacy, which was punishing and painful, to distance, which had been scary for her as a young child. In adulthood she was replaying the only attachment pattern she knew, which alternated between coming close and backing away.

The disorganized/fearful attachment style is defined by EFT as:

- Caregivers scary or harmful
- No safe place for child
- Disruption in the attachment system, with no relief for the child
- "Come here/go away" behaviors
- Attachment figures both sought and feared
- Often traumatic backgrounds

- May feel like a failure
- Inability to trust
- Cannot tolerate ambiguity
- Sudden shift in moods, inner chaos
- Lack a sense of safety

Thus far we are building a library of theories and models that help us understand the matches we are attracted to. In a ReMatch process adults will want as much information as they can get to help them understand who they are and why they are attracted to particular matches. Coming out of graduate school in 1982, I read a book by Dr. Harville Hendricks titled *Getting the Love You Want* that deepened my understanding of attraction and the unconscious forces driving us in adulthood. Let's look briefly at Dr. Hendricks's model, which has proven to be very effective for my clients.

## Kerry, Kim, and Unconscious Attraction

Kerry was the all-American guy. Growing up, he was the family hero, played sports, excelled in the classroom, obeyed all the rules, and was a leader in student government. He was never in trouble and was given a four-year ride to a state university, where he planned on majoring in pre-law and coming home to join his father's law firm. His life was goal oriented and achievement based.

When he met Kim in college, she was active in sorority, and he was drawn to her outgoing, fun sense of style and humor. Born into a successful family, Kim had been raised in a social atmosphere with her parents hosting community functions at their large house. She made decent grades, but what set Kim apart was her outgoing personality that could connect with anyone quickly. Kerry was smitten, and Kim found him to be a guy who "really knew where he was going in life."

Their relationship quickly progressed, and in their senior year of college they were dating exclusively, . . . but then things started to veer off track. Kerry and Kim were at a party, and Kerry noticed that Kim was entertaining all his frat buddies with her stories and funny jokes. She was basking in the attention, and he felt a twinge of jealousy creeping in. What had once been very attractive—Kim's entertaining personality—was now getting on his nerves.

Later that week the couple was studying for a Business Law exam together in the library. After several hours Kim suggested that they take a break and get coffee and chat. Kerry brushed off her request, countering that he "needed to keep hitting the books." Alone in the coffee shop, Kim wondered why Kerry had to be so rigid and uptight, why he couldn't relax a little and enjoy life. The guy who knew where he was going was beginning to grate on her nerves. Had Kerry and Kim done a poor job of choosing each other to date? Or was there something deeper going on that might explain their concerns?

Dr. Harville Hendricks correctly suggests that we all grow up in a family context in which some of our needs are met, while others, even in the best of families, are not attended to. Those unmet needs live in our "old brain," the amygdala, which is the seat of the "fight or flight" response. The amygdala is unaffected by time, meaning that an old hurt or wound experienced in childhood can reemerge in adulthood with the same power it exerted when we were young.

Certain aspects of ourselves are supported and encouraged by our families, while other facets of our personalities are discouraged or simply not attended to. Kerry's parents had encouraged responsible behavior and were less concerned about his being social and having a good time. In Kim's family, on the other hand, these social traits had been highly prized and encouraged because they helped her function as a child in a world filled with adult conversations. Kim had learned to be fun and entertaining, while Kerry had learned to be serious and achievement oriented.

When certain aspects of our sense of self are not developed, they morph into what Dr. Hendricks terms "the Lost Self." Those parts of us do not go away but remain immature and hidden in our unconscious. "The past is alive in people's memories and unconsciously continues to influence their lives in powerful ways," Hendricks concludes.

We choose partners in life whom we expect will provide us with what we didn't receive from our parents or caregivers. This is the old brain trying to recreate our childhood and get it right this time. So, the marriage has a fundamental conflict, according to Hendricks. We match with someone we are intensely attracted to but who cannot fundamentally give us what we are lacking from childhood. "Our dream person is our worst nightmare," Hendricks states.

Kim was rewarded for being social but had cut off access to her own more serious sense of self. She was attracted to that sense in Kerry, but it was at the same time that piece of him that drove her crazy. Kerry had been rewarded for being responsible, but in his trek up achievement mountain he had forgotten to develop a fun side. He was attracted to that quality in Kim, but it was at the same time the very piece of her that evoked his jealousy.

Both were dealing with wounded aspects of their amygdala, explaining why they could go from zero to sixty in a short time and have an argument fueled by the fear living in the "old brain." It was as if the old brain were asserting, "I chose you to give me what I need. I should get it because I didn't get it before. I shouldn't have to tell you—you should know!"

According to Dr. Hendricks, the first phase of Kerry and Kim's relationship was the Romantic Phase, during which they experienced four highly intoxicating characteristics that connected them:

- Recognition:   "We just met, but I feel like I already know you."
- Timelessness: "It has been a short time, but it feels like I've known you forever."
- Reunification: "It's like a part of me has come home."
- Necessity:     "I love you so much I can't live without you."

These messages make complete sense when one remembers that their source is the "old brain" trying to recreate the conditions of childhood and "get it right this time." "Two similarly wounded people may be drawn to each other," notes Dr. Hendricks, "hoping to get their unspoken, unconscious needs met through projecting them onto the other person. Thus, each person is trying to find in the other the parts of themselves that were lost in infancy or childhood."

A second phase of the relationship, the Power Struggle, began when Kerry and Kim made a commitment to each other. The expectations that each would fulfill the other's needs went up significantly, . . . and the once highly desirable traits in the other now made each unhappy. In this phase the partner is expected to fulfill all of our unspoken needs and to do so perfectly—without being told. Negative qualities began to surface. Both Kerry and Kim began to see traits in the other that reminded them of past caretakers, parents, or lovers. Each wondered, "Why do I keep picking the wrong person?"

Hendricks notes that the "Weapons of Love" in the Power Struggle are:

- Becoming emotionally distant
- Becoming critical

- Becoming irritable
- Old brain (amygdala) kicking into gear
- Repeating old behaviors over and over again

Couples come to me complaining of having the same old argument over and over. They are stuck in their dance of conflict and can't seem to find the way out.

In one of the finest descriptions of a mature marriage I've ever read, Dr. Hendricks describes the work each partner needs to do in order to move to "a more conscious relationship." The qualities of a Conscious Relationship are dependent upon my activating my higher order thinking and not getting hijacked by my amygdala. I learn to tolerate discomfort and listen to my partner without reacting out of anger and fear. I come to view them as a fellow wounded struggler, not as someone who is intentionally trying to sabotage me or the relationship. I also learn that I am responsible for fulfilling some of my own needs; no one else can do all of that for me.

Dr. Hendricks recommends that:

- We plug into a new brain to replace our old brain.
- In most interactions we are safer to lower our defenses than to raise them. This allows our partner to become an ally, not an enemy.
- We realize that the marriage has a hidden agenda: to heal childhood wounds.
- We develop an accurate picture of our spouse as another wounded soul.
- We take responsibility to communicate our thoughts and feelings.
- We do not let the amygdala take control of the situation.
- We value our partner's thoughts and wishes as much as we do our own. They can't meet all our needs magically; we'll have to do some or the work ourselves.
- We embrace the darker side of our personality.
- We work on our wholeness.
- We accept the difficulty in building a healthy relationship.

If Kerry and Kim can learn to move through the power struggle into a more conscious relationship, they will come to value each other for who they are and take responsibility for doing their own work. Rather than blaming and accusing each other, they can slowly gain insight into themselves and take personal responsibility to do their own work. Extended adulthood becomes a prime time for people to stop and take a good, hard look at themselves; the families they grew up in; and the unconscious messages they may be projecting onto their partners.

## Practical Advice during the Attraction Stage of Dating

### Make it your goal to date, not to get married.

Too many people come to the first date armed with their list of "must-haves" and treat the meeting like a job interview screening potential applicants for a marriage license. This approach is drudgery and is destined to fail. View dating as an exploration, an adventure, an opportunity to learn about yourself and other people. Date in order to date, and let the destination emerge organically from your experience with that person.

### Be yourself.

The best advice I was given was to be myself. Don't give up the cool; unique; and, at this point in life, hard-earned qualities that have made you the person you are. If you don't care for riding on the back of a Harley, . . . own it and say that's not your thing, even if I get my kicks this way. You will encounter dates who want everyone to drop into their little box of reality and conformity. My advice: run the other way.

### Decide ahead of time what's important to you.

I've been talking a lot in this book about your Pocket List of Non-Negotiables. Those are essential, especially before you begin dating. The reason is that it is very easy to get caught up in the rush of an attraction to a new person and throw out some of the key qualities you are looking for. It's easy to go quiet on our non-negotiables because we like someone and don't want to risk running them off. In actuality, risking authenticity and vulnerability as you own who you are may be a gift to that person.

### Delayed disclosure enhances attraction.

Have you had a date during which the person begins sharing their most intimate family secrets with you before you've learned where they work or how many kids they have? Premature disclosure can be off-putting to other people, especially new matches. Dr. Richard Stuart, a pioneering marriage and family therapist, explains the concept of Measured

Communications. He discovered that attraction actually increases when someone peels off the layers of another person in measured doses rather than dumping their whole story in one coffee date. I recommend peeling the onion carefully to avoid tears.

### He or she reinforces your view of yourself.

We are attracted to people who make us feel generally good about who we are in life. My students in counseling are normally compassionate, empathetic, intuitive and curious. They possess a genuine concern for helping other people do better. Most of their partners reinforce that self-image, knowing that their spouses are working adults going back to school full time. We want to be with someone who respects and reinforces who we are and what we are trying to do with our lives.

### Forcing attraction does not work.

Caitlyn was reflective and sad during our session. She had been dating a guy she had met at a work conference who was attentive, had great manners, and was motivated to date her. "The problem was I was just never that attracted to him. I kept waiting for the burner to turn up, but it never got off low heat. He's a great guy, but he's not the one for me." We've all been in that situation. One person's burner is on high, and the other is waiting for theirs to fire up. And it never does. While this situation is momentarily uncomfortable, the best advice is to "put on your track shoes and get moving." The other person will find someone who thinks they are amazing . . . and you will, too.

### Online dating empowers women and those with reserved personalities.

Women who are interested in dating are empowered through online dating because they have the ability to initiate contact and control more of the communication. Twenty years ago, marriage and family textbooks openly bemoaned the fact that social norms worked against women calling men and asking them out on dates. The texts suggested that women who initiate might be looking for different qualities in a relationship than men are looking for. While my experience is that both sexes can be very superficial when it comes to dating, online dating gives women the option of sending a message, flirting, swiping, or signaling, "Hey, I find you interesting—let's connect." That is in my opinion a very good thing.

The other group that is served well by online dating, especially in extended adulthood, consists of both men and women who are shy. "I haven't dated in twenty years. What would I say if I just walked up to a woman?" the introverted man may ask. When I started out dating, I read a popular dating book at the time that encouraged me to initiate conversations with women I didn't know at the rate of five per week.

I was not happy with this advice but committed to working the author's program. I was circuit training at the gym one day, and an attractive woman was following me around the circuit. We were the only ones there. Feeling like a coward, I didn't say anything and afterward beat myself up for not initiating a conversation. The next day I was working out and the same woman was there. She smiled and followed me around the circuit.

When we finished, I built up my confidence and struck up a conversation. She talked easily, and we chatted for a few minutes, at which time I decided to go for it. "Would you like to grab a coffee after the workout?" I asked. Her expression completely changed, and she voiced a firm No and turned and walked away. I learned that, for me, a saving grace of online dating was that every woman on that site was interested in dating. They might not be interested in dating *me*, but they were definitely interested in dating someone. Getting that first hurdle out of the way was priceless to me, and I went back to working out in peace.

In this chapter we've looked at many of the theories and models around attraction and mate selection. You've gained some insight into your template of attraction. In the next chapter I will extend our discussion to practical tips and strategies for dating and on how to survive in the world of online dating.

# CHAPTER 10

# A SURVIVAL GUIDE TO DATING

## "You Are Not the One"

I was unpacking the boxes in my new apartment in Las Colinas when I noticed that I'd gotten an email from eHarmony. I had just moved to Dallas to begin a new career as a traveling consultant for Accenture and decided it was time to "get out there" and start dating after my divorce. I signed up for eHarmony, completed their massive questionnaire, put up my profile, and waited.

"You have a match!" the enthusiastic email stated. "Let us introduce you to Chloe, a match picked out just for you based on our highly successful compatibility assessment. Send her a message now and get the conversation started!"

I opened Chloe's profile, and there was, indeed, an attractive woman of about my age who had similar interests and background. Interestingly, her profile listed her as also living in Las Colinas. I thought to myself, *Wow, this matching system is impressive!* Before I could finish reading her profile I received my second notification from eHarmony: "You have mail!" An Icebreaker message had arrived from Chloe, wanting to initiate communication. I thought once again, *Gosh, these eHarmony folks have matches that get things rolling.*

I opened her email, which contained a cute icebreaker question: "If you were alone on a desert island, what one thing would you take with you?" Since a rescue cruiser from the Coast Guard was not one of the options offered, I made another selection and sent her my own icebreaker question in return. Then I returned to unpacking my boxes.

It wasn't long before I received another notification from the good folks at eHarmony. "Congratulations, Don. Chloe has decided to continue the conversation! Answer her questions now, and you are one step closer to finding the love of your life." This email contained a series of four more surface-level questions with multiple choice answers from which I could select. Once I'd sent her my answers, I could select four questions to send to Chloe for her to respond to.

The eHarmony model contained a series of questions that moved a match from surface level communication to sharing deeper, more profound information about themselves. The questions moved me from sharing information about my preferences on the subjects of working out and eating to a highly personal list of "must-haves and can't stands"—information I wouldn't normally share with someone I'd never met. I decided to go along with this because these were the "dating experts," . . . right?

The entire process of exchanging five or six rounds of questions, I discovered later on, normally took days or even weeks to complete. My motivated match, Chloe, was in a hurry, and we completed all six rounds of the pre-scripted communication in one day. When we moved to "open communications," where we were now trusted to be adults and manage the highly dangerous process of actually communicating on our own, she suggested that we meet for coffee the next day.

I hadn't finished unpacking my boxes or worked my first day on the new job, but I had a first date! I thought, *What's the big deal everyone's complaining about regarding how hard dating is in middle age? This is a breeze!* Probably no dumber thought has ever passed through my cerebral cortex.

Chloe and I met at a Starbucks close to both our apartments. She looked exactly like her profile pictures, and we visited for a while. In the end we agreed to meet for dinner, where we could continue our conversation; she suggested two days later, and we agreed to meet at a restaurant we both liked. Being a guy who "likes to get things done," I thought this was impressive. New city, new job, new apartment, and maybe a new girlfriend all in the first week. I was on a roll!

Chloe suggested that I come by her apartment before going to the restaurant to see where she lived. I got the grand tour of her place and learned more about her background as she showed me some family pictures. Over dinner we discussed jobs, her growing up years in Dallas, and where we liked to work out.

The evening seemed to be progressing nicely, and I thought I was making a good impression. The waitress had just returned to our booth with my AMEX card and the check. As I signed, Chloe reached her hand across the table and shook my hand. "Don, I've enjoyed our two dates— Thank you. You are not the one!" And with that she stood up, gathered up her purse, and left the restaurant without another word.

A seventy-two-hour whirlwind "romance" with Chloe that ended with "You are not the one!" constituted my introduction to dating in the second half of life. I smiled to myself and thought, *Well, young man, you think you know a lot about dating. You have a lot to learn!* In the coming years I would be excitedly talking to my daughter about a new match I was communicating with, and she would gently chide me, "Remember, Dad, you are not the one!" This oft repeated caution turned out to be very good advice.

After we navigate a divorce or the death of a spouse and do our healing work, at some point we say, "I'm ready to get back out there." Tired of being alone and ready to share our lives once again with a partner, we decide that it's time to step into the world of dating in the second half of life. An effective ReMatch process helps us understand the brave new world of dating—especially online dating—and prepares for the new challenges and opportunities that will present.

There was no one right way to go about this and no foolproof matching system, I discovered with eHarmony, that was going to do the hard work for me. There would be no shortcut to searching through profiles and answering the same question a thousand times—in my case typically something like, "When we're talking, are you psychoanalyzing me?" I learned from my first encounter with Chloe that I had a lot to learn and that my old dating patterns from twenty-five years earlier needed to be tossed into the trash.

## Propinquity in Decline

"Cari, you've got a phone call. It's Don," I heard the college girl who answered the phone yell down the hall. Then there was a long pause, followed by the sound of a door closing and steps down the tile floor as a freshman girl approached the phone to say hello. It was 1975, and I was a freshman in college calling Cathcart, the freshman woman's dorm, to talk to a girl I'd met in English Composition to ask her out on a date to a concert.

Freshman girls lived sixteen rooms to a hallway, thirty-two eighteen-year-old young women all sharing one central phone on their dorm floor. Today this arrangement would be considered purgatory! Guys would nervously call in, hear their names announced by the dorm hallway self-appointed telephone operator, and then wait, hoping not to hear a chorus of laughter from faceless woman now learning that "He wants to ask her out! Omg!" Mercifully, by the upper-class years the dorm rooms came equipped with private phones, allowing self-respect to be somewhat restored.

A generation ago, dating was based on propinquity. You dated the people you were around. You met someone in class, ate lunch with someone in the cafeteria, or met someone at a fraternity or sorority function. High schools, colleges and universities, and even churches sponsored elaborate social events to "mix the kids" and get them dating. My university sponsored an annual Sadie Hawkins week, during which the dating protocol was reversed and the girls were tasked with asking the boys out. The annual spokesman for the event was a beleaguered fellow who never got a date.

"Propinquity" is the sociological term for "the people we are around," and it has worked well as a catalyst for romance for thousands of years. People date and marry the people in their proximity. What a novel idea! Doctors date nurses, coaches date athletes, scholars date folks studying in the library, and salespeople date customers. The concept is powerful and effective.

As I go through my life, I'm thrown into social circles in which the likelihood of my meeting someone with a similar background and interests is higher. If our template of attraction goes off, we might be off to the races. By the way, in my clinical work as a therapist, propinquity is also the highest predictor of extramarital affairs—a discussion for another time.

Propinquity is not dead, but it is certainly in decline. With the explosion of online dating sites, people are not limited to their network of friends and coworkers. They can explore matches in a five-, fifty-, or five-hundred-mile radius of their home. Online daters can select sites that focus on certain types of matches, such as Date Greek Women, certain values (Christian Mingle), or certain age groups (like OurTime for mature daters). Online daters can also select the amount of control they want in the dating process. Early on, eHarmony was highly controlled and restrictive with regard to communications and the number of matches they would send. Swiping apps and dating sites like Match, on the other hand, give almost all the control to the user and provide little or no guidance in the matching process.

When I hear clients say, "I'm done with online dating. It's a zoo. I'm going back to meeting someone organically," they are talking about returning to the traditional use of propinquity. When someone says, "I'm going to be open to meeting someone organically, but I'm also going to use Match or Bumble," they may be expanding their use of propinquity while at the same time expanding their opportunity for success in meeting the love of their life if they can enjoy the world of online dating.

## Twelve Types of Online Daters

As I dated online, I began to have similar experiences with different matches. I would journal about my experiences and noticed that there were patterns emerging. My academic brain kicked into gear, and over time I began assembling these patterns into a series of repeating categories. Here are some of the online dating types I encountered:

### In a Hurry

Chloe, my first match on eHarmony, was definitely in a hurry. There was a pool of potential partners out there, and it was her self-appointed task to get through them as quickly as she could. Try one out, reel him in, and pitch him back if he doesn't work out. I noticed through the years that matches who tended to ramp up very quickly often departed just as quickly. Matches who came on strong, with lots of new partner energy and enthusiasm, would often disappear just as quickly. I had to learn to avoid either getting too excited at the beginning or overly disappointed at the end. Interacting in a good relationship is going to feel like sliding a button through the buttonhole of a finely crafted shirt. My encounter with Chloe had felt more like the grating of Velcro—quick on and quick off.

### Pen Pals

Hal is on Match, but he rarely meets anyone for a date. In fact, it's been almost a year since he's actually been on a date, though he communicates regularly with several women through emails, texts, and an occasional phone call. Hal is a lazy dater. He really doesn't want the headache of getting cleaned up; putting on nice clothes; making reservations at a restaurant; or, worse yet, having to show up and admit that his photos were taken ten years ago.

What Hal really enjoys is being a pen pal with women. He likes to write to them and engage them in "a relationship" that really is nothing more than a myth in his mind. Hal's attachment style is dismissive/avoidant; he uses online dating to connect with women but keeps them at an emotional distance. His frustrated female matches wonder, "What's wrong with this guy that he'll never meet?"

### HR Directors

Connie shows up at each first date armed with her list of "Must Have's" and a key list of questions to ask each new victim of her dating interrogations. She grills the guys on their background, family, finances, and religious and political beliefs, boldly laying out her expectations with a "take no prisoners" attitude. In her brief silences she isn't so much listening as she is pausing to catch her breath.

Connie attended a divorce recovery seminar at her church taught by two lay members who had never dated in midlife, and they trained her in how to conduct these initial interviews. After six months Connie had never been invited on a second date, even though she had encouraged a few men to "call me, and let's get together." She couldn't understand why men didn't find her to be a fun woman to date.

### Group Therapy Twins

Mike and Monica met in a divorce recovery group. They were both coming out of long-term marriages and going through nasty divorces. After they had each shared their story during the first night of attending the group session, they were drawn like moths to a flame to one another's stories: "This person's been through what I've been through." They connected after the session for coffee and two weeks later dropped the group in favor of dating. "I've found my match—isn't that the best recovery?" they both rationalized.

Pain made for a dramatic, and at times chaotic, bond between them . . . and this worked for a time. Eventually, however, as the dust settled on their divorces, they were left to discover who they were as a couple when they were not managing a crisis. Mike and Monica split up a year later after discovering that each had short-circuited their own recovery process and had to go back and do some individual counseling.

### Mr. and Ms. Google

I often encountered "Google Dates." I would show up to meet some-one for the first time, only to discover that they would come in armed with a bibliography of information about me and were ready to ask follow-up questions about my life. "I must confess that I looked at your website." "I went out the listened to some of your YouTube videos." "I googled you and have been reading your book."

This never bothered me. In fact, I was flattered that they had taken the time to do their research. Good for them! It's all there, right? Today most of us check the social media footprint of people. My kids who are police officers regularly do this to catch bad guys. What I liked about this approach was having a match use the information as a springboard for a conversation. That was helpful. What was discouraging, however, was when a match showed up believing that they already knew who I was.

*You watched a YouTube I recorded for my university class, and you think you know me? I don't think so.* Social media is a vital adjunct for helping us get to know someone, but this shouldn't be a replacement for the Bargaining Stage of attraction, during which we slowly pull back the layers of someone's story and enjoy the process of getting to know them.

### Placeholders

Craig had been dating a woman he had met on Match for two years. They and been broken up for only a month when his best friend encour-aged him to get back online and meet someone else. "The best way to get over a relationship is to get another one," his friend confidently assured him. Craig met Connie and they began dating. While she was excited about dating Craig, however, she noticed that he seemed to be "not that into me."

Connie would initiate most texts and phone calls and even plan dates. Craig was "there" but seemed to be on the sidelines. After six months of frustration Connie ended the relationship, saying that she could tell Craig was emotionally stuck on his old girlfriend and not yet ready to date. Craig needed to work through his grief, not run out and find an-other girlfriend to date. Connie deserved more in a relationship than be-ing a placeholder so Craig could heal and move on.

### Pre-Daters

As a therapist I have clients in what I call "Pre-Therapy." They don't make appointments regularly, don't follow through with homework, and aren't engaged in a change process. They are attending sessions but haven't involved themselves in the process because they are not ready for therapy.

The same dynamic occurs with online dating. There are people online who, for a wide variety of reasons, are not yet ready to date. A man may be transferring from one city to another and decide to go online, create a profile, list the new location as his home city, and begin dating "as if" he lives there. He wants to get a head start on his social life in his new town.

That may be fine for him, but what about the poor matches who invest time and effort into meeting him, only to discover that he really won't be living there for another year? He has made the decision for both of them that a long-distance relationship is fine. Unfortunately. that wasn't his decision to make individually—although it happens all the time.

A common practice is for matches to begin dating while they are still in the process of getting a divorce. In fact, I would vote that this should become a new category in the dating profiles: "single" or "single again, still waiting on the attorneys." The common rationale is something like, "My spouse has been dragging this thing out, and I got tired of putting my life on hold." While this may be a perfectly reasonable explanation, the key question to ask is how they have navigated their divorce adjustment, since they are still in the middle of it.

The third category of Pre-Dater I encountered were the group I refer to as "Just Passing through Town." A woman would contact me, excited about opening up communication. She would be a long-distance match who would be coming to Dallas soon and was anxious to get together. There were assurances that this trip would be a part of a larger move to the area in order to be closer to her family or a new job—or some other rationale.

I would go to the trouble of planning a date, meet the match and enjoy the evening, but then never hear from her again. I learned quickly that there are women—and men—who aren't interested in dating but just want someone to take them out for the evening because they are traveling or haven't been on a date for a while.

Just as with my Pre-Therapy clients, the Pre-Daters proved to be a frustrating waste of time. They take no responsibility for their actions, even though they create a highly negative experience for other online daters. At the core they were simply very selfish individuals. These people are incapable of a loving adult relationship, and I learned to steer clear of them.

### Damsels in Distress

Karl and Karen met on the North Dallas Turnpike after Karen's SUV had broken down. Karl stopped and saved the day, and Karen was so impressed with his take-charge attitude and so grateful that he had come along that she invited him to coffee. One thing led to another, and they started dating. Karl soon discovered that a disabled SUV wasn't the only crisis in Karen's life. In fact, their dating seemed to move from one major or minor drama to another. Two years and thousands of dollars later, Karl took off his Superman cape and ended the relationship.

In family systems classes we talk about "the Karpman Triangle" proposed by Stephen B. Karpman. In this relationship one person is the "Victim" trying to manage unsuccessfully the struggles of life. The other person is the hero or "Rescuer" willing to come in, take control, and save the day. The victim may have grown up in a home where they learned that they were not competent to handle life, and the hero may have learned to be over-responsible.

Eventually this dynamic changes. The victim decides that she is tired of being controlled by the hero and moves to the "Persecutor" role. "Stop telling me what to do—I can manage things just fine." Or the hero moves to the Persecutor role by demanding that the victim take some responsibility for her own life. Both need to learn to move into an adult role and take personal responsibility for their own lives without being either dependent or codependent.

Unless Karl and Karen take a look at the roles they play in their dating, they are likely to get hooked into the same dynamic over and over again. Karl will complain about "all the needy women out there," and Karen will carp about "all the controlling men there are." Both need to step back and do the core work I describe in Step Two of the ReMatch process.

### Recruits

Recruits don't really want to date. They show up for a first meeting, go through the motions of having a conversation about dating, and at the end confess that their son or daughter signed them up for the service. "My daughter filled out my profile for me and picked out the pictures. I had nothing to do with it," was a common confession I heard from first dates who really hadn't wanted to be there. They had been recruited to date and were there to test the waters and see if this was something they wanted to do. I was convinced on a number of occasions that their

"Recruiter" had picked me out, saying, "This looks like a good guy. Let's try you out on him!"

There was no interest or attraction whatsoever, and I had wasted time, money, and effort. *That's a Saturday morning I'll never get back!* I learned the hard way to gently inquire if dating was really their idea or whether someone else was pushing them to try. The Recruits would do better waiting until the individual has the internal motivation to get out there and date. This readiness cannot come from external encouragement, no matter how well intended.

### Burnouts

I remember my first It's Just Lunch date in Dallas. I was to meet a woman for drinks at an upscale restaurant and bar in Addison after work one evening. I arrived at the restaurant early, nervous and excited because I didn't know what to expect. When I met my match at the bar, I found her to be an attractive woman of about my age who worked for American Airlines as an executive at their headquarters at DFW Airport.

We chatted easily, but there was a sadness about her. It was clear that there was an energy differential: I was excited about meeting her, and she was simply "worn out from dating," as she put it. "This is my last date," she announced. "It's Just Lunch asked me to meet you and I agreed, but I'm really done with online dating. It's too much work and, no offense, but the men are just too disappointing. You seem like a nice guy, but I'm just over it. I get all fixed up and go somewhere to meet a guy who is nothing like his profile and nothing like someone I would want to date."

She nursed her glass of wine, sharing her sad history of dating failures, and I slipped on my therapist cap and tried to listen empathetically. Dating in the second half of life had worn her out. Dating online had worn her out. Dating using top-flight dating services had left her cold, and she was done. This was my first date . . . and her last.

That evening made a big impact on me. I remembered it well at those times when I became discouraged, took down my profile, and swore off dating for long stretches of time. It was more peaceful to be alone than to search through profiles, answer emails, arrange first dates in towns where I'd never been before, and arrive to discover that this was someone I'd never look at a second time if I were to meet them on the street. What sounded like an easy path to romance quickly became a stressful part-time job.

In time I found that I had become closer in spirit to that American Airlines executive than I was to that guy who had so long ago met her for a first date. Discouragement and burnout became a constant reality as time went by. I reached the point, as she had, when I entertained the option that "this may never happen," that I might never find someone . . . and I was at peace with that.

### CPAs

My dad was a CPA and taught accounting. He lived in a world of debits, credits, and balance sheets. He knew how to balance the books at the end of the year. There are people dating in the second half of life who are looking to balance the books, too. The first half of their life has been devoted to a relationship that was not satisfying, so in the second half they are determined to find someone who can "balance the books" for them and make up for all the years of disappointment they've experienced.

Their profiles are usually easy to spot. They are written in a stressful, almost commanding tone, telegraphing, "I have been through this. I'm not taking it anymore." You can almost hear the strains of "We're not going to take it" humming in the background as you read. This preamble is usually followed by a long list of their wonderful qualities, followed by another rather extensive list of requirements for anyone lucky enough to get a first date with them. Swipe left.

I understand the drive to "balance the books" people bring into the second half of life, and I certainly don't recommend that people repeat patterns of the past. However, I need to be careful that I don't place the responsibility for my happiness squarely on the shoulders of someone else. That's more than anyone can bear.

Dr. Richard Stuart, a pioneering marriage and family therapist, articulated the Principle of Personal Responsibility. It states, "I am responsible for creating those circumstances, actions, and attitudes that lead to my own fulfillment and happiness." In other words, "I am responsible for my own happiness, not everyone else." Spending time looking for the perfect person to perfectly fill all of my needs will only lead to disappointment, discouragement, and despair.

### Crusaders

"You need to have all your students buy my book. They all need to read it." *Excuse me . . . what?* Maggie was a new match and an "author" who had reached out to communicate with me. We had barely begun communicating online when she informed me that her new book on positive psychology was a "must read" for my students. Ignoring the fact that I barely knew Maggie, that she held no formal degree in psychology, and that the only license she held was a driver's license, I politely and firmly thanked her and said, "No, I set the curriculum for my classes, not you, and we are doing just fine right now. Have a great day." I got a scathing email in return, to which I did not reply.

Maggie was a Crusader. She was online to sell books. She was online to convert everyone to her brand of personal fulfillment. Actually, she was online to get some ego needs met, and when I didn't play along her real personality presented itself. Maggie, like most Crusaders, is a bully, and she was using the theater of online dating to throw her virtual weight around. I've met Religious Crusaders: "You need to come to my church and believe what I believe in order to date me." I've met Social Crusaders: "Why are all three of your kids cops? Don't you see how they abuse people? What we really need is to defund the police!" And I've met Political Crusaders: "Don't contact me if you voted for this candidate!"

Crusaders miss the life lesson that we don't have to be "identical to be intimate." They think that everyone else needs to think, act, and feel just as they do. Did I mention those fourteen-year-olds walking around in fifty-year-old bodies? Crusaders are at the top of that list.

A number of years ago I worked with a terrific couple whom I've mentioned before. They were entertaining, engaging, and a lot of fun to talk with in sessions. Politically, they were polar opposites—and both did politics for a living! He was the Chairman of the Republican Party in the State, and she was a well-respected Democratic lobbyist working in DC. Politically they were as different as they could be, but they found ways to build "intimacy without being identical."

Crusaders, in contrast, go through life thinking they have the answers for everyone else, and they find in the second half of life that there are fewer and fewer people listening to their sermons or putting up with their bullying tactics.

## Getting Ready to Get Out There

When I played schoolboy football, pre-season was the time we got ready for our first game. My shoulders and neck were sore from the pads and weight of the helmet. I had to run wind sprints in full pads to get used to moving in all that gear. And I had to get mentally tough to take a hit and give one back in return. Before the first game there was a lot of physical, mental, and emotional work that had to be done. The same could be said of dating in the second half of life.

There are people who attend a high school reunion, reunite with an old flame, strike up a romance, and never go online to date. There are couples who met through a friend for whom things just fell into place organically. These romances happen all the time. However, there are a large number of would-be daters—I would even argue the majority of men and women in extended adulthood—who have no options in their friend circles and will have to conduct either an online or a traditional dating search. Before paying the fee, putting up a profile, and getting into the game, they may want to do some pre-season training.

### Develop an Alligator Skin

Sly Stallone was asked how he had survived all the disappointments leading up to the premier of *Rocky*. He replied, "I developed an alligator skin." Stallone had learned to deal with rejection. Dating in the second half of life is about rejection, and dating online, particularly, is filled with this experience. A new match comes in. You open the profile and are excited about this new person. You craft an email, and it is answered quickly and with enthusiasm: "Thanks for reaching out."

Or they reach out to you first. You spend the next several days exchanging messages, and communication with other matches drops off due to the time you're investing. You start imagining what dating that person might be like. You begin sharing more personal information and flirting openly with them. Then, at about the time you think *This has some wheels*, they ghost you and disappear, leaving you back at square one. This process is repeated hundreds of times for the veteran online dater.

I have noticed in my forty years of counseling individuals, couples, and families that people differ greatly in their ability to bounce back. Some people get hit by life once, walk over to the sidelines, pull off their helmets, and sit down on the bench. They are done with the game and not going back in. They keep living but are done with the romance game, thank you very much. I've had other clients who have gotten knocked down repeatedly by life and love but keep getting back up. They have a higher degree of resilience. I call them "the Invulnerable Ones." They don that thick alligator skin that will allow them to deal with rejection and the battles life throws at them.

### Dating Wing Man and Wing Woman

I recommend that people interested in dating in extended adulthood equip themselves with a trusted man and woman to be their Wing Man and Wing Woman to help advise them during the dating process. Having a member of the opposite sex play this role can be invaluable as we try to understand communications from the opposite sex. "Is she flirting with me?" "Was he joking, or was he trying to be serious?" Our dating Wing Men and Women can help us interpret what's going on from outside the relationship without getting caught up in the emotion of attraction.

A good Wing Man and Woman will know you very well. They will be familiar with your marital or dating history and will know some of the typical mistakes you tend to fall into and help you avoid them. Do I tend to be a rescuer? Do I tend to fall for someone who promises to take care of me? Do I rationalize away big red flags when I'm first attracted to a match? A wing person will remind us of who we are. It is important that we give them permission to speak candidly to us when they sense that we are headed into the ditch.

The Wing Man and Woman can encourage us to think beyond our own choices and consider other matches. They may move us beyond our comfort zones and encourage us to date someone we would ordinarily overlook. They can also be on the watch for people who might prey on our good intentions. "I'm not sure I like the sounds of that guy and what he's saying to you" may be a statement we need to hear when our judgment is clouded by the rush of attraction.

I was fortunate to have a great Wing Man and Wing Woman, Dr. James Cail and Dr. Margaret Pinder, both veteran therapists with a quick sense of humor. Neither was afraid to put me in my place when I needed it. Dr. Cail had an expression for my "not so great ideas." I'd come in with some great new idea for my life, my search for love, or my career. He'd listen patiently, and then the phone would go very quiet.

"You want me to comment on all that?" he'd ask. Yes. "Don, that sounds like a mouse fart deal to me." I was stuck in my own head, creating drama and about to do something stupid. I needed someone charged with the task of telling me that I was about to do something to really mess up my life.

### Check the Mirror

I had a doctor come through my class several years ago who operated a bariatric clinic in Dallas. He told me after class one day that his clinic was filled with men and women looking to lose weight because they were getting ready to date again and wanted to look better. I was not surprised. Physical attraction is usually the first signal in our template of attraction that goes off. For adults looking to date in the second half of life, checking the bathroom mirror may be a good place to start.

### Do I need to get into shape?

Men and women are attracted to people who are in shape or making an effort to get into shape. Get a membership to a gym, hire a personal trainer, and check with your doctor first. We don't have to look like the cover of *Muscle and Fitness* Magazine, but we can look our best. My matches would often ask what kind of exercise routine I followed. One of my interests was to find a partner who enjoyed going to the gym to lift with me.

Extended adulthood is a time when partners are interested in the long-term health of the other person. Am I going to be a nurse for the next twenty years? We all will encounter medical issues as we age, but matches who are working to keep themselves healthy and who look attractive will find that they have an easier time meeting new people.

### How's my wardrobe?

I had matches show up for first dates who had obviously put time and thought into their outfits. Their ensemble flattered them and made a great first impression. I've also had matches show up looked as if they had just rolled out of bed. Clearly, dressing well was not high on their agenda. With me being a guy who likes to dress well, it was clear that we were not going to be a match. Guys especially often need some help in updating a tired wardrobe, picking out clothes that are flattering to their body type, and choosing colors that complement their complexion. I learned to lean into a few outfits I enjoyed wearing and felt confident in on a first date, so that clothing was the last thing I needed to worry about.

For men who are not "GQ " and want to do better, there are clothing services and stores that offer custom advice, tailoring, and styling for a guy with any build. They can help improve a man's wardrobe with a few quality pieces without breaking the bank in the process. As men age our bodies change. The clothing that looked good on us when we were thirty probably doesn't flatter us anymore. Men's dress clothing and the new casual wear are designed to hide "imperfections" and present more flattering lines as we get older.

Yes, girls, I know you suffer from the same maladies! Consider some repackaging as you prepare to get out there and date. Let your wardrobe compliment your body and make a quiet statement about your sense of style. Matches will definitely notice.

### How's my grooming?

While personal grooming is something we often take for granted, this is an area I hear people complain about a lot. Do I need to update my hairstyle? Do I need to change cologne or perfume to something more flattering? How do my hands and nails look, and might I need a manicure? Then there is the unstated importance of dental health. People reading this will likely roll their eyes and protest, "You have to mention that?" The answer is "Absolutely."

I've heard so many complaints from women and men about matches who are oblivious to the way they present themselves. When people meet, they are projecting themselves into the image of the other person. Could I see myself with this person? What would it be like to hold hands, touch, caress, and kiss? Do we look like as if we go together as a couple? People are consciously and unconsciously aligning themselves with the other person, and when the perceived alignment is strong, they speak of the connection as an "instant click."

### How are my listening skills?

Good daters are good listeners. It's as simple as that. There is no shortcut. Good listeners make great partners because they hear us and try to understand us. If you're dating someone in extended adulthood and they are great talkers but don't know how to listen well, you're not going to change that. If life hasn't taught them to listen by now, I doubt it's going to happen. They will talk, and you will listen.

I was matched with a woman who was a therapist like myself and decided to open up communication with her. The first time we talked on the phone we chatted for about an hour, with her doing most of the talking. She never asked me a question, and I finally interrupted her and inserted some information about myself to see what she would do. She paused for a moment and then went back to talking.

During our second conversation I tried an experiment, wanting to see how long it would take her to ask me a question. We talked again for an hour, and once again she had never asked me a question. This time I did not offer anything about myself to see if she would initiate a question. She never did.

It was incredible to me that a person who ostensibly "made her living" asking questions and listening was so self-absorbed, or perhaps so anxious to share about herself, that she had no self-awareness of how she was coming across. The ability to listen as much as talk made it onto my "Pocket List of Non-Negotiables." I offer the gift of listening, and I do it very well. I was going to demand that my partner do the same in return, or I was definitely not pursuing the relationship.

### How are my speaking skills?

Dating is about communications, both written and oral, and good daters are engaging conversationalists. What can you do to up your "Dating Conversation IQ"? Consider the following tips to get started:

- Get your "elevator speech" down pat to briefly introduce yourself, your work, your family, and your interests.
- Anticipate the common question someone will ask after reading your profile. "You're a therapist. Do you psychoanalyze all your dates?" was one I must have answered a thousand times.
- Extroverts, you're used to pontificating. Try to limit your speeches to about a page of verbiage so your date can have a turn.
- Introverts, you're used to giving short answers. Try expanding your conversation by giving at least a paragraph's worth.
- I would read a profile and make some brief notes about my date's interests.
- Read the profile and craft two or three questions you'd like to ask that you think they'd enjoy talking about.
- Save the "big ticket items" for later on down the road. You don't need to know their marital and divorce history over the first cup of coffee.
- Be careful not to over-communicate. We know that attraction is heightened by a degree of unknown that is yet to be explored.
- Approach the conversation like a tennis match in which the goal is to volley with each other, not to have one person acing with each serve!

### How are my writing skills?

In today's online world dating is all about writing. Profiles have to be written, along with emails to introduce ourselves, answers to questions, quick flirty responses to texts, . . . and the list goes on. Successful daters, whether online or traditional, will be able to express themselves in written forms. I've tried many approaches to writing an online profile based on other profiles I have read and been impressed with.

I've tried short and sweet—a brief paragraph or two with a statement at the end inviting more discussion if interested. I've tried longer descriptions of myself flavored with some humor to show that I don't take myself too seriously. Neither approach proved to be more successful than the other. In the end I opted for a shorter profile that included some interesting information about myself, written in an open and inviting way.

I let several people read the profile before I went online, and I also paid attention to comments I'd get from matches who would share what they liked about the profile. I never used the online writing services and don't recommend them. All of their profiles come out sounding the same, and it was easy to spot one that had been professionally produced. I preferred hearing a match's description of themselves in their own words. This was much more effective in my opinion.

Having said that, it was not at all uncommon to meet a match who had been a lively online pen pal but who ended up struggling as a conversationalist. The virtual world has created the phenomenon of people who are capable of having an "online personality" that is very different from their actual personality. That's why I think of online dating as an introduction and nothing more.

You don't really know who that person is until they show up "in the flesh," and even then, it will take a long time to peel back the layers of who they really are, especially when adults are in the second half of life and have a more complex history. Keep your expectations reasonable. You don't know if that new "perfect guy" is going to be as good in person as he is online. My best advice is to see if the writing matches real life.

## Making Arrangements

I was dating in the massive Dallas-Ft. Worth Metroplex and getting matches from across Texas. I learned very quickly that a large chunk of my time would be spent locating where my match was, finding an appropriate place to meet her, and making arrangements for a first and perhaps subsequent date. This became an ongoing logistical challenge I constantly struggled to achieve.

Some matches preferred a simple cup of coffee, very low key, in a quiet, casual atmosphere that allowed for easy conversation. Others wanted something more creative and were put off by the traditional cup of coffee date. Still others were hoping for a spark of excitement for that first date and wanted to have "a meeting and a memory," all in one. The expectations were a moving target, and regardless of how hard I tried I would occasionally miss the mark.

There were several habits I developed that helped me with arrangements. First, I built a list of restaurants, coffee shops, and cafés in the areas I routinely used for dating purposes. I generally picked out places that were quiet to allow for easy conversation, public and safe, and easy to find and park around. Second, I added to the list as I met matches in different areas and explored new places. I researched the restaurants and checked websites and menus.

Third, I built dating into my monthly budget. Simply put, online dating is expensive. I was brought up with the belief that "the guy was the guy," so I paid for easily ninety percent of the expenses, even with dating services that instructed matches to "split the check." I appreciated the thoughtful woman who would pay, but for the vast majority of dates I funded everything.

Fourth, I made sure my match had my full name and contact information before meeting the first time, even if I had only her first name. I saw her being armed with information about me as a nod toward her security. Finally, I would text her when I was leaving and again when I had arrived because in the world of online dating, we've all arrived for a first date only to have the other person fail to show up and refuse to take our calls. This is a terrible practice but one that is common among both male and female daters, I have discovered.

## Sites, Services, and Matchmaking Friends

Just do a Google search on dating services or search the App Store for dating sites, and you will be busy for the rest of the day. The number and variety of sites is overwhelming, especially to someone who is dating for the first time in many years. With some time and guidance, you can pick one site or several that meet your needs, fit your personality, and offer the kinds of features you'd like to have from a dating site or service. I will not attempt to review the sites or services here but will offer some general principles for using any of them effectively.

## A Numbers Game

Any of the sites will work in the sense that ultimately it is about two people meeting and determining whether there is enough attraction to continue the dating process. With that in mind, that can be done by swiping an app, joining one of the major dating sites, a referral from a good friend, or meeting someone at a yoga class. The rule is to "keep fishing" and have enough dates to maximize the opportunity that one of them will eventually lead to attraction in a match. It will happen!

Daters later in life get discouraged because of the age-related change in their time perspective. Many were accustomed to being in a longstanding relationship, and the thought of carrying on the dating process long term may seem daunting. But it is necessary. All of the sites will match you, but they will do so in different ways and at different speeds.

## Degree of Control in Date Selection

The inflight magazine offered high-end, customized matchmakers who screened their elite clientele for the finest matches nationwide—once one paid their hefty fee and then turned the selection process over to two glamour queens who knew about as much about mate selection as I do nuclear fusion. Another service offered twelve highly personalized dates, one per month over the course of a year, assuring the searcher that each one would be highly matched to their individual preferences. Thirty dates later I was yet to meet a match who came close to my preferences or description. But once again, the experts were in charge.

Then there were the wide-open sites where I was in total control. I could look at profiles; search for matches by distance from my home, height, education, or interests; and reach out in a wide range of ways, such as a virtual wink, an icebreaker question, or a personal message. Between these two styles were services and sites that offered matches based on an internal criterion they had developed. Daily they doled out matches like cards from the bottom of the deck, and I was expected to follow up on them.

For those who prefer immediate gratification, there were the dating apps on which I could swipe right or left, depending on the first impression I got from a picture, and hope the match swiped right on my profile as well. The operative question is how much control you want in the matching process. I tried them all. I began with using the highly controlled services and sites and eventually abandoned them entirely when I realized that I knew more about this topic than the people to whom I was paying a service fee. They were simply salespeople with no interest in my preferences. For them it was all about signing me up, and they offered only a limited "pool" of available women to date.

## Profiles, Profiles, Profiles

There are two numbers I would like to know: how many miles I've run in my life and how many online dating profiles I've read! When you first start dating online the profiles are the exciting part of the process. Checking out the prospects can be addictive. Maybe the next one is going to be "the one." We start searching the profiles or swiping incessantly, searching for Mr. or Ms. Right. We also begin building our own profile. What pictures do I pick? Does this picture make me look fat? We write and rewrite our profile a dozen times, trying to pick just the right words and phrases that will communicate what a wonderful guy or girl we are! We get the profile written, go to bed, and then get up the next morning and are horrified at how bad it sounds. Welcome to the world of online profiles.

Over the years I developed an attraction to certain well-constructed profiles that shared some characteristics:

- A straight-forward, honest, and fun tone to the writing
- A clear description of who the person is and how they see themselves, along with some of their interests
- A basis description of the kind of person they are attracted to
- A simple statement of what they are looking for in a relationship: dating, something serious, marriage, travel partner, etc.
- A head shot taken within the last two months
- A full body shot taken within the last two months
- Verification of the member's identity (available on some sites)

I discovered that profiles fall into certain categories I do not find engaging:

### The Lifestyle Profile

This profile featured an impressive album of pictures of the person around the world pursuing their latest adventure. Here I am getting onto my private jet. This is me sunbathing on my private beach. A picture in my wine garden—my vineyard is just the best; isn't yours? This is me on the mountain in Tibet discussing the meaning of life with a monk during my two-year retreat from the States after the death of my Yorkie almost destroyed me. I was never sure if lifestyle matches were looking for a partner or a travel agent. Perhaps both would have been the ideal match.

### The Bass Pro Profile

This profile also featured an impressive array of pictures and usually an economy of written text. "This is me on the bass boat with my two best buds—Ernie and Duke. I'm the one in the wife beater t-shirt, if you can't tell. This is me hunting bear last fall in Canada. I'm looking for a gal that likes to field dress deer. This is me at the Sweetwater Rattlesnake Roundup. I won it two years ago and have a collection of rattles hanging in my garage." To be clear, I have nothing against hunters or fishermen, and I respect people who deal with snakes. What I hear the girls complaining about, though, is a guy's profiles on which all they see is him holding a line of fish in front of the pickup truck with a pair of sunglasses on. We would all do well to show multiple sides of ourselves, not just showcasing one hobby or interest. Also, the girls love to see a man's eyes.

### Preachy Profiles

Preachy profiles were an automatic delete for me. These individuals used their profile to preach at members of the opposite sex. Sadly, they used their platform to berate men or women, whichever the case might be, for all the wrongs they had endured in past relationships. The rant would normally go on and on about what they would not put up with ever again. This was usually followed by a stormy critique of how members of the opposite sex wrote their profiles. "I WILL NOT RESPOND to you if you are NOT within a five-mile radius of my home and are NOT at least 6 ft. tall and obviously workout because I DO so and if you voted for THIS CAN-DIDATE DON'T EVEN SEND ME A MESSAGE. BTW-I am a CHRISTIAN and

I TREAT EVERYONE WITH LOVE, SO DON'T BOTHER ME IF YOU ARE NOT THAT WAY." These poor angry souls obviously have some core work to do.

### The Group Profile

"This is me at my high school reunion with twelve friends I graduated with. This is my work team picture of us ziplining—I'm the third one from the left in the helmet and goggles on the back row. This is me with seven other runners covered in mud after completing the all-endurance mud-a-thon marathon." Perhaps it's a social thing. Perhaps it's insecurity over how they look. Whatever the reason, the group profile will feature a wide assortment of pictures of the person with family, friends, teams, and colleagues and leave potential matches searching to pick out which person they actually are. Dating sites always advise the subscriber to the site to post one good, recent headshot and one recent full-body photograph at a minimum, without exception.

### The Hot Friend Profile

Insecure about your looks? Simply have your picture taken with four of your hottest looking girlfriends or very cute guy friends. Then hope daters searching will attribute the good looks of your companions to you. Sociologists call this the "halo effect." We attribute admirable characteristics to attractive looking people, and these dating candidates are hoping this effect will bleed over to themselves! Note again the profile picture rule just stated: one head shot, one full body shot, and drop the groups and hot sidekicks, please.

### Me And My Kids/Grandkids

Some profiles make it very clear that the match's first priority is their children or, in the case of extended adulthood, their grandchildren. The profile pictures are a collection of shots of Grandma with all her grandchildren or Grandad posing as the family patriarch. I have no argument with parents prioritizing their parenting responsibilities, especially when they have been doing it alone. That is admirable.

But two problems can occur. First, a child or teen may enter the adult subsystem. They can become Mom's or Dad's sidekick or friend, and the parent-child roles are lost. When a new partner comes along, that parentified child can detonate the relationship fairly quickly if they decide to. Second, most adults, regardless of their age, want romance, to fall in love and enjoy an adult love relationship that is more than "being Grandma" or "being Grandpa." Not getting a lot of matches? Consider whether you might be coming across as a girlfriend or boyfriend or as the director of a childcare center.

## William Vaught, CPA/Matchmaker

Bill Vaught was a partner in a major accounting firm in Dallas and had studied accounting under my father in college. Our families had been friends for years, and I had gone to high school with his daughters. When I became Vice President at Amberton University, we reconnected because Bill served on our Board of Trustees. I was recently divorced and had moved back to Dallas to work at Amberton and was thrilled with the opportunity to be back in academics. We had a new president who was in her first year and building a relationship with the Board.

Bill decided to make me his "dating project." He decided that I needed help finding the next love of my life and pursued that mission with great enthusiasm. I would get regular phone calls at the university from Bill: "Don, how's that dating going? I've got a wonderful woman I want you to meet. I told her all about you, and she's dying to meet you. Here's her number—give her a call." Bill was a force to be dealt with. I would be in meetings when a call would come in. "Dr. Hebbard, you have a phone call from Bill Vaught on line one." People in the meeting would look at me, wondering, "Why is a board member calling you?"

I found my circle of friends to be highly supportive but very little help in terms of matching me to potential dates. This occurred for several reasons. First, those in my circle of friends were either married or did not have their attraction radars turned on. They would regularly say, "I just don't know anyone to recommend to you."

Second, I found it very difficult to communicate to someone else what I would find attractive in a match. The woman reported to be "lovely" would end up being someone I was not in the least attracted to. Then I was in an awkward position with the date and my friend who had recommended her. It was a no-win proposition. Finally, even the so-called "professionals" who worked for the dating services were terrible at listening to what I was looking for. It was all a sales pitch to get me signed up.

In the long run I found that the only one I could rely upon to effectively and accurately match me to dates was me. I was going to have to take personal responsibility and work through the ocean of online pro-files. I also learned to listen to my own inner voice when it came to at-traction. If there was a connection, I was not going to try to analyze it to death. I learned to accept the allure and enjoy it. If there was no connec-tion, I refused to feel guilty about that or try to double-think the situa-tion. Attraction does not need an explanation. It just is.

## Ghosting

Ghosting is the common term for the disappearance of an online match that is normally unexpected and often without explanation. Dianna has been communicating with Dameon for several days on the dating site. They have been exchanging messages several times a day, and the messages have gotten longer and more frequent. They are both writing more and asking more questions of the other person. The questions have become more per-sonal, showing an obvious interest, and are becoming clearly flirtatious.

Dianna's time and attention have moved off several other matches she had been communicating with and have focused on Dameon as the number and intensity of messages has increased. She finds herself get-ting excited about meeting him and looks forward to the announcements that a new message has arrived. Then, five days into the communications, Dameon goes silent. Dianna is anxious and checks the site throughout the day. No message. The next day when she wakes up his profile is gone. She is surprised and disappointed. Dianna was ghosted and will never know why.

Welcome to the world of online dating. There is often no explanation. Nor is there anything solid you can put your foot down on. It's all a gam-ble, and the prospect very often disappears; in fact, that will be the rule, not the exception. In time Dianna will learn to keep the communications going with her other matches, lower her expectations during the early stages of communication, and develop a thicker alligator skin.

A bright spot in the online jungle for me were the occasional matches who approached communicating with respect, tact, and a willingness to explain their actions: "Don, I'm going to cut off communications. I'm not ready to date." "Someone I used to date has come back into the picture." "My membership is running out. Can we move off this site?" It was al-ways refreshing to meet someone who acted like an adult, regardless of whether we were attracted to one another.

The other practice I decided to follow was to allow a match to reconnect if she chose to do so. We were matched and had communicated for a time, but then the woman disappeared or the communications went cold. If she reached out a few weeks or months later, I made the conscious decision to open up communication again. I did not know why she had ghosted me or gone quiet, but I was willing to hear her explanation. She may have pursued another match. She may have had a family emergency. There may have been issues with the site. The goal was to meet eligible matches, and we had connected for some reason. I was willing to give it another try if she was.

## The Pipeline Model of Online Dating

Christine always seemed to have plenty of matches and a variety of men to date. She had a great profile and was engaging and funny with an attractive style without being a "cover girl." When guys would press her for a dating commitment too quickly, she would firmly but kindly explain that she was dating around and wanted to give things time to develop. She gave herself the gift of time and the opportunity to learn about other matches. When I asked her about her success, she described it as "the Pipeline Model."

Many online daters want to focus in on one match and put all their "eggs in that basket," she observed. Then when they meet and there is no chemistry, or they are ghosted, they have to start back at the beginning. In the meantime, they might have lost a connection with a really good potential match because they had locked too early into a "pseudo-dating relationship." They were building a life together with someone they'd met for coffee only once or twice, and she rightly saw this as "crazy." "I call that the 'one and done model,'" she finished.

Christine built her dating "pipeline" (similar to the funnel image described earlier) in three phases. In the first phase were the matches with whom she was in the initial stages of communicating online through the sites. This part of the pipeline was fairly open to a wide range of men she could conceivably be attracted to or who found her attractive, though she wasn't sure the attraction would be mutual. Her goal in this first part of the pipeline was to make contact and communicate.

The second phase of Christine's pipeline was designed to increase communication, learn more about the match, exchange information and more pictures, and see if there were any disqualifiers. Does anything about this person eliminate him/her from meeting in person? The third phase was meeting for a date or dates to see what would happen in person and if the two would want to see each other again after an initial meeting. Phase three was about exploring the relationship in person.

Christine was smart. She realized that the vast majority of matches would never lead to a first date. She also realized that the majority of first dates would end up being men she would not want to pursue in a relationship. So, she developed an approach that fed prospective dates into her dating pipeline and allowed her more power over the entire dating process.

Most of her friends who followed the "one and done" model—I have one match, and I'm going to follow it through until it's done—were repeatedly disappointed and found themselves feeling powerless in the online world. Christine reversed the order, accepting that she had to keep fishing, and empowered her dating with an abundance of choices. When she was ready to follow her heart and date a guy exclusively, she knew it because she had not allowed herself to be locked in too early in a pseudo-dating relationship.

As I've talked with clients, I've repeatedly heard that this is one of the hardest transitions for adults raised with a more traditional view of dating. The "one and done" approach may be more comfortable, but it is actually limiting the person. Dating widely can be positive and powerful for adults in extended adulthood who have spent years married to one person or haven't dated much.

Remember that the goal at this point is not to get married. The goal is to date. And dating helps us learn about ourselves. Many of us discover that what worked for us in a relationship in our twenties and thirties would never work for us in our fifties and sixties. Dating allows that exploration to take place without undue pressure or a premature commitment.

## Those Who Cannot Date Online

There will be people who, after reading this chapter, will decide that they cannot or will not date online. The scenario simply does not fit their style or personality. I was asked by the television station KTVT in Ft. Worth to do a Valentine's Day interview on the world of online dating. Also interviewed that day was a woman who had been dating online, had a bad experience, and decided this was not for her. That was certainly her choice, and I wished her much success doing what was comfortable for her. Those who do not pursue online dating typically fit into one of seven categories:

### Burned

The guest on the morning show had been dating online, had experienced a negative outcome, was burned by the process, and chose not to do it again. What is interesting about this category of daters is that their stories are usually no more dramatic or disappointing than others I've heard, but still, they choose to use them as a rationale to exit online dating. This is certainly a valid choice for them.

### Traditionalist

The Traditionalist will say, "I want to meet someone in the course of my life, and I want the encounter to be organic and natural. I don't want to feel like I'm having to force something." Again, this is a credible position, and there are large numbers of adults who meet at work, through hobbies, or at community events.

### Anti-Marketers

A big complaint I hear from the Traditionalists is, "I've filling out this profile, posting pictures of myself for strangers to look at, and I feel as if I'm just marketing myself like a piece of meat at the butcher." Anti-Marketers react to the idea of having to promote themselves in a dating pool and be compared to other men or women. The program feels far too crass to them.

### Talked Into It

The "talked into it" crowd generally does not last long with online dating. "My daughter talked me into getting on the site, helped me write the profile, and picked out my pictures." They show up for a first date insecure, tentative, and afraid this whole endeavor has been a big mistake. For the "talked into it" group, it definitely is.

### Too Lazy

I have a saying in couples' counseling: There are some people who are just too lazy to be married. The same holds true for online dating. The requirements of working the program can be somewhat the equivalent of having a second job, and some people will just be too unmotivated to make a good dating candidate. I always showed tremendous respect to the women who had taken the time and trouble to go online, communicate with me, get fixed up and looking their best, and meet up with someone they had never met before.

### Thin Alligator Hide

Online dating in extended adulthood will include rejection. That is a given. Some people will be able to roll with that reality, not take it too seriously, and move on. Others will feel deflated and decide, "I'm just not going to put myself out there." One of the great side benefits of dating online for me was the development of a thicker skin and the ability to be firm and direct with my boundaries.

### Reuniters

Reuniters meet each other at the high school reunion and reconnect, or they are at their college homecoming and run into an old flame. They connect on Facebook and rekindle a lost relationship. The reuniting stories are all around us, and when they do occur, they are some of the most hopeful and engaging dating stories we can hear.

In this chapter we have explored some of the positives and pitfalls of dating in extended adulthood. By now you've begun thinking about your own approach to dating in a ReMatch process. Are you ready to get out there? Would you date online, traditionally, or in combination? Have you imagined what your profile would say and look like? If you have, then you have begun to build your dating strategy. What if you could assemble a team of experts in dating to help you get started? What would their best advice to you be? In the next chapter I will open the door of the therapy room and bring you into key conversations I've had with top dating coaches as they answered some of the toughest questions about finding love in extended adulthood.

# CHAPTER 11

# THE DATE COACHES SPEAK

"She is what she is." The words hung in the room like a trapeze artist hanging from a wire with no net below. I was very quiet as I weighed the words. "I can't tell you what to do. The decision about any relationship rests with you, the client. My best advice to you would be to evaluate the relationship as it is at this point in time. Don't measure it against something you hope it will be. She is what she is today."

I was in a session with Dr. Maureen Lumley, a gifted Jungian analysist who was working with me on a dating relationship matter. Because I work in the marriage and family therapy field, I was fortunate to have access to some very impressive clinicians whom I invited at times to speak into my dating experiences. These "date coaches" provided me with a view of my dating life that prevented me from getting stuck in my own head. They suggested perspectives I had not considered.

Dr. Lumley was speaking to me about the rollercoaster ride I was currently on. Growing up in Dallas, my favorite ride at Six Flags over Texas had been the Runaway Mine Train. The train would start out innocently enough, gliding out of the railway station. Within seconds, however, the riders would be whipped around in a neck-jerking runaway mine train experience. "She is what she is" was a reminder that my date was a rollercoaster. She had always been a rollercoaster. My trying to change that would be about as successful as an attempt to turn the Runaway Mine Train into a Ferris wheel.

This chapter will explore some of the key conversations I've had with my dating experts and the valuable perspectives they have offered as outsiders looking into the world of dating in extended adulthood.

## Quick is Sick

"I just need to tell you that I've fallen in love with you, and I can see us being amazing together as a couple." David stunned Denise with this statement, not so much because he was sharing from his heart but because this was only their third date. Denise was enjoying getting to know David, but falling in love with this new guy had not even entered her mind. David was in a hurry to be in love, but his pace was sending up red flags to Denise, as it should have.

Moving too fast is one of the most common problems among people beginning to date again. They meet someone, experience an initial rush of excitement, and lock into the relationship quickly, only to discover within a few months that this is not the "ideal match" they thought they had found. Why do people move quickly? There are a number of reasons:

- "I've been unhappy for so long, and it's my turn to be happy."
- "The clock is ticking. I'm not getting any younger."
- It can be easy to mistake infatuation for real love.
- Moving quickly can mask deeper problems that will emerge later.
- Daters with impulsive decision-making styles will move fast in dating.
- Some individuals have an intolerance for being alone.

The inability to be alone and be satisfied often drives people from one relationship to another. A mature, functioning adult is able to be both connected and separate. I can be alone and contented or enjoying the company of my partner and fulfilled. Good marriages have a healthy balance of separateness and togetherness. Fast-paced daters like David often have a difficult time being alone and will move from one dating relationship to another. That same pattern may carry over into marriage, impelling them to move from one marriage to another. The issue is not with the partners they are selecting but with a core wound they carry that needs to be healed.

When I first started doing couples' therapy, my professors taught me to ask an engaged couple to wait at least one calendar year before moving on to marriage. That would give the two twelve months to see each other in a wide range of situations, as well as time to adjust to the daily routine of life. In my judgment that timeframe should be longer in extended adulthood. Mature couples need more time, not less, to put their own lives in order before blending them. There are a number of important reasons a longer period of dating and engagement is wise in extended adulthood:

- Couples have more history to meld at fifty or sixty than they did at twenty-five.
- Blended families may be formed with children from multiple marriages.
- Long-distance relationships can slow the development of the couple relationship.
- Decisions may need to be made about where the couple will live, what jobs they will take, who will travel, and for how long.
- Financial decisions may need time to evaluate as couples bring more complex financial situations to the table.

A major reason I counsel my couples that "quick is sick" is that a longer engagement allows for the possible emergence of red flag issues than can be successfully hidden in a whirlwind romance. Getting swept off one's feet can be result in issues being swept under the rug. Certain personality disorders can be masked for a brief period of time, but eventually they will emerge. Addictions may be denied, but in time their effects will be seen. Uncontrolled spending may not be obvious, but the bills will come due. Sexual triggers as a result of sexual trauma can be hidden, but eventually the dysfunction will emerge. We will look at these problems in depth in the next section.

I have found that "quick is sick" is the pattern of choice among those individuals who do not want to do their own core work and believe their own relationship failures are everyone else's fault. David needs to take a look at what is driving his addiction to falling in love. If Denise taps the brakes, he will either continue pressuring her or will move on to another match and dismiss her as "someone who didn't know a good thing when she saw it." Denise is the adult in this relationship, and she is being wise not to allow David, a very new match, to dictate her timetable.

## A Man Who Likes Women . . . A Woman Who Likes Men

As I've shared earlier in this book, I was sitting on the back porch with Dr. James Cail, my mentor, talking about starting to date again. "Do you have any advice for me?" I asked. "Yes," he said. "You need to find you a woman who likes men . . . and likes the kind of man you are." I thought, *What a strange piece of advice. A woman who likes men? Don't they all? And what's not to like about me?* In time I discovered that his first piece of advice was his best one. The principle goes both ways. Ladies, find a man who likes woman . . . and likes the kind of woman you are.

Dr. Cail's advice was clear. You are going to run into members of the opposite sex who are dating but really don't like members of the opposite sex. Entering extended adulthood, we all carry baggage from our previous relationships. These experiences shape our outlook on the opposite sex and our attitudes toward marriage.

Oddly enough, there are indeed men and women who clearly do not like members of the opposite sex but go into the world of dating anyway. Perhaps they are seeking the "perfect match" that will change their minds, or maybe they're looking for someone who can "pay them back" for all the bad times they've had in the past. I've seen men and women date and then find an excuse to dismiss every potential partner for reasons large and small. My belief is that they were trying to prove to themselves that no man or woman was really good enough for them to date.

To illustrate this dismissal and even hatred of an entire gender, I was teaching my course in Marriage and Family Therapy and asked my students to write a reflection paper on the kind of clients they would enjoy working with. One woman wrote that she was adamant she would never do therapy with a man. She could not relate to them and saw no reason to force herself to have any kind of relationship with them. I found this both sad and alarming. She had just dismissed half of the population. How she had managed to get into a graduate program in marriage and family therapy was a mystery to me. Men and women like this in some cases do date for short periods of time in order to confirm their belief system that no man or woman is good enough for them.

## No More Mr. Nice Guy

Alice Cooper in the seventies wrote the lyrics, "I used to be such a sweet, sweet guy till they got a hold of me, no more Mr. Nice Guy, no more Mr. Clean, No more Mr. Nice Guy." The song referred to a tragic man who spent his entire life trying to please everyone until he reached the point at which he couldn't take it anymore. His overly "nice" people-pleasing was his undoing, and he went over the edge.

Dr. Clif Davis is a pioneering psychologist and marriage and family therapist in Dallas who has spent decades advising clients in matters of the heart. Clif advises his clients, "Do not be altruistic in your dating. You need to decide the kind of person you want to be with and go after that unapologetically." Dating is not a time to be dishonest. It is a time to be honest with yourself first. People pleasers, like the tragic guy in the Alice Cooper song, spend their lives dancing to the songs other people write for their lives. They never learn to make their own music and end up in relationships that may be good for their partner but are less than ideal for themselves. Dr. Davis's suggestions for the man in Alice's song would include:

**Don't succumb to magical thinking**. Magical thinkers believe that "It will be quick, and it won't take much work."

**There is no such thing as instant intimacy**. True intimacy takes time to build, and quick intimacy may be an early warning sign of trouble coming later on.

**Some bring too much baggage to recognize health**. Some daters have become accustomed to being mistreated. Chaos or conflict is all they know. Put them with a good guy or good woman, and they don't know what to do. Often, they will sabotage the heathy relationship and return to a dysfunctional one.

**Managing anxiety with consistency**. A person who cannot manage the anxiety of being alone will reach out for a dating partner, any partner, to help them deal with their apprehension. They have to have someone, anyone, in their life, even if that person makes them miserable, sad, or angry.

Dr. Davis's mantra is simple: Don't Settle. People who put in the time and do the work often spend years in the dating world. They wonder whether true love will ever show its face, often coming to terms with the idea that love may not be in the cards for them. Yet when they do find the love of their life, they are thrilled that they were able to maintain their search and their optimism.

## Possession vs. Love

"There is a big difference between loving someone and possessing another person." Dr. Margaret Pinder, past President of the Texas Association for Marriage and Family Therapy and beloved Professor of Counseling at Amberton University, was talking to me about the difference between immature and mature love. "Real love gives each person room to be authentically who they are. It supports the person in their identity, dreams, and goals. People who want to possess their partner are all about control. Love is not controlling—it is freeing."

Dr. Pinder was speaking about the difference between sharing a life with someone and building a life together versus one person being controlled by another in a relationship. High control people cannot love well because loving well is about giving up control. A high level of control may feel very "flattering" to their partner at first: *He makes all the decisions. I don't have to think about anything.* The take-charge style feels so reinforcing. Until the first disagreement. Then attention turns into control.

Partners can try to control using a variety of techniques. I can over-talk you and drown you out. I can be stubborn and make every decision painful if things don't go my way. I can control the information in the relationship and not let you in on key things we both need to know. I can even use my weaknesses, addictions, or extended family members to exert outside influence, all with the purpose of maintaining control in the relationship. There are individuals who are wired for relationships based on a power exchange, and they will be very difficult to date, much less carry on a long-term relationship with.

Good life boundaries are like a backyard fence. They protect what is in my yard. They are not offensive but defensive. Things that "belong in by backyard" that I do not have to explain or defend include:

- My body
- My sexuality and sexual expression
- My hopes, dreams, and desires
- My preferences about whom I spend time with
- My beliefs and values
- My energy and need for rest
- My time commitments
- My right to say No without guilt
- My likes and dislikes

In a great relationship couples teach one another, honor their respective boundaries, and learn to enjoy their similarities and respect their differences. Relationships built on a control model say, in effect, "This is my yard—you are welcome to come into it and abide by my rules, but leave your own boundaries outside the fence." The controlling person's idea of a "relationship" is in effect an immature arrangement suitable for only one person. In my experience the association normally does not survive.

## Listen to Your Gut

Maddie and Mark had been dating for fifteen months when she discovered that Mark was living a double life. He traveled for his job and, while out of town, had a girlfriend in another city. He had smoothly convinced her that she was "the love of his life," only for her to discover when a girlfriend found his dating profile listed in another city that all his promises were lies. As we talked, Maddie tried to come to terms with the fact that some people lie as easily as they breathe. She confessed to having had "a gut instinct about Mark" she didn't quite like at the beginning, but he was so charismatic and convincing that she had just turned off the voices in her head. Those voices had proved to be prophetic.

Through the years I have encountered countless clients who have shut down the voice of intuition in their heads. They have driven through the warning signs and ignored the red flags, have turned down the volume of their best judgment and ended up believing a pack of lies. When the lies come out, and they always do, they kick themselves for having been so taken in by the deception. The didn't listen to their gut and ended up, like Maddie, paying a high price in time, emotion, and energy.

I firmly believe that life gives us an internal gyroscope that can sense the truth or smell lies when we hear them. When we hear truth, it feels solid. It has a tone of authenticity to it. We feel as if we can put our weight down on it and count on what the person is telling us. Conversely, lies alert our early warning system. I can almost feel when a client or graduate student is lying to me because I have been lied to so often. We can feel the duplicity, can sense their untruths, can track the parts of their story that just don't add up.

Dr. Paul Faulkner, founder of the Marriage and Family Institute at Abilene Christian University, used to speak about "the collective wisdom of the common man." He firmly believed that you could take a sampling of fair-minded people and expose them to a problem or situation and their innate common sense would kick in to resolve the issue. He believed that we possess collectively that inner sense of knowing what is true, right, and fair. When we ignore our inner voice, we put ourselves in peril.

One final note in this discussion. There are individuals who are masters at lying and hiding their true identity and motives. In Maddie's case, we learned that Mark had a long history of lies and deception and was masterful at presenting a fake image. While Maddie did turn down the volume of her own better judgment, Mark was an expert at helping her along in that process. We will look in depth at some of the masters of deception in our next section on Red Flags in Relationships. My best advice is this: when your gut alerts you of a problem, don't ignore it; reach out to a trusted friend or professional and have a conversation about what you are feeling. That could be the best decision you'll ever make.

## Come Close, Get Away

Kim had activated and deactivated her dating profile so many times that it looked like a revolving door. Following a breakup, often at her initiation, Kim would swear off dating and get busy building her own independent single life. She was done with dating, and that was it! Then, after some time had passed, she would start to long for a dating relationship. She was lonely and didn't want to be alone.

The profile would be reactivated, and off she'd go into the world of dating. Each time she'd connect quickly with a new match who promised to be different from all the others. A whirlwind romance would follow, and the two would act more like a married couple than two people dating. Then one morning Kim would wake up and feel trapped. She was lost in this other person and felt engulfed by the entire relationship. In a few days or weeks, she found a reason to end things and found solace once again in being alone. Until the pattern started over again.

Murray Bowen, a founding father of family therapy, talks about this pattern of bouncing between isolation and distance or engulfment and fusion. Some people crave their independence. Once they have it, and the isolation that comes with it, however, they begin to crave connection. Because they lack internal balance, they overreact and rush too quickly into a new relationship. The connection feels good for a time . . . until a new fear emerges. "The fear of engulfment" Bowen spoke of can cause someone to run from a relationship because they fear losing their own sense of self. Like Kim, they can find themselves bouncing between the two extremes of isolation and fusion.

Kim doesn't intend to send mixed messages to her partners, but she does. She sends a "come close get away" confusing mix of signals. Her dates are confused because she is confused. She would be wise to pause her dating, devote time to working with a trusted therapist, and delve into the pattern that drives her both toward and away from true intimacy. All too often it is easier to blame the dates for the repeated opening and closing of the dating profile.

## People Who Can't Do Relationships

One of the largest shifts I've made in teaching therapists over the past decade has been to discuss with them that some people have a very difficult time being in a relationship. I used to believe that with enough teaching, training, therapy, and work, almost anyone could learn to be in a satisfying relationship. While I still believe that the majority of us can enjoy a healthy bond, there are many people I've worked with through the years who lack the "basic wiring" to make a relationship work.

What are those basic wiring deficits some people lack?

*Reciprocity.* To be in relationship means to not always get one's way, and there are some people who simply have to be in control. They are going to be hard to remain in relationship with over time.

*Empathy.* Empathy is the capacity to recognize human need and then respond in an appropriate manner. Some individuals are low on the empathy scale and are very difficult to live with. When their partners encounter difficulties, they do not know how to respond in a compassionate, effective manner.

*Emotional Regulation.* To be an adult means that I must learn to control and regulate my negative emotions, especially when I'm in a complex relationship like marriage. Someone who "goes off the reservation regularly" is going to be very difficult to live with.

*Mentalizing Skills.* High on the list are good mentalizing skills. This refers to my capacity to sit in the presence of someone who disagrees with me, shut down my own arguments, and listen to their perspective. Great spouses have great mentalizing skills. They want to understand where the other person is coming from.

People who cannot play fair in a relationship, lack empathy and compassion, are constantly upset, and couldn't care less about seeing anything from another's perspective might make fine politicians in

Washington, DC, but they should have their license to date revoked. They are fourteen-year-olds in fifty-year-old bodies.

## Long-Distance Dating

Paul and Paula picked me up at the Midland airport to drive me to my speaking engagement. They had volunteered so they could tell me their story. They were newlyweds, although they were both in their late sixties, were clearly crazy about each other, and related that they had met online two years earlier. Paul was running a large homebuilding business in West Texas, and Paula was a Florida girl living along the panhandle near Destin. There was no chance their paths would have crossed in person, but when they both decided to give long-distance dating a try, they were shocked to discover that they'd each found the love of their life several states away!

Paula was retired from a career teaching high school math, and Paul was knee-deep in a large, family-owned construction business. Paul couldn't leave Midland without taking an enormous financial hit, but Paula was game for becoming a Texan. They both commuted for a time, and that allowed Paul to understand the world Paula had built in Florida. He spent time getting to know her kids, who were more than a little shocked that their mother was online dating and had met "this guy from Texas."

Paul and Paula were smart. They had both been in long-term marriages and had seen the value of compromise and remaining flexible. They took their time, built the relationship first, and then let the details of location, finances, and extended family begin to take shape. They knew there was no "right picture" of what marriage should look like for them at this time of life, so they built a new marriage around their unique needs and style. It took some time, travel, and more than a little intentionality, but they confirmed in the car that day that they had each met "their person."

At this point in writing, I have just married after a three-year long-distance relationship. I currently live in Dallas, and Lisa, my wife, lives in Houston. We have kept Interstate 45 busy on a weekly basis and now believe we have each been blessed to have "found our person." Because my work teaching, counseling, writing, and speaking can be done both in person and online, it now makes sense for me to relocate to her home in Houston. Lisa has a beautiful home and is a lifelong resident of Houston, so I did not want to distance her from her network of friends there. She has been the ideal match for me to build this long-distance relationship with, and along the way we have both learned some important lessons.

Looking back, there were some key factors that made long-distance dating work for us, and I saw those same qualities in Paul and Paula when we visited:

- A willingness to look beyond the normal geographic area and be open to matches from other locations
- A willingness on the part of both to travel and come to the other's home
- An interest in getting into the life that person has built in order to understand them better—friends, family, home, habits, and traditions
- Both partners prioritizing the time and energy it takes to build a relationship when not in the same town
- Keeping in regular contact with each other throughout the week when apart
- Setting aside funds to "travel and date" and seeing that as a positive investment in their shared future
- Flexibility on the part of both partners when considering plans for the future (my way, your way, and our way)
- Making the relationship totally safe—no secrets or lies, allowing trust to be built

## Settling Due to Fear of Moving On

Grace knew her mother very well. She knew when her mother was in love. This was not that. Grace had watched her mom in several relationships over the years and could tell when she was "excited about the idea of falling in love." This time she was going through the motions, hoping that the spark would somehow ignite into flame. It wasn't happening—and it wasn't going to happen. Her mother was "comfortable" but not in love. She was afraid to pull the trigger and end the relationship. Grace kept saying, "Mom, don't settle," and her mom kept rolling her eyes and saying nothing in return. Why do people stay in relationships they know are really not what they want?

*Avoidance of Pain:* It is painful to end a relationship. To have the conversation. To be honest about one's feelings. People go along in order to avoid being uncomfortable.

**Placeholders**: Sometimes we get into a relationship coming off a bad breakup. We know the relationship doesn't have wheels, but it is there to fill the space until time passes.

**False Hope**: We hope that one day, magically, we will wake up and possess that intense attraction to the other person that seems to be missing.

**Fear**: We may fear that this person may be "my only shot at happiness."

**Denial of Needs**: We may be denying our own needs and desires and being too altruistic in our dating.

A very wise therapist once told me that, when I am true to my feelings and release another person, it may be painful at first, but I am allowing them to find their person and me to find mine. William Bridges, in his excellent book *Managing Transition and Change*, notes that we all hate endings but that it is those very endings that can lead to new beginnings.

In this section we have looked at some important strategies you can use to build an approach to dating that will work for you. I've presented some models of attraction that help explain why we fall in love with the people we fall in love with. We've also gone into the therapy room and consulted with key dating coaches to discover ways to avoid common pitfalls of dating in extended adulthood.

"I should write a book." I've heard it hundreds of times from the mouths of men and women dating in extended adulthood. They've gotten out there, dated, gotten burned pretty badly, and walked back to the sidelines and sat down on the bench. "I'm done. If that's the way it is out there, you can have it. I'm not going through anything like this again." Then they relate their story to me. I listen carefully, and even though the exact details will change from person to person, I began to see them falling into several distinct categories. I call these Red Flags in Dating. Because they are so common in dating, I have devoted a separate section to them and assigned them an entire stage in the ReMatch process. My intent is not to be shocking or dramatic but rather to describe the common patterns I have seen or worked with in therapy.

# RED FLAGS IN DATING

# CHAPTER 12

# THE EMPATHY RED FLAG

Dale was not a woman to write a guy off quickly; in fact, she was known to be quite tolerant. But her recent first date with David had been such a disaster that she had quickly written him off and refused his offer for a second date. What alarmed Dale so quickly? In my terms, it was the absence of an "empathy chip" in David's hardwiring. They had agreed to meet at a restaurant for dinner at 7:00 p.m. Dale arrived a few minutes early and waited at the bar as they had agreed to do. Seven o'clock came and went with no sign of David and no text saying he was stuck in traffic and running late. By 7:15 Dale was wondering if this was a classic ghosting standup. Moments later a large man blustered through the front door and loudly yelled to the hostess, "Where the hell's the bar?" He was saturated with rain and was obviously frustrated at the delays in traffic around the restaurant.

David made his way toward Dale as she lifted her hand to signal that she was his date, and he came over; gave her a wet, rainy hug; sat down and quickly ordered a drink; and began to complain about the sudden rainstorm that had upset his timing. A brief but sincere acknowledgment of his tardiness never came, and Dale noticed the oversight on his part.

After sharing drinks and initial conversation, he asked if she were ready to eat. He approached the now somewhat overwhelmed hostess once again and in a loud voice that could be heard across the room demanded to know when their table would be ready. The hostess assured him that it would be soon, reminded him that he had been slightly late, and promised to seat them just as quickly as possible.

Dale noticed that David stiffened at what he perceived to be an insult and quickly informed the poor woman that he was a regular customer of this establishment and expected to be treated better than this. Once again Dale observed David's lack of perception, realizing that the hostess was doing the best she could and that David himself was to blame for the delay in being seated.

Dinner went from bad to worse. Dale would ask David a question about his life, which would lead to a long-winded dissertation going on for ten or fifteen minutes. He was blurting too much information too quickly. When he had finally finished, she waited for him to reciprocate with a question about her. It never came. An awkward silence would ensue until Dale would ask him another question, which would lead to David once again pontificating about his favorite subject—himself. When the evening mercifully ended, Dale noted that he had never asked her one question and that when she had offered up interesting tidbits about her life, family, or work, he had nodded, gone back to eating, and resumed talking about himself.

The wait staff had endured a challenge in human relations management. The server could do nothing right. The chef had prepared his steak wrong. The dessert was not what he had ordered, and the bill had been miscalculated. It seemed to Dale that David needed to be wronged so that he could be offended and straighten out everyone else around him—and then tell a war story showcasing how incompetent everyone else was. Dale sat there, politely enduring the meal and counting the minutes until she could escape this scene of dating disaster.

The "cherry on top" for the evening came when David made an observation about Dale: "I almost didn't recognize you at the bar tonight. You looked younger in your pictures. Have you put on weight or something? I know a lot of women photoshop their pictures." Dale was done! Strike three, and you're out. She couldn't wait to get out of there and felt as if she needed a bath when she got home to wash off the toxicity of the evening. She deleted his profile, blocked his number, and seriously considered giving up dating entirely. How could someone be so rude? How could he not see the effect he was having on other people? Worse yet, what kind of life would she have had being married to a man that shallow and callous?

When Dale and I visited, I told her that she had spent the evening with a man who was "missing the empathy chip." David's computer did not have any software to process anyone's wants, needs, opinions, or emotions other than his own. He may have been fifty-two years old chronologically, but he was about nine emotionally. His world revolved around David.

## Empathy—A Working Definition

Simon Baron-Cohen gave us a definition of empathy, calling it "the ability to identify what someone is thinking or feeling and respond to their thoughts and feelings with appropriate emotion." This, he explained, requires two skills. He proposed first that empathy involves recognition. One must recognize the condition someone else is in and realize when they are in pain or distress. In David's case, he failed to recognize Dale's alarm that he was running late or the hostess's stress from waiting on customers in a frenetic environment. It also didn't occur to him that Dale was entitled to time sharing about her own life in the dinner conversation. David failed the recognition test.

The second aspect of empathy is response. Empathetic individuals are able to see a situation and then respond in a compassionate manner. David's responses all evening were angry, frustrated, defensive, and self-absorbed. It never crossed his mind that Dale had carefully selected an outfit to wear that evening, had thought carefully about some questions to ask him, and had been looking forward for several days to sharing something about herself with him. David was there—but, then again, he really wasn't. He was on a date with himself, and Dale just happened to be sharing the table with him. Since Dale had a highly developed sense of empathy, she noticed the mismatch immediately and ended things quickly, as was appropriate.

## The Empathy Scale

Baron-Cohen was studying what makes people commit terrible crimes affecting other people. What makes people climb a tower and gun down a hundred people with a rifle? What caused the Nazis to murder over six million Jews and other "deplorables" they deemed worthless? He determined that the cause was the absence of empathy and developed a highly practical Empathy Scale to judge the level of human empathy, publishing his findings in an excellent book titled *The Science of Evil*.

What does all of this have to do with dating in extended adulthood? It's simple. One of the first things Dale noticed about David was his low level of empathy. Was his empathy radar turned on? Did he even have the empathy chip? It is my observation that people are drawn to individuals who rank higher on the Empathy Scale and that, even if one's date is not a "keeper," the date itself will be more enjoyable the higher they score. Conversely, lower scoring dates will leave the individual tired, frustrated, and ready to pack it in.

### Level 6: Remarkable Empathy

Individuals with remarkable empathy have their empathy radar turned on all the time. They are constantly aware of the thoughts and feelings of others around them and are eager to respond in an appropriate way. They are quick with an encouraging word, a kind card of sympathy, or a text at just the right moment when we are down and discouraged. Many of my counseling students are at Level 6 on the Empathy Scale. They came back to graduate school because they observe that, everywhere they go, people are telling them their problems. Oftentimes, partners with remarkable empathy are a joy to be in relationship with because they intuitively know what their partners need.

Characteristics of Level Six include:

- Continually focused on others' feelings
- Empathy radar never turned off
- Aware and responsive in a beautiful way
- Remarkable leaders
- Add wisdom and sensitivity to life

### Level 5: Just Above Average

Joan was a hard-driving manager of a highly productive sales team. She knew how to get results, and her team regularly received awards for exceeding their goals. But the thing that made Joan so unique was her ability to turn off the engines and take care of her people. A team member was admitted to the hospital while on assignment, and that night Joan had flown in to be at her bedside and make sure the company insurance was paying for everything. She was highly oriented to both production and people. Joan, as a date, would be perceived as a Level 5, Just Above Average on the scale. People with this level of empathy don't have it on all the time, but they can turn it on when the situation requires it and transition to Level 6 quickly. They can make excellent partners and entertaining date companions.

Characteristics of Level Five include:

- Can turn on empathy radar when needed
- Friendships based on emotional support
- Can hold their opinions and not rush to judgment
- Sensitive and willing to take their time with people
- Not afraid to lean into the "messy people stuff"

### Level 4: Low Average, Slightly Blunted

A few weeks after Dale's date with David, she had a first date with Mike. who was the manager of the local Honda dealership. A nice guy and very easy to talk with, Mike shared that he had been through several losses during the past year, including those of his mother, a longtime employee, and his best friend and motorcycle riding buddy. When she gently pressed him for details or inquired how he was doing, he offered a perfunctory "fine" and quickly changed the subject. She learned over the course of several dates that Mike was much better at sharing the concrete details of selling or riding motorcycles than he was the emotional intricacies of his own grief. Mike processed his emotions by declining to talk about or explore them, and he preferred not to process his partner's emotions, either. He was a successful individual in many ways, but he preferred not to get "all bogged down in emotional stuff you can't do anything about anyway."

Characteristics of Level Four include:

- Slightly blunted emotion that doesn't affect their daily life
- Prefer conversations that do not deal with emotion
- Family and relationships more activity or task oriented
- Modus operandi trying to fix the problem, not get into a long discussion about it
- Prefer not to be expressive about how they feel—or may not be aware

### Level 3: Mask or Compensate

As Dale and I talked and she learned more about the Empathy Scale, she shared with me the details of a very unusual first date she'd had several years earlier. She and Drew had met online and, although his profile was rather brief, found that they had some things in common and agreed to meet for a drink after work. He arrived precisely on time, dressed nicely but understandably nervous. He confessed to not accepting many matches or dates. He could carry on a conversation, but something was "off." It was as if his responses were scripted, practiced, or prerecorded.

She remembered as a girl going to the Dairy Queen, putting a dime into the juke box, and watching the automatic arm pulling out the selected 45 record. She felt with Drew as if her questions were the dime and his responses the pre-scripted answers. It was an interesting date, but Dale left with an odd feeling that she hadn't met the real Drew but just a scripted version of him meant for public consumption.

There are individuals who are somewhat aware that they lack the empathy and people skills to navigate society. Navigating emotions is a nightmare for them; even casual conversation can be a challenge, making the world of dating in extended adulthood very difficult for them. They may create a highly developed series of scripts to assist them in casual conversation as a way to engage in public and manage social relationships.

The problem comes when a date is interested in pressing past the rehearsed speech and wants to delve more deeply into a topic. In Drew's case, when Dale politely asked a follow-up question he struggled to answer, leaving him embarrassed and her unsure of how to proceed in the conversation. Dale and Drew's differing levels of empathy were actually increasing the mismatch, and Drew was relieved when the date was ended.

Characteristics of Level Three include:

- Somewhat aware that they have difficulty with empathy
- Masking or compensating for it
- Avoiding people or situations that require empathy
- Pretending to be normal with regard to empathy
- Finding small talk uncomfortable
- Preferring to be home and alone, finding it a relief to be by themselves

### Level 2: Blunders through Life

As she and I together explored empathy, Dale observed that we had not yet touched on David's style. Then when we came in our discussion to Level 2 her interest was piqued. There are those individuals who do not possess any empathy and blunder through life committing both large and small relationship wounds. They are unaware of the effect they have on other people, or they may be aware and just not care. "That's the way I am—take it or leave it!"

They can be highly successful men and women with the trappings of wealth and fame, but they leave bodies in their wake. They can do more damage in one phone call, text, or meeting than the average person would do in a year. Often, they are partnered with someone with a highly developed sense of empathy who spends their life running around after them cleaning up the messes.

They will do life on their terms, and other people's weak little feelings can go to hell. My expression in therapy for these individuals is that "they rub the cat's hair the opposite direction." David was on a Level 2. It wasn't necessarily the case that he was unaware that he had made Dale uncomfortable, the hostess stressed out, the waiter frustrated, and the people around him in the restaurant annoyed; it was that he didn't care!

If Dale had pursued this relationship, she would have found herself in one of three final destinations. First, she might have found herself in constant conflict and embarrassment from having to live through all of David's little tantrums. Second, she could have informally decided to take him on as a fixer-upper project. "I'm good with people. Maybe over time being around me will change him for the better." No, Dale, we call that crazy thinking.

Had she pursued the relationship, she would eventually have landed at destination three: "fed up and exhausted." I would have gotten a call in a year or two from a frustrated Dale, angry at David for "being such a jerk and for me for being so stupid thinking I could fix him—and look at all the time I've lost on this worthless relationship."

Characteristics of Level Two include:

- Major problems with empathy
- Leaving casualties in their wake
- Spouses and others cleaning up the interpersonal messes they leave behind
- Short with others, becoming angry and saying hurtful things
- May realize they hurt others but don't care
- Blundering through life saying and doing all the wrong things

### Levels 1 and 0

Levels 1 and 0 are inhabited by individuals who have no emergency brake on the things they say or do. They commit crimes like assault and murder and destroy property. They show little or no remorse, and since there is no conscience development they have no moral sense of right and wrong. There is no limit to the harm they can do to another human being because they see humans as objects or as deserving of their violence.

When triggered, their limited brain circuitry shuts down, and they attack. These people need to be in jail to protect the rest of society from their evil. Pointing out their misdeeds and the hurt they have caused is useless because they totally lack the empathy chip. They cannot recognize the suffering they have caused or respond in any appropriate manner. It was individuals on these two levels that Simon Baron-Cohen found to be responsible for the evil in the world.

I am, as discussed, the father of three police officers. They live in the world of Levels 1 and 0, and I hear a steady stream of stories of the vicious acts of criminals, both men and women, who exist without empathy and do unimaginable things. The "thin blue line" exists as society's only protection against Levels 1 and 0. If we are a nation of laws, then they must be enforced quickly and effectively with those who are incapable of self-regulation.

The current political insanity of the "defund the police movement" is a most ridiculous and dangerous idea because it encourages the dismantling of the only social structure America has in place to protect her from and effectively deal with those who inhabit these two lowest levels on the scale. In my counseling practice I say, "If you abuse your access to someone, you are denied access." In the criminal's case, law enforcement must deny persons on these two levels access to normal society.

## Red Flag Review

Dale discovered that the absence of empathy was a red flag for her. David, while a successful businessman, was still on "training wheels" when it came to emotional development. He was not interested in changing and in fact saw no reason to change: "What's wrong with everyone else walking around with their feelings on their sleeves?"

Dale also learned some things about herself. She learned that she was a person operating somewhere between a Five and a Six on the scale. She had a rather sophisticated radar and wanted a partner who could match it. She was not interested in a fixer-upper project and now had a new quality to add to her pocket list of non-negotiables for her match.

In my own work, not only as a therapist but also as a consultant to businesses, universities, and churches, it is the presence of high levels of empathy on the part of leadership that leads to long-term success. Conversely, it is the absence of empathy that sows the seeds of institutional destruction. That destruction may not come quickly, but it will come. The price for not dealing with people's emotions, whether personally or organizationally, will be paid, and it may cost the life of the institution.

# CHAPTER 13

# THE BORDERLINE RED FLAG

I was sitting around a large conference table with twelve older couples, all of whom carried a sad, grim look on their faces. We were a part of an "invitation only" support group sponsored by the National Institute of Health for Parents and Partners of Borderline Personality Disorder sufferers that was touring major cities. The group was offering support to family members with children, spouses, or dating relationships with people diagnosed as having BPD.

Over the next three months I would hear tearful stories from exhausted parents who had spent years trying to rescue their children, usually daughters, from the consequences of their destructive actions. One couple, a highly successful couple from Dallas, had gone so far as to build their daughter a separate small garage home behind their large mansion. She would rollercoaster between living there and trying to hold down a job and living on the streets.

Our two clinical facilitators were experienced in working with BPD and were there to gently offer healing and some new information about how treatment might proceed. I'll never forget the first night when they said, "Research in the coming years will reveal that there is not one form of BPD; there may be as many as 250 varieties we are running into all the time. We are just learning about this complex personality disorder."

We went around the table introducing ourselves. Each couple described their life and that of the individual in their lives suffering from BPD, oftentimes a now grown or high school age daughter, and the effects

BPD was having on their lives. All of the children with BPD represented in that group happened in fact to be girls. When it came my turn, I introduced myself, I stated that I was in a dating relationship with a very successful woman who suffered from BPD and that I was there to learn how to be a better boyfriend.

The room grew very quiet. When I said that I was just looking for someone to enjoy life and go to the movies with, the place broke out in laughter. The other participants knew better than me how impossible my expectations were with this particular dating partner. In time I would come to understand the rollercoaster ride I was on and why my emotional exhaustion had led me to this group in the first place. I would also come to understand why this particular red flag had hooked my own core wound and made me particularly vulnerable to women with this personality disorder. I would learn as much about myself as I did about BPD.

## A DSM Definition

The *Diagnostic and Statistical Manual of Mental Disorders* 5 states that "borderline personality disorder is a pervasive pattern of instability of interpersonal relationships, self-image and affects and marked impulsivity, beginning by early adulthood and present in a variety of contexts." It includes many of the following characteristics:

- Frantic efforts to avoid real or imagined abandonment
- A pattern of unstable and intense personal relationships characterized by alternating extremes of idealization and devaluation
- An unstable self-image or sense of self
- Impulsive behaviors in the areas of sex, spending, binge eating, substance abuse, and reckless driving
- Recurrent suicidal behavior, threats of suicide, or self-mutilating behaviors
- Reactive moods followed by periods of anxiety
- Recurrent intense anger, difficulty controlling anger, frequent displays of temper, and recurrent physical fights
- Stress-related paranoid ideation or severe dissociative symptoms

I drove by Carrie's house one Sunday afternoon to see her. She had custody of her two boys that weekend and was spending time with them.

When I got into the house, I found that the boys were playing video games in the living room and Carrie was taking a nap in her bedroom. The boys and I talked for a few minutes, and then I informed them that I was headed to the store to pick up a tie for a funeral I had to attend the next day.

As I was leaving out the back door, I heard the bedroom door open and Carrie coming out sleepily from her nap. When she learned that I was leaving she rushed to the back door, frantic to stop me. "Where are you going? Why are you leaving me?" I explained to her that I was just going to the mall to pick up a tie and would be back in a few minutes. At that moment a switch flipped, and she turned angry and attacked me verbally.

"Go ahead, leave me—go do whatever it is you have to do. Leave me just like everyone else leaves me. In fact, go back to that f@*#— ex-wife of yours and see if I care!" With that she ran to the bedroom screaming, slammed the door, and I heard things being thrown against the wall. I waited and a few minutes later opened the bedroom door to find her curled up on the bed crying and begging me not to leave. The boys outside on the couch were silent, terrified, having seen this little drama play out repeatedly through their entire lives.

Why does someone behave that way? How does this happen? And how could they ever be in a dating relationship, let alone a marriage? In this chapter we will look at some of the unique factors that make dating the individual with a borderline personality so seductive and destructive at the same time. We will also explore how this personality is a natural hook to certain other personalities and why it is so difficult to end such a relationship.

## No Safe Place

Healthy families give their children a sense of secure attachment, and the children find their parents consistent, safe, and easy to get close to. Secure bonds in childhood mean that people can experience secure emotional and other bonds in adulthood. At the other extreme are families in which the caregivers are scary and harmful. The child has no safe place because the parents or caregivers one day are reliable and approachable and the next day angry or abusive. The child never knows what to expect and is powerless to leave the family system. They are also dependent upon these scary, inconsistent parents for the only love they hope to experience—which never comes.

There is often trauma in these homes of a wide variety. The child lives in a state of fear and chaos and may retreat internally just to survive. Dissociation may be their only hope for survival. They personally experience a sudden shift in mood states that parallels the family chaos they are experiencing. They grow up without a sense of safety and can easily trigger, going into fight-or-flight mode not only as children but later as adults.

Carrie grew up in a poor working-class family, the older of two children with a younger brother. She was smart and pretty and had a naturally inquisitive nature that would lead her to a successful career in nursing later on. Her mother, who probably also had borderline personality disorder, was a walking time bomb. Intensely jealous of her pretty daughter, she would constantly berate her and in public introduced her as "my ugly duckling daughter."

Carrie lived in fear from the beatings her mother would inflict on her with anything that was handy—a broom, a skillet, a brush. She would run to the perceived safety of her father and looked forward to Saturdays when they would work together on his truck. When Carrie turned eleven, however, her father began sexually abusing her, and that continued until she graduated from high school. She could remember her confusion from her father coming into her room and having sex with her and then later hearing him do the same with her mother through the thin walls in the next room. Carrie never experienced one day of safety or any form of healthy attachment in her family growing up.

## Repeating the Pattern

I discussed earlier that the roots of attraction are formed in the family dynamics we experience growing up. Oftentimes we repeat the same patterns we experienced early in life. It is as if our primitive brain is trying to get that particular need met, but we keep running back to the same familiar old well that has already run dry.

In Carrie's case, she married as quickly as she could to escape the chaos, picking a man she thought her mother would approve of. "Pick a man with money, honey, and you'll be fine" was the soundtrack running through her mind. She did—and he turned out to be more abusive than her parents had been, combined. The marriage ended quickly, and Carrie returned home to her mother's judgment and abuse.

In nursing school Carrie met Carl and began hanging out with him. They became good friends, and, although there wasn't any attraction on her part for him, Carl was crazy about Carrie. After a year of his persuading her, she agreed to marry him, convinced that his drive to be successful would get her out of the poverty she'd been brought up in.

Maybe she could learn to be attracted to him . . . but that never happened. The couple built a financially successful life together, but their sexual relationship suffered. Carrie rejected Carl sexually and instead would spend money, run up debt, and often fly into unexplained rages at him and the children. Her emotional life was a rollercoaster of depression, anxiety, anger, and self-loathing. She would tell Carl, "If you think our life is chaotic, you should be inside my head." Carl had an affair, Carrie was devastated at a now real abandonment rather than a perceived one, and the marriage ended.

## Dating the Borderline

What happens when a person with BPD fills out a profile and enters the world of online dating? What happens when a friend says, "I know this really nice woman where I work, and I'd like to introduce you to her"? Are there some telltale signs of this personality disorder? Remember, people with BPD are often in highly responsible jobs and fields. The disorder is one of attachment and relationships, so they may function well in one area of their life, such as work, but struggle in their love life where the close attachment bonds are expected. These bonds can be made with a lot of therapeutic help, but often the BPD sufferer will not get the help they need or will blame everyone else for their struggles.

What are some of the signs of someone with BPD?

### A rollercoaster of emotional intensity and relational chaos

The romantic relationship will be intense emotionally, sexually, and intellectually, and that will be a part of the hooks it puts into a dating partner. The intensity can be intoxicating, but with that intensity comes a rollercoaster of emotion. One week we are doing fine, and the next we are in chaos. It's that combination of intensity and chaos that eventually leads the partner to declare, "I want to get off this ride!" But it is very hard to end the ride, as we shall see.

### Lies, manipulation, and gaslighting

Getting to "the truth" entails a confusing minefield of mixed explanations and fabricated stories. You never know if you are hearing the truth because the truth is a moving target. Truth for the individual with BPD is whatever is convenient for them at that moment in order to achieve their desired results. At any given time, the desire may be to stay attached to the partner or to punish them, but trying to get to the real story is like nailing Jello to the wall. Gaslighting is common when the most obvious reality is denied, and the partner is left wondering if they are really seeing the truth or going crazy.

### Wonderful and awful

The DSM noted that people with BPD bounce between idealizing their partners and devaluating them. One day the partner is Mr. Wonderful, her prince charming, the answer to all her dreams, and all her friends hear about what a great guy he is. But if the abandonment trigger goes off, as it did the day I needed to buy a tie, Mr. Wonderful becomes the Jerk, just another of the lousy men who have paraded through her life using her for their own purposes. Her partner will never know whether he is Mr. Wonderful or the Jerk from day to day.

### Painting black

After helping Carrie through graduate school, I attended her graduation, only to discover that her friends wouldn't speak to me and the faculty members looked at me as if I had two heads. They had heard horror stories from Carrie about what a terrible boyfriend I had been while she was struggling to work fulltime and take classes. In reality I had paid for car repairs and helped her with tuition and books. But I had been "painted black"—my dating partner had destroyed my reputation to exact vengeance for my perceived wrongs in the relationship.

### Rage

If you have never experienced a person with BPD raging at you, you will certainly remember the incident. When Carrie would trigger from an event, either real or imagined, her amygdala would fire off, and she would go into fight mode. I've got a fairly thick skin. I've had accusations thrown at me from angry students, clients, church members, and seminar attendees for years, but nothing comes close to the vicious anger that spews from the mouth of a sufferer from BPD. It is mean, personally targeted to the partner's exact vulnerabilities, and spat out with an intensity that is powerful and intimidating.

### Triangles

In couples' therapy I talk about triangles. Two people are not getting along, so one reaches out to a third party and downloads his dissatisfaction over the relationship. We now have three people in the mix—no longer a dyad (two parties) but a triad (three). Healthy relationships require dyads to resolve difficulties. People with BPD come into dating with lots and lots of triangles to which the date is drawn in. They are still involved with their ex and are still communicating with a one-time boyfriend . . . or two or three. You're wanting a simple dating relationship but find all these other men hanging around, with her refusing to clean up the mess. Thus, it is impossible to build trust.

### Plan B mentality

Carrie's mother convinced her that she would never attract a good guy—so she had better have a backup plan. Carrie always had that Plan B. There would always be other men hanging around, waiting in the wings for their time with her, because deep down she didn't feel worthy enough to keep a "good guy." "The good guys will leave me, so I had better have a backup plan for when that happens." The individual with BPD is terrified of being alone, and the partner dating them constantly senses that there is a "missing piece" being hidden from them. The problem at this point is that the lies, manipulation, and intensity mask their better judgment.

### Avoidance of help

A coastguard cutter comes plowing through rough seas in the North Sea. Ahead of them a woman is bouncing in the waves, about to drown. They pull up alongside her, call out for her to hang on, rush to throw her a lifeline, and pull her up on deck. The crew runs for blankets to prevent her from freezing. When the woman is stabilized the kind cook directs, "Wait here on deck; I'm going down below to make you some coffee."

When he returns, much to his surprise the woman has thrown off the blankets, jumped overboard, and is now once again in peril in the North Sea. This was the story I saw in the eyes of those parents that first night in the support group. They had steered their lives over and over again through rough seas to save a child bent of self-destruction, only to find the child quickly leaping back into harm's way.

## Styles of relating to their date

I discovered a useful model that describes the various roles a date with BPD may take on. They may, in fact, shift among several of these roles repeatedly over the course of the relationship.

- *Witch* represents the mean persona (angry and vengeful) the personality takes on.
- *Waif* represents the helpless or hopeless persona, intended to elicit a "knight in shining armor" response.
- *Queen* represents the entitled persona with the mantra, "I deserve anything I can get."
- *Hermit* represents the scared persona who often hides out to avoid the world.

## A Map of the Love Relationship

While attending the support group for parents and partners of individuals with BPD, I became acquainted with the website *Welcome to Oz*, a specialized site for families and partners of those dealing with issues of BPD. One particularly helpful article by Roger Melton described the various stages through which a love relationship with someone with BPD may progress. I found the article to be helpful and accurate, and when I share it in my classes it invariably sparks discussion and affirmation from my adult students.

### The Vulnerable Seducer Phase
- The female Borderline at first appears sweet, shy, vulnerable, and in need of rescue.
- She may "overshare" the details of her life early on to engage her date in the tragedy of her situation.
- This engages the man's Knight in Shining Armor gear.
- She conveys to him, "No one understands me but you. You are special!"
- The world has betrayed her, she intimates, but you understand her like no one else—and so quickly!

- Her gaze and interest are both razor-focused on the man.
- She craves listening to him, and he feels this to be his dream come true.

The key characteristic of this phase is its fast startup. The man feels that he has met his dream woman, and her focus is all about him. Many Borderlines, as well as narcissistic individuals, have an uncanny knack for perceiving the motivational patterns of their partners and using them to manipulate them. The intensity of the relationship is intoxicating, and if sex has started, which it almost certainly has, it is off-the-charts focused on him and becomes a strong hook in the relationship. The new dating partner feels as though he has met the woman of his dreams.

### The Clinger Phase
- The intense interest in the new partner subtly shifts to a focus on herself over time.
- The focus must be on her needs, her desires, her struggles, her life.
- For the partner, empathy becomes confused with love. He empathizes with her situation and is drawn to the sex, but this is not real love.
- Adult love is based on reciprocity or two-way care and concern—it is not about a one-way rescue.
- The Borderline has an innate radar for identifying partners who will be sympathetic and come to their rescue.
- Physical complaints emerge and then disappear at a rapid pace. There's always something wrong and a new ailment to be treated.
- She is depressed and then anxious or detached and indifferent as her moods shift from hour to hour.
- The partner is lost in confusion, trying to figure this woman out or trying to defend himself from being blamed for the last tirade.
- The sex and intensity will be wonderful for a while, until he becomes aware that it is being used as a tool in the manipulation.
- She is a black hole of needs that are never filled. There are emotional needs, financial crises, and physical ailments, and the partner is trying to fill a black hole.
- Her "I love you" really means "I need you to love me."

During this phase the rollercoaster ride officially begins. Relating to her is an ongoing ride alternating between stability and chaos, and she is an empty pit of needs that cannot be filled. Of special note is that at this phase the Borderline will isolate their dating partner more and more from family and friends. Children, best friends, and exes are all subtly painted black and begin to fade from the man's life. This gives her more control over his attention and energy. Anyone else is perceived as a threat.

### The Hater Phase

- At this phase the angry persona appears in full form, to the surprise of the partner.
- This Dr. Jekyll and Mr. Hide personality is both intensely intimidating and intensely confusing to the partner.
- The actual rage trigger is difficult for anyone to see. To the Borderline it is very clear: "You did this—you caused me to act this way."
- The rage will always be justified by blaming her partner for having hurt her.
- The rages are always unpredictable and unexpected.
- The rage can occur in public or in private.
- The wrath will tear down the partner over time.
- The raging can be extremely dangerous, leading to assaults, driving accidents, and embarrassing public demonstrations.

## Slot Machine Reinforcement

Scientists attempting to discover the most addictive behavioral pattern took mice and put them in front of a pellet machine with a key. Every time the mouse would press on the key, the pellet machine would expel one pellet for them to eat. The mice loved it! Then the researchers set the key to two strikes before a pellet would emerge. The smart mice learned to hit the key twice. They increased the keystrokes again and again in response to their favorite meal. Finally, mice were pounding the keys twenty or thirty strokes to get the pellets, with no apparent thought to the number of strokes they had to make.

Then the scientists changed the rules of the game. Instead of one stroke or five strokes, they set the key to random strokes. One time the mouse would hit the key twice and get a pellet, and the next time it would have to hit it twenty times to get the pellet. The reinforcement schedule was no longer regular or interval but was now random. When the researchers identified the mice who returned to the key at the highest frequency, it was always those that were on the random reinforcement schedule. Something about never knowing when the good-tasting pellet was going to return in the tray was very addicting.

What does this have to do with dating, and in particular dating and BPD? In the early phase of Vulnerable Seducer, the partner is getting high levels of immediate positive reinforcement. Her stories are fascinating, the eye contact is adoring, and the sexual encounters are passionate and all about him. The dating partner feels that they have met their dream woman and that this is going to continue for the rest of their life. They are hitting the key and a pellet is shooting out . . . and, man, does it taste good!

By the time we move to the Hater Phase, the episodes of anger have now replaced all the adoration. The Borderline bounces between loving their partner and hating him. The partner is on a rollercoaster ride between adoration and disgust from their BPD partner. Occasionally the adoration kicks in, and they go back to the "good ol' days" of Phase One, but those intervals get further and further apart. The partner longs for the intensity and passion of the Seducer Phase all the time, but it may happen only once a month or less. What they fail to understand is that Phase One, with all that adoration, fulfillment, and attention, was a mirage. It was all about meeting the needs of the Borderline.

But breaking off the relationship at this point is very difficult. Like the mice who are addicted to hitting the keys, they believe falsely that the next strike may put the relationship back to where it once was. They are addicted to periodic reinforcement, as with the mouse hitting the key one or one hundred times. One good day will keep them hopeful for another month or two that it's all going to work out fine. That's a lie. The real work of change hasn't even begun. In fact, the partner may be standing in the way of that change by remaining in the relationship.

I call this dynamic "Slot Machine Reinforcement." I met Jack Binion, the founder of the Horseshoe Casino, on a flight to Shreveport one afternoon. He talked about his life from the early days of gambling in Las Vegas. People, he pointed out, will sit in front of a slot machine all day long and feed coins into it because the system is based on periodic reinforcement. Just as with the mice and the pellets, these gamblers are addicted to the idea that the payoff may come with the very next coin. So, they can't walk away.

A relationship with a Borderline can be addictive in the same way. The addiction for her partner is to the idea that maybe he can turn her around and be the knight in shining armor, that the relationship may go back to the intensity of that early phase of seduction. The rollercoaster can become an addiction that destroys the rider!

## Exhaustion and Stumbling, in for Help

These clients stumble into my office confused, exhausted, angry, and feeling guilty for not having been able to figure out this complex and confusing dynamic. Many of them have been on this dating coaster for several years with a Borderline partner and have no idea what is going on. All they know is that they are worn out and cannot go on like this.

"Dr. Don, I'm a pretty smart guy, or at least I thought I was, but I have no idea what I've gotten myself into here. I am lost and need some help." They download a story that sounds very similar to the three phases I've just described and will often ask how they could be so astute in their business dealings and yet get involved in something this dysfunctional. "I feel like an idiot," they confess.

Actually, the very fact that they are high functioning may have led the Borderline partner to be attracted to them in the first place. Not all mental illness is roaming the streets begging for food. Some of it is walking the halls of our most respected institutions in highly responsible positions. The individual with BPD comes out only in their interpersonal relationships.

In my experience these relationships do not end overnight or easily. Couples tend to break up, stay apart for a while, and then reconnect and try it again. They attempt to go back into Phase One but find it impossible to do so. Every attempt to reconcile, without a serious and sustained approach to therapy on the part of the Borderline, will fail and end up exhausting the partner even more. By the time they reach my office, partners have normally been bouncing in and out of the relationship many times and are running on fumes. Other areas of their lives, including work, children, finances, and health have all suffered because of the rollercoaster effects of periodic reinforcement.

## Hooking the Knight in Shining Armor

If you are reading this chapter and wondering why anyone would put themselves through this kind of relationship drama, let's go back and look at the models of attraction we discussed earlier in the book. One of them was based upon the needs, both unmet and met, we experience in our families growing up. Our family of origin is the first experience most of us have with a love relationship and can be key to understanding who it is we will fall in love with later on and why we pick the partners we almost unconsciously do. This model is key to understanding the powerful hooks that a Borderline romance can have on a partner.

I was relinquished by my parents at birth and placed in the Vermont foster care system in 1957. This meant that there was no bonding with my birth mother, resulting in an attachment wound at the most vulnerable point in my life. I was adopted into the Hebbard family, and it was assumed at that time that the adjustment into a nurturing family would automatically resolve any earlier negative experiences I might have had.

This was, as we know today, an incorrect assumption. The co-fears of abandonment and betrayal had been poured into the foundations of my personality from the very start. It would be years before I would come to realize their impact.

My adoptive father was a CPA, a hardworking, dedicated churchman who was deeply devoted to my mother, the love of his life. My adoptive mother, unable to have children after multiple miscarriages, longed to be a mother. The couple had already adopted a daughter from the state of Connecticut and wanted to round out the picture with a son. Vermont was contacted, and I was the child agreed on.

My adoptive mother had two sides to her personality. There was the adoring side that would cook meals, clean clothes, and escort us to every team practice event. Then there was the volatile woman who would rage at my sister, at me, and even at unsuspecting store clerks who did not do what she wanted. I had been adopted by Mount Vesuvius. I have very clear memories of the sound of my father's dress belt coming off the top shelf and the experience of her wailing on my legs in a fit of rage over something I had said or done. Most of the time I had no idea what that was.

Our family dynamics were predictable. We all coped with her in different ways. My father escaped into work, teaching college and conducting church work. Whenever she turned her guns on him, he would give in because he knew it was pointless to try to "fight city hall." Dad was a conflict avoider. My older adopted sister dealt with my mother's raging and unpredictable behavior by running away. The hippie culture had hit the East Coast, and Greenwich Village was the scene of the new drug culture, so she rejected my mother and escaped there.

It is of note that she and my father had been very close, and that relationship had been the source of intense jealousy on the part of my mother. I've had numerous Borderline women tell me that it was a good thing they'd had boys because they couldn't have managed having a girl around the house who looked younger and cuter than they did.

That left me with my mother. My job was to follow her around and clean up the messes she made in public by verbally abusing people in stores, hospitals, and restaurants; interestingly enough, she would turn off this behavior at church. I was the family "fixer," the designated knight in shining armor who could make everything okay and take the focus off her rages and misbehavior.

Unbeknownst to me, I became accustomed to being with someone in a loving relationship (an adoptive mother) who also had a serious mental disorder. I couldn't escape the problem and got very good at covering it up. Remember that this was all happening unconsciously. By high school I had tired of all the drama at home, and when I graduated, I left home and returned only for brief visits.

Dr. Clif Davis, one of our dating experts in the last chapter, was discussing this dynamic with me one day in session. He was describing the impact it had on me unconsciously in terms of my selection of women to date: I was always picking fixer-upper projects.

The danger for me, Clif pointed out, is that I might fail to perceive my own contribution to this dynamic and keep repeating the pattern over and over again. But here was the good news: Once I had seen and owned the pattern, that perception would start to unplug its power over my attraction radar. "When you do your own work and heal that core wound of abandonment, betrayal, fixer, and knight in shining armor," he encouraged, "eventually that attraction will disappear. You won't be attracted to that kind of woman, and, interestingly, they won't be attracted to you. It's as if the two of you are two poles on a magnet that are repelling each other. If you do your work, you will begin to attract a whole different kind of woman and have a whole different kind of relationship."

You can now see that the attraction cycle to a Borderline partner was a natural fit for our respective core wounds. We were both dealing with issues of attachment and abandonment, though in very different ways. Ours was a match made with hellacious consequences for both of us. We were trying to build a relationship not on strengths but on dysfunction. We both needed to separate and do our own work, which thankfully we both did.

## Key Questions to Ask if Dating a Borderline Partner

When partners come in for help, therapists offer support and education and will often ask clarifying questions to help the person come to some kind of decision about their situation. Certainly, if the partner with Borderline Personality is committed long term to therapy, there are multiple new paths of treatment that can be effective if the person is willing to do the work.

Having a committed partner to do that work with them can certainly help the process. However, my experience has been that Borderline clients tend to bounce in and out of treatment, making heartfelt promises one day and then flippantly blowing off treatment the next. The proof is looking at what the other person is doing and not listening to what they are saying at times.

Dr. Maureen Lumley, one of our dating experts from the last chapter, suggests three important questions to ask the dating partners when they are on the rollercoaster of emotions and getting worn out:

1. Do you trust her?

2. Are your needs being met? In other words, is this relationship fulfilling you overall?

3. Can you accept her as she is right now, recognizing that this is likely all the relationship will ever be?

The answers to these questions can open up a conversation about where the relationship needs to go and, perhaps more importantly, the internal core work the partner needs to look at regarding what led to the attraction to begin with.

In this chapter we have looked at some of the dynamics of borderline personality in relationships. There are many more, and entire books devoted to them. In the next chapter we will explore an often-related red flag that is very common—sexual abuse and its effects on dating and relationships.

# CHAPTER 14

# THE SEXUAL TRAUMA RED FLAG

Mark came to me confused, tired, and bewildered by the dynamics in his marriage. "My wife, Michelle, won't come. She says the issue is all in my head and it's all my fault. So, this is my last stop—I don't know what else to do." He explained that their four-year marriage had gone from enchantment to disenchantment to absolute confusion. He and Michelle had met through some mutual friends and had begun dating. Both were in their late fifties, having been married before and with adult children who were delighted with the match.

Early dating was exciting. They discovered that they enjoyed many of the same things and felt that their dating dynamic was more one of "likes attracting" than "opposites attracting," at least to begin with. They traveled well together and enjoyed sports and an active social life. Having a partner made everything so much better for each of them.

The early days of the relationship were affectionate and warm, and the chemistry was obviously present for both. Mark had been brought up in a family that was openly affectionate, and his parents had a healthy view of sex as a vital part of a relationship. In his first marriage Mark and his wife, who had died of cancer, had enjoyed a healthy sex life and an easy, affectionate connection they had both enjoyed. He was looking for the same dynamic in his next marriage. Michelle informed Mark that she, too, loved sex and affection and that he need not worry because that area of their relationship would be one of the strongest—just trust her.

Mark started attending church with Michelle, and they became involved in the large community church's singles program. One day in class the singles' pastor made it clear that sex of any form before marriage was a sin and that anyone wanting to be a part of their group had to sign a purity covenant or risk being expelled from the ministry. Michelle had already signed it and told Mark in no uncertain terms that, if he expected to date her, he would have to agree that sex would begin only after they were married.

Mark, who had also grown up with a strong faith, was hesitant, but his love for Michelle convinced him to agree, so he signed the document. He thought it rather odd and possibly unwise, however, to take two mature people who were sexually experienced and dial them back developmentally to a time when they were young.

The marriage began with a ceremony for all their friends, great celebration, and hope for the couple. Everyone was excited that they had each "found their person." Their honeymoon to a relaxing beach was all-inclusive and an explosion of sexual passion. The pent-up chemistry from months of dating poured forth into days of sexual excitement, to the point that they found it difficult to keep their hands off each other and their clothes on.

Michelle especially seemed to flip a switch and became insatiable sexually, easily achieving multiple orgasms with Mark. Mark was in heaven over having found a woman who was his "best friend, lover, and partner in crime," and to celebrate their love and passion they bought a large antique apothecary jar and small cinnamon heart candies for the bedroom. Each time they made love they put a heart in the jar to commemorate their special attachment to each other.

Only a few months into the marriage, however, the situation began to gradually change. They were having a disagreement one night over an upcoming trip, and Mark noticed that Michelle seemed to freeze up, going glassy-eyed and seeming to disengage from the conversation. It seemed as if she really wasn't present any longer. He ended the conversation but noted that she stayed silent and more reserved for several days.

Their affectionate relationship began to cool, and they became more distant. Michelle didn't seem to want him to hug her, touch her, or at times even hold her hand. Then other days she was back to the same warm, loving woman she had been when they dated. He exhausted himself trying to replay in his mind what he might have said or done to garner these contradictory reactions, even going so far as to keep notes on his calendar about their conversations to make sure he hadn't said something to upset her. There was no evident pattern to her engaging and withdrawing, however, as far as he could tell.

Sleeping together had become an interesting experience of "come close and get away." Some nights Michelle would snuggle up close to him, and they would fall asleep in each other's arms, mutually enjoying the comfort and closeness of human touch. On other nights, however, she would sleep on the edge of their king size bed in a fetal position, with a wall of pillows between the two of them. Once again Mark was at a loss to determine what he might have done to cause this reaction. His questions were met with a blank stare, or in the morning she would hug him while he shaved, as if to say, "I'm back to being connected to you now."

Sex had become a confusing minefield for Mark. They had waited to have sex until their honeymoon, as she and her pastor had requested. But what had started out on the honeymoon with fireworks and a promise of good things to come had turned into a revolving door of sexually mixed messages. There was the passionate Michelle who loved sex, would do anything Mark and she desired, and was easily orgasmic in a variety of ways. This persona emerged on occasion, and when it did their sex life was dynamic.

Then there was the cool and aloof Michelle. She didn't want sex or affection and quickly rebuffed any advances on Mark's part. It became clear early on that Michelle had to be in control of everything sexual in the relationship: when they had sex, how it was done, and on whom the focus would be—which was ordinarily her.

Finally, there was the tough Michelle. Any attempt by Mark to approach her and talk about difficulties resulted in the tough girl persona emerging. Affection and sex went from a regular part of their relationship to the occasional outcome of a guessing game. They would go through periods when they would have sex daily, with Michelle enjoying every minute of it, to months during which they would engage only once or twice. During those confusing times there was no visible relationship rupture that might be keeping them apart.

It was during such a period that two additional patterns emerged in their relationship. First, Mark noticed that when he pleasured Michelle in certain ways this would immediately trigger her to shut down and end sex or to simply freeze up and lie there motionless. He noticed that any stimulation around her neck and shoulders tended to result in this reaction. He also noted that she did not wear jewelry around her neck or clothing that gathered around her neck. As an experienced lover, he tried to be conscious of her preferences and to avoid doing anything that might shut her down even more.

The other interesting change was in Michelle's public persona. In the past when they had gone out in public, her focus of attention had been on Mark. She was clearly proud of him and proud to be seen with him. Now when they went out it was as if a light switch had gone off and Michelle had to be the center of the attention of all the men in the room.

Driving to an event, she would be quiet and tired appearing, hardly talking to Mark. When she got there, however, she would light up and engage the men in flirtatious conversation while Mark sat back and observed the show. Driving home, she would return to the introverted, tired woman and would crawl into bed in the fetal position, not wanting to be touched. Mark wondered what was happening to his "party girl" once they were alone. Why did every other man in the room warrant all the attention? In his first marriage he had not been known as the jealous type, although he had been married to an attractive woman.

Mark learned over time that there were always other men hanging around. Clif, Michelle's boss for the past seven years, was an important fixture in her life—a non-negotiable part of her social system. He had helped her buy a car when she had needed help. She managed some of his investment properties, and they would often meet at the rental homes after work to conduct business. She received expensive jewelry as gifts from Clif on her birthday, and at the holiday party Mark observed that Clif's wife obviously disliked Michelle and the relationship she had with her husband. Michelle blew this off and thought of Clif's wife as a controlling, spoiled bitch.

But there were other men, too, "hangers around," Mark called them— who were always in Michelle's circle and had some history with her. She was constantly talking to her ex-husband and giving him "dating advice" about the women he was seeing.

Mark happened to read an email her ex had sent her with a sexy pic attached. When Mark hit the ceiling, Michelle defended her ex, protesting that the email had been a mistake; he had sent it to her by mistake, and there was no reason for him to be so paranoid. Mark even observed Michelle talking intimately with her college-aged daughter's boyfriend and then seductively taking him by the hand to "tour the house" with her.

It was during these months that Mark noticed the disappearance of the love apothecary jar, which was never to be seen again.

When Mark would try to discuss the situation with Michelle, she would shut down and freeze up or become angry and defensive, lashing out at him for being jealous and an over-sexed jerk who didn't love her and wanted only to use her body. Mark was speechless. When he offered to pay for counseling, Michelle retorted that she had been to counseling with her singles' pastor and had worked through all of her "issues"—now he needed to do the same thing. She was fine, and he was the problem with his high sex drive and jealous personality. She had just finished reading a book and had decided from it that he was a narcissist. She phoned her singles' minister and informed him of Mark's sins, asking to have the group "pray for their marriage to be healed."

Mark was not only stuck when it came to therapeutic options but was also stuck sexually. He was married to a woman he was intensely attracted to and with whom he had experienced a passionate relationship for a brief period of time. What was he to do with his sex drive? He wasn't going to have an affair and was committed to making this marriage work. When Michelle walked in on him masturbating one night, after one of the many times he'd lain awake waiting to see if she was going to initiate sex, she declared him to be a sex addict in need of intensive therapy.

Mark stumbled into my office tired, confused, and angry, reporting that he had thought he'd "done everything I was asked to do, but I feel like I'm in a washing machine on the spin cycle." Relationships in extended adulthood were supposed to be fun, he lamented, but this was anything but. What Mark failed to understand is that there had been forces at work that far preceded his relationship with Michelle but were powerfully controlling many aspects of that relationship, including communications, trust, sex, and conflict resolution. In my experience the case of Mark and Michelle is not unusual but normative for couples dealing with the long-term effects of sexual trauma.

## How Common is Sexual Abuse?

When I opened my first counseling center in Irving, Texas, in 1982 I was treating a wide range of couples, from affluent couples from the new and upscale Las Colinas development to working-class couples from the warehouse and industrial section of south Irving. By the end of the first year, I was keeping another therapist busy with referrals for sexual trauma that was impacting the marriages I was working with.

About one in three couples, I was treating were dealing with this issue. I have come to believe that child sexual abuse is the most ignored and untreated mental health crises of my lifetime. Its effects on the victim's normal development, the marriage, and the entire family system are undeniable and unprecedented. My judgment is that, in our current socio-cultural climate, the problem is getting worse rather than better and will be an issue for adults dating at any age. It is of special concern in extended adulthood, as we shall see.

Statistics indicate that one in four women will have been sexually abused by age eighteen, as well as one in six men by that age. Men report sexual abuse less often than women, and it is my belief that in the coming years we will see the number of men increasing as barriers to reporting come down for them. Two-thirds of victims do not report the crime until their thirties, if at all.

The profile of the victim is not limited by age, race, socioeconomic status, religion, education, or neighborhood. Sexual abuse knows no bounds. There are approximately 730,000 registered sex offenders in the United States. Male to male sex offenders will average 150 victims before prosecution and male to female offenders 52 victims. The average age at which a perpetrator starts is thirteen or fourteen, while the average age at which they may first face prosecution is somewhere between thirty and forty—meaning that they have been victimizing children for upwards of twenty-seven years. Tragically, we believe that less than 3 percent of abusers will ever encounter the criminal justice system. Criminal background checks are not the silver bullets, identifying as they do less than 10 percent of perpetrators. Hence my belief that this is the critical mental health issue of our time.

Identifying the perpetrator by "stranger danger" simply does not work. It's impossible in advance to spot these people. Ninety percent of victims are abused by people they trust, either in the family or as trusted friends with access to the family. Sometimes the parents know the abuser well and actually "bless" their time with the child, assuming everything to be alright. The abuser has gained access to the family and garnered their trust. It will be difficult to suspect that this person could do this; they are camp counselors, coaches, pastors, teachers, volunteers, and music instructors. They are inside the fence.

We understand now that not all molesters are male and believe that upwards of 10 percent may be female (compared to about 90 percent male). The female may be a counselor, music teacher, coach, or church pastor who has access to children and has gained family trust. Also, the rate of peer-to-peer sexual abuse is on the rise, with a 300 percent increase in peer sexual abuse within the past eight to ten years.

The abuse normally occurs with someone trusted by the child and the parents, breaking the trust bond that is forming developmentally for the child. "The people who love me protect me" messaging is now replaced with "the people who love me abuse me." This blight in poured into the foundation of the personality and will continue to operate in adulthood like a software program running in the background. It isn't opened up on the screen but is constantly running through an invisible script. This was the dynamic Mark ran into with Michelle. It wasn't visible at first, but the abuse was running the show.

The abuser, a friend or relative, will gain access to the child and separate them from the group or family so they can have private time with the them. The grooming process will include creating the image that the child is special and introducing them to pornography and sex talk. Every case-one law firm in Ft. Worth encountered cases involving the use of pornography. This reinforces two powerful motivators for the perps, which are secrecy and arousal.

Eventually sexual touch and nudity are introduced, and even though children have a sense of what is appropriate the abuser learns to gently push them through the boundaries. Michelle as an adult had a hard time setting sexual boundaries or even knowing what those might appropriately be. Her normal boundary development had been violated by sexual abuse.

Tragically, about two-thirds of sexual abuse victims don't tell until adulthood, even if then. They are inhibited by threats that they will be blamed for the assault. Sexual predators commonly explain away their behavior, countering, "The child was being seductive with me and wanted this, so it was not my fault."

The number one reason children do not report the abuse is that they do not believe anyone will take them seriously. This is a stinging indictment on the condition of parenting in our country today. Children are left with no one to trust. It is common for children who do make an outcry to be ignored or minimized: "This is a good family; we won't hear of such a thing." Yet the Center for Disease Control notes that 92–98 percent of all cries for help are legitimate, even if the intimidated victims later recant.

As a clinician I have found that many of my clients whose lives and marriages were dramatically impacted by sexual abuse take a nonchalant attitude, rationalizing that the abuse "just happened back then. I've put it behind me and moved on. It's not affecting me now, and I'm not going to think about it."

In actuality, the wound of abuse is running on the laptop of their life every day, taking up a massive amount of space on their hard drive. It is affecting the function of other programs, such as marriage, relationships, sex, intimacy, communications, and emotional regulation. But because it is minimized and not manifesting on the home screen, the victims choose to power on through life and ignore it. They and their spouses are both the losers in that decision. But the core work in this situation is something most people will refuse to do, as Mark had found out.

Long-Term Impact on Children:
- Depression
- Suicide
- Eating Disorders
- 98 Percent of Prostitutes Sexually Abused
- Substance Abuse, either Legal or Illegal
- Seductive or Promiscuous Behavior to Get Attention
- STDs
- Excessive Modesty, Females Layering Up

## Inhibition, Disinhibition, and Bifurcation

How may sexual trauma walk itself out in adulthood? Dr. Heather Mac-Intosh in *Principles and Practices of Sex Therapy* suggests that sexual trauma may present in one of three ways in adulthood or in a combination of the three. She calls them Inhibition, Disinhibition, and Bifurcation. We will look at all three and apply them to the case of Mark and Michelle.

### The Inhibition Style
The inhibition response to sexual abuse will suppress, restrain, or avoid normal sexual feelings and responses. This approach can manifest

itself in avoiding relationships altogether or attempting to date and then pulling back when the partner expresses affectionate and sexual advances. It may demonstrate itself in behaviors that would tamp down the natural sexual attractiveness of a person through excessive weight gain or loss and a layering up of clothing to conceal the body. The inhibition style can be found in the dating population in people who may want a member of the opposite sex "around" to fulfill companionship needs but may not be interested in a sexual relationship. Or they may experiment with dating and then run from the relationship when the dating partner begins to be affectionate toward them.

### The Disinhibition Style

The disinhibition style addresses the core trauma wound in an opposite manner than the inhibition style. This style telegraphs the person's sexuality through dress, behavior, pictures, and dating profiles. The victims have learned at an early age to relate to the opposite sex from a sexual standpoint, and that set of behaviors has carried over into adulthood. The disinhibition style may be flirtatious and outgoing, and the person may dress in a provocative manner. They may give off the impression of being somewhat histrionic, needing the attention of everyone in the room to be on them. Interestingly, a combination of the Inhibition-Disinhibition style may emerge, with the survivor being sexually provocative in public but inhibited in private, as we saw in Michelle.

### The Bifurcation Style

The bifurcation style results from a splitting of one's sexuality. The victim may be sexually inactive or periodically active with their primary partner, while carrying on an active sex life with other lovers that is kept secret from their spouse. The effect is an ongoing sense of uneasiness in the marriage, evoking an uncomfortable suspicion that there is a "missing piece" in the relationship. When the secret affair or sexual liaisons are discovered, the rupture can cause irreputable damage to the marriage.

The victim of the abuse does not know how to walk into the memories of the trauma, and the spouse is traumatized by the revelations of the hidden sex life of their spouse. To make this even more challenging, there is no one predictable pattern. Dr. MacIntosh observes that "Some survivors switch from one to the other over time, and clinicians should not assume that a survivor avoiding sexuality with their current partner has always been avoidant, or that they are avoidant with all potential sexual partners."

In the case of Mark and Michelle, she was a survivor who was manifesting the Bifurcation Style. After a brief interlude of sexual relations with Mark, her core wound would emerge to erect the closed boundaries that would keep her safe but alone. Occasionally and without explanation those boundaries would come down and the couple would connect, but then the software of abuse that was running in the background of her computer would kick in again and drive her away from him. The message that "the people who love you hurt you and can't be trusted" had been poured into her foundation at a young age, and the fact that Mark was a kind and loving husband actually triggered more avoidance in her.

Michelle's bifurcation continued with an active and casual sex life through casual encounters with men she met through her work and church life. Clif was a classic example. He fit Michelle's type; was safe in that he needed anonymity because he, too, was married; and gave her positive reinforcement as a sex partner and through his gifts to her. Mark lived in a constant state of confusion, looking for reasons in their relationship that might explain the perplexity, when in reality the undercover abuse software was running the show. If he'd had the benefit of being privy to those thirty years of her history, he would have seen this pattern repeated many times.

Michelle's stance was the typical one I encounter in therapy. Mark was blamed for being controlling, overly sexed, and an insensitive partner who needed to do his work in therapy. Michelle was not interested in looking at her wound in a slow, careful, and respectful manner with a trained therapist. And at this stage in her life, I found it questionable to assume that she as a survivor would choose to do the work and heal the wound. It would be easier for her to just end the relationship with Mark and to power on through life with clenched teeth. Michelle would spend enormous emotional and psychological energy keeping a lid on all that pain.

## Effects on the Relationship

### Trust

When people are traumatized in childhood, especially by those close to them, this can impact their ability to trust their partners in adulthood.

### Closeness

Because being close to someone in childhood brought pain, closeness to one's partner in adulthood can be a scary thought. Childhood trauma can cause feelings of shame, guilt, insecurity, and self-criticism. These feelings can make it very difficult to draw close to another person in adulthood.

### Sexuality

Because sexual trauma occurs during the critical periods of childhood development, normal sexual development can be arrested. The survivor is uncomfortable in their own sexuality, and certain positions, ways of touching, or other stimulation can trigger old memories that retraumatize them.

### Emotional Regulation

Childhood trauma can make it very difficult to understand, feel, and tolerate the victim's emotions and those of their partner. When you or your partner is upset, it may be very difficult to tolerate those feelings or know how to respond.

### Communication

A child may have been brought up in a family in which being clear, direct, and honest was very dangerous and might have triggered more abuse, resulting in the child never learning how to express themselves in a relationship. They struggle as adults to know how to communicate, and some, like Michelle, simply freeze up and don't know what to say.

### Confusion

Partner confusion and exhaustion is the hallmark of this relationship. Spouses and partners may not even know there had been sexual abuse in the past or the extent to which it actually occurred. Partners like Mark may be anxious to help but may sense that there is a missing piece to the whole story.

### Confederate Fillers

People do not go through life with an internal psychic hole in their emotional lives. They are going to fill the void with something else if they choose not to heal the wound. Some of those substitutions may on the outside look positive, while others are clearly destructive. People try to stuff that hole with drugs, alcohol, excessive spending, or gambling away the family savings at the racetrack. They may cram it with seemly positive activities like exercise, getting another college degree, taking care of children, raising animals, or excessive work. For a time, this seems to work, but it's like going to the convenience store to buy Thanksgiving dinner. You may get some junk food to fill you up, but you haven't satiated the real need.

I have practiced in the world of organized religion throughout my whole life. I am trained theologically and take spirituality very seriously, but I have seen people try to use religion as an excuse for failing to do the hard work of therapy. Will you go in for counseling after your third marriage has failed? "No, my pastor met with me and prayed, and I've been delivered from my past. I met a great partner and my whole life has changed."

Really? What about the hard work of facing one's attitudes, behaviors, and emotions? I've worked with countless Christians who meet with me a few times but bolt for the door as soon as we get close to the core issues they need to look at. Luke's Gospel makes pretty clear the way God looks at change. John the Baptist enjoined his audience to "Bear fruit worthy of repentance." In other words, "don't tell me; do the work and show me."

## Addicted or Abandoned

Many partners of survivors who bifurcate find themselves in a difficult, no-win situation. Like Mark they have made a serious commitment to one person, and that commitment includes their sexuality. They are trusting that person with their sexual needs and for sexual fidelity. "You are the one I want to have sex with, and that excludes everyone else because you fulfill me in every way," is their message. That's a great approach when it's working and reciprocated.

However, when the rollercoaster of bifurcation starts, any spouse finds themselves in a position of having no control over their sex life. Their partner is on one month and off the next, and there may be ongoing hints of affairs. There may be unexplained flirtation, messaging, and texting and an ongoing sexual drive on the part of their spouse that is not being met. Every day comes the nagging question, "I wonder if we are on or off today."

Men and women with a moderate to high sex drive who may expect daily sex several times a week become especially frustrated. The thwarted spouse may ask in bewilderment, "We talked before we got married about how frequently you wanted to have sex. What happened to those discussions?"

Men and women, especially those who have been married before and experienced an active, healthy sex life, will often turn to routine masturbation to assuage their biological needs while waiting on their bifurcating partner to initiate sex. Mark found himself resorting to this practice and felt confused, guilty, and resentful.

When Michelle walked in on him masturbating to an adult video or some other erotic stimulation, she was hurt and confused. She quickly assumed that Mark was a sex addict, labeled him as the "problem" in the relationship, and even reported his behavior to her singles' pastor, who recommended treatment. Mark was labeled and blamed for having what amounted to a normal cycle of sexual arousal, and Michelle was able to fly under the radar and keep her wounds hidden yet again. Mark was not addicted; he had been abandoned.

## Advice for Dating in Extended Adulthood

We have covered the following advice earlier on in this book, but I feel it bears repeating.

### Go Slowly

One of the reasons I recommend that people move slowly in their dating in extended adulthood is to allow all aspects of the other person's personality to emerge. Sometimes that takes a little time.

### Minimize and Maximize

Some survivors will minimize the impact of the abuse. "The computer program is still running in the background, but it's been minimized on the screen. Other survivors will maximize the story. It's their lead story, and they download all the history on the first date. The abuse has taken center stage and has become synonymous with their identity. A healing approach may be signaled by someone who is able to address what happened and suggest steps to mitigate the problem in a way that is measured and appropriate to where the relationship is at that time.

### A Two Gets a Ten

One of the telltale signs of trauma in my work is a situation in which a level two (minor or routine) event or comment elicits a level ten reaction. We will be discussing something that on the surface seems to rank at about a one or a two in importance, and the emotional reaction I get is at a level of eight, nine, or ten. That often is a signal that there is something deeper going on there that could have to do with a traumatic event.

### Getting Rid of Old Lovers

We can and must cut off old boyfriends and girlfriends. They can and should get the clear message that "I am in a committed relationship, and there's no flirting or texting around." I have a simple rule for relationships: Anyone seen as a threat to the relationship is gone. The bifurcation partner may have lots of exes hanging around, and that is in my estimation a deal killer.

### Freezing Up

Every time Mark would engage Michelle in a problem-solving discussion, she would get glassy eyed and freeze up. Her amygdala would go into fight-or-flight mode, and she would be back in that panicked victim state. She lacked the wiring to walk into conflict, so every serious discussion ran the risk of her reverting to panic mode.

### Mentalizing Skills

Mentalizing skills refers to my ability to listen to what someone else is saying even when I disagree with them—to hear them out. These skills are essential for a couple's communication. Trauma can short circuit one's ability to mentalize and prevent them from stepping vicariously into the other person's shoes. Without doing her work, Michelle was lacking the skills to hear anyone who might trigger her fear reaction.

### Predictability in Sex

Sex in extended adulthood is very important because the partners come into a relationship with very different sexual histories. I will devote an entire chapter to this subject, but it is important that this area of the relationship develop as normally over the time of dating as any other areas in order to determine whether the two are sexually compatible and if sexual trauma will be an issue in the relationship. As we've discussed, for the person manifesting the bifurcation pattern this may take time to emerge, and it may happen subtly.

## Epilogue

What happened to Mark and Michelle? The relationship might have gone a number of different ways. Michelle might have blamed Mark, continued to insist that he was the problem, and retreated behind her defensive walls. He might have sought treatment for the presumed sexual addiction or refused it entirely, and the marriage might have ended up going parallel, with the two of them pursuing their own lives in tandem.

Another possible scenario is that an affair or affairs on Michelle's part went public and blew the marriage apart. As the details of Michelle's secret sexual life became known as Mark's friends shared stories about her that they had held back before, he might have felt traumatized by the enormity of the problems. The rollercoaster had already left him exhausted and struggling to make sense of it all.

However, Michelle might have had enough insight to recognize that she had married well. Mark, in fact, was a man who deeply loved her and would be committed to joining her in a healing process. If she could gather up the courage to take the first step, she would discover that she was not alone. Trust could be found, and healing could come about within the confines of a healthy, committed relationship. The choice was up to her.

Stage Five brings us to the area of sexuality and intimacy. By this point in life adults will have an extensive sexual history that will inform their attitudes, wants, and desires related to sex in dating. In the next chapter we will explore the varied sexual styles someone may encounter as they begin dating in extended adulthood.

# SEXUALITY

# CHAPTER 15

# DATING AND SEXUAL STYLES

Craig was confused. After a difficult divorce and giving himself time to heal, he had decided to date and had been online and using some dating services locally. His profile was attractive. He was good looking, owned a successful medical sales company, and enjoyed a large circle of friends. Financially secure and emotionally healthy, he had expected that dating would be a breeze, but he couldn't have been more surprised. He had been dating for almost a year when we visited, and I asked him what was so difficult. "I go on dates and the expectations sexually are so vastly different. I never know what to expect." I asked Craig to describe some of the dates he'd been on, and he shared the following stories to illustrate his confusion:

"I had a first date with an attractive, successful woman I met online. We had emailed, texted, and then talked on the phone and decided to meet for coffee. Up until meeting, things were fairly casual and relaxed. When I met her at Starbucks she sat down, and it felt like the interview had begun. She worked her way through a long series of questions about me and my life. That was fine—I was happy to share, but I felt like I was being interrogated more than in a natural flow of conversation. After she finished her questions, she ticked off a number of things she reportedly 'must have.' She didn't want to acquire someone's debt. She wasn't interested in raising someone else's kids, and she wasn't going to have sex before she got married again. She presented all of this with a 'take it or leave it' attitude.

"Another woman I met was quite different. She was a music teacher, and we connected over my love of Classic Rock music. We met for dinner one evening, and after the prior first date I was better prepared with answers to all of the key questions I might be hit with. Instead, we ended up talking about all the great concerts we'd attended over the years and who are favorite artists were from live performances. I was enjoying her company but really didn't feel that much attraction to her, though we could have become good friends.

"When the dinner ended, she offered to drive me to my car, as it was raining and I was parked a distance away. As we kissed goodnight, she slipped her hand into my slacks and began to jerk me off. I was so surprised that I didn't respond—which didn't bother her in the least. After meeting the first woman with her list, I hadn't exactly been prepared for this date.

"I had a rookie-meets-a-veteran kind of date that went very well. She had been dating online on and off for a couple of years. When we connected online, I didn't feel rushed, and she was always timely and polite with her messages back to me. I was impressed by her confidence and the comfort she felt in her 'own skin.' She seemed to know who she was and what she was looking for.

"As we began to date the subject of sex didn't come up immediately. In fact, most subjects seemed to just emerge very naturally in the conversation as we got to know one another. When we did talk about sex the conversation was very open, honest, and comfortable. She shared that her approach was to 'let things walk out organically. Let them develop as the relationship develops.'" Craig shared his relief that he did not have to resort to a list to respond to or try to torque his chemistry to match someone else's attraction to him.

Craig continued, "Probably the most interesting evening I spent was with a woman who was in 'the lifestyle,' as she expressed it to me. We had come across each other's profiles online and had both sent messages, so we knew there was some mutual initial attraction. After drinks one evening she shared that she was looking for a man who was educated, successful, and attractive. She wanted a serious, committed relationship with a man who was open to her lifestyle. She had several men she enjoyed having sex with and wanted to continue that as a couple once we were together. She had decided that I would be an ideal match for her if I were open to a committed but open relationship."

Craig was not alone in navigating the brave new world of sexuality and dating in extended adulthood. Many women I spoke with voiced the same confusion, complaints, and concerns. "He thinks that because he buys me dinner, I owe him sex." "I feel like my profile is expected to be an advertisement of my sexuality, and I'm much more than that." "I want to meet a guy and get to know him and not have to be fighting him off me." "Why won't the men take the initiative some? I have to be in charge everywhere else. I want the guy to be the guy." "No, I don't want a dick pic, thank you very much!" The girls spoke to me with frustration and resentment. Many had abandoned dating entirely because they were tired of needing an NFL referee to throw penalty flags on men without manners.

I've spent most of my adult career talking to people about their sex lives. I teach courses in Sex Therapy and Human Sexuality, so I thought I'd have some basis for understanding this area of dating in extended adulthood. For the most part I was wrong. As I began observing sexuality and dating various matches, a number of styles and approaches began to emerge. As my client Craig learned early on in his dating experience, different dates could show up with vastly different attitudes and expectations around sexuality. This chapter will explore some of those approaches and styles.

## Four Sexual Styles in Dating in Extended Adulthood

As Craig discovered during his early months of dating, people come into the dating world with a vastly different range of experiences and expectations. When two people date, as a part of the Bargaining Stage of Attraction they begin to share and compare their expectations for sex and intimacy in the relationship. As I listened, I came to note four distinctly different primary orientations to sex and to dating in extended adulthood that people seem to adopt: No Sex, Quick Sex, Developmental Sex, and Adventurous Sex. Combinations of the four are also used. Let's look at each one and how they impact the relationship.

## No Sex Before Marriage

There are individuals who choose to wait to have intercourse or oral sex until after they are married. They may hold deep personal or religious convictions around beliefs about premarital sex and believe that "Sex before marriage is simply wrong because God designed sex to be exclusively within the context of marriage." I am very familiar with this perspective, having grown up in a conservative Christian church. I often encounter this approach among daters coming out of first and/or long-term marriages in which they may have had sex with their spouse exclusively for many years. Sex existed for them only within the confines of their marriage, and the prospect of now opening up that boundary in any form of dating or committed relationship was firmly declined.

Often these daters will lay out that boundary on the profile or early on in dating to clarify with matches what they will and will not agree to sexually. The difficulty comes in the actual implementation. As couples date, intimacy and passion naturally grow, and it is often difficult in the heat of the moment for the partners to control themselves sexually, leaving couples to end up in a battle between guilt and desire.

That's understandable. In extended adulthood people are experienced lovers, and it can be extremely difficult to stop the natural flow of sexual expression and arousal—especially when the partners are used to full sexual expression. That's like hitting one note on the piano when used to the entire keyboard. It's likely that such couples will cross those boundaries at times and then have to compassionately reset and try again.

### Observations regarding this style

- You may want to date someone with religious or personal convictions about sex that are similar to your own.
- It may be helpful to draw up your own sexual history and look at the key variables that have shaped your sexual identity.
- It may be helpful to expand your theology and explore the Bible's healthy view of sexuality.
- Be aware that someone's choice to delay sex may be an excuse to avoid sex entirely and establish a "low-sex" or "no-sex" relationship. In such situations religious or personal convictions are being used to mask a deeper core wound.

## Quick Sex

Craig discovered early on in his dating that there are some women, like the music teacher, who are ready to go from the first date. She liked Craig, was attracted to him, and saw no need to wait to express herself sexually by giving him a hand job to say goodnight. Her startup was faster than the expectation of Craig, a rookie dater who found himself taken off guard by the sexual assertion of this new woman he'd just met. He was flattered and yet confused that his first and second dates could have been so different.

As we talked, it became clear that Craig did indeed have a strong sex drive. He loved sex and could have it daily with the right partner. Three things had happened to him in the front seat of her car that night. First, he learned that he couldn't fake his template of attraction. As much as he had enjoyed her company, the sexual chemistry wasn't there for him, as it evidently was for her.

Second, he discovered that he needed some warm-up time. He needed to get to know his date before things turned sexual. Sex was a part of a much larger mosaic of intimacy and attraction that in his experience had many sides.

Third, and this was very important, because he had been married before he viewed sex as accompanying a level of commitment. He wasn't going to be a rock star bedding down new women in every town. Craig was going to need some commitment built around sex in order to relax and perform sexually. That was a part of his nature.

### Observations regarding this style

- Quick sex is a stage some of my clients go through coming out of a difficult divorce or a bad breakup. "I've been miserable," is their message, "so I'm going to go out and enjoy myself and screw around and have some fun because it's been so bad for so long."
- Quick sex can be so intoxicating it can overshadow the development of other areas of the relationship. Couples become great sex partners but fail to develop other aspects of their relationship. Down the road those underdeveloped areas may take down the marriage.
- Quick sex can be a mask for certain personality disorders or unresolved trauma. The match may have learned early in life that sex is their main way to connect with their partner, or they may use sex as a powerful reinforcer to keep a partner in a highly dysfunctional relationship. "I know he's a bit crazy, but the sex is so good!" may be the explanation.
- Interestingly, individuals who do not want a highly sexual marriage may begin with quick sex, and then the frequency and intensity decline over time, to the confusion of their partner. Sex in this instance is a control mechanism.

## Developmental Sex

A developmental approach to sexuality in extended adulthood sees sex as one part of the overall formation of the couple's relationship. It grows and evolves over time, just as do all areas of their relationship, and though it is not the only thing that holds them together it is an essential part of the relationship that must not be ignored. Many of my clients come out of marriages in which sex was a minefield of dysfunction and disappointment. They have never experienced a satisfying adult sexual relationship and are adamant that the next marriage will bring them the opportunity to experience and offer all forms of intimate expression, including communication, affection, and sexual interaction.

Individuals who have been in marriages where sex was controlled by their partner, for a wide range of reasons, will gravitate toward the developmental approach to sex. They may have waited until marriage to have sex and then discovered that their spouse was not the right match for them sexually, or they may have gotten caught up in quick sex early on, ending up at the same mismatched destination. These people will want to take their time to see if their new partner is not only a financial, emotional, and decision-making match but also a good sexual match.

Craig found himself comfortable with his match who took a developmental approach. She was open to discussing sexuality, her past sexual history, and her hopes for a great relationship. Her comfort allowed him to share authentically, and they found that they had much in common, not just sexually but in other areas as well. Both agreed that they wanted to be in a "committed relationship" before deepening the sexual connection rather than rushing into that phase too quickly. They were also able to discuss issues of aging and physical health and explore how that might impact them in the future.

### Observations regarding this style

- The developmental approach places sexual adjustment as a part of the couple's overall adjustment in many areas.
- It trusts the wisdom of each couple to approach their sexual life together in a way that is respectful, practical, and meaningful to each of them.
- It is a good fit for the stage of development in which adults find themselves during their fifties, sixties and seventies.

- It places sex in the confines of a committed, developing relationship that is not based solely on sex.

- In practice, some couples in the "No Sex before Marriage" camp evolve into the developmental approach in a committed relationship as it becomes more serious.

## Adventurous Sex

Craig was surprised by the offer to enter a relationship that would include more than two people. He had heard about open relationships and swingers but had zero frame of reference when confronted with the invitation by his fourth match. As he did his research and reflected on his attitudes toward a wide range of options from people in "the lifestyle," he discovered that it was more common than he had ever imagined.

There are people from all walks of life, economic backgrounds, races, and religions involved in more adventurous sexual lifestyles. Clubs, websites, and even orientation courses provide information and introductions to couples interested in pursuing this option. While this is nothing new, and I've seen couples in open marriages throughout my time in practice, this option does seem to be more openly discussed than in times past.

### Observations regarding this style

- My experience clinically has been that often one partner, man or woman, is drawn to this lifestyle and introduces their partner to it.

- Podcasts and orientations to open marriages center around a theme of dealing with partner jealousy, setting agreed upon boundaries, and secrets and communications issues.

- This choice definitely increases the complexity of a couple's dynamics psychologically, sexually, and emotionally with the introduction of multiple partners to the marriage.

As Craig embarked on his dating career in extended adulthood, he realized that there was a lot to learn, not only about his matches but about himself. One area we began to look at was the role he saw sex playing in his future long-term relationship.

## High Desire, Low Desire

I was attending a training seminar with Dr. David Schnarch, author of *The Passionate Marriage*, with a room full of psychotherapists. As he began to explain his model of High Desire and Low Desire in sexual adjustment in marriage, everyone in the room sat up and began to take notes. We had all seen this playing out in our practice many times and felt his explanation to be right on target.

Dr. Schnarch explained that there will always be a high-desire and a low-desire person in every aspect of the marriage. There will always be one person who wants to do something more than the other, whether it be sex, cleaning the house, or paying the bills. This creates a default power struggle. The person who wants something less is more in control, and the person who wants something more feels that they are either waiting on the other or trying to convince them do come along and join in.

Low sexual desire is not a gender-specific issue. There are marriages in which the woman has a higher drive than the man, and vice versa. I have had many female clients say, "I have the sex drive of a man, and my husband can't quite keep up!" Lower sexual desire can be impacted by a wide range of factors, including physical health, use of drugs and alcohol, anxiety and depression, relationship problems, feelings of sexual inadequacy, and a past marred by sexual or physical abuse.

Dr. Schnarch recommended the following steps to help a couple navigate the differences between high and low desire:

- Recognize that there may be differences and that this is a normal area to be navigated by healthy couples.
- To reduce the pressure on the high-drive partner, the low-drive partner should at times agree to sex. Once they are engaged, sexual arousal will take over and they will enjoy themselves.
- The low-drive partner can help by initiating sometimes so that the high-drive partner does not always feel that they are initiating. Share the initiating role.
- Keep an atmosphere of affection in the marriage. Affection is the atmosphere, and sex is the event.

In extended adulthood I've found that many individuals are seeking a "likes attracting" relationship, especially in the area of sexuality. If they have been the high-drive partner in a long-term relationship, they may have grown tired of "constantly waiting or chasing my partner for sex." They may be looking for a mate who is more like them in terms of style and drive. In this case a developmental approach to sexuality may be helpful. Couples will be able to see over time how their sexual styles match in terms of frequency, intensity, and quality.

## Agreement in Five Key Areas

When he is counseling couples, Dr. James Cail encourages them to come to an agreement around five key areas of sexual adjustment. Discussions around these areas open up conversations that start when we are dating and can continue and evolve for years into the marriage. His five key areas of conversation are:

- Frequency and Intensity: How often do we want to have sex, and in what ways? What is the intensity and style of sex we each want to experience?
- Orgasm: How can you achieve a delay in the male orgasm so that the female can achieve orgasm or multiple orgasms?
- Alternatives: What additions to sexual intercourse do we want to experience—oral, anal, mutual masturbation, dominance, toys?
- Talk: There should be lots of sexy talk, both descriptive (Let's try this) and erotic (I want to do . . . with you).
- Fantasy: Dr. Ian Kerner notes in his book *She Comes First* that active fantasy in marriage is a key part of a healthy sex life for couples.

I discovered in my own dating that women were not only open to discussing these key areas but anxious to have the conversations about sex, as many of them had been in marriages that were not sexually satisfying, and they did not want to repeat the past.

## Sexuality in Extended Adult Dating

### The Conversation

Sex educators, counselors, and therapists all recommend having a conversation regarding safe sex and practice prior to commencing sex with a new partner. This sounds like a perfectly reasonable thing to do. In practice, I found it to be variously appreciated or discounted and awkward. Some dates appreciated the opportunity to discuss healthy sex and engaged in the conversation openly, while others treated the conversation as an unnecessary box to check before beginning sex. Still others wanted no part of the conversation, which, of course, was a cue to other problems. This is an area in which texting and emailing can come in handy. Matches are sometimes more open to exchanging information when they are not sitting eye to eye.

### "Can You Still Perform?"

As men and women age, the question of performance takes on greater significance. The older I got the more relevant and common this question became from potential matches. Do you like sex? Is that something you're good to go with? With the enormous popularity of Viagra, Cialis, and other sexually enhancing medications, men will be able to achieve and sustain an erection for much longer. Women, too, experience changes in their sexual responses with changes in drive, wetness, and orgasms. Again, an openness to having those conversations, acquiring new information, and working together as lovers to achieve mutual satisfaction will be key in this stage of life.

### Natural or Enhanced

One woman told me, "I'm going to age naturally, and I'm not into plastic surgery. If a man doesn't like the way I look, that's his problem." Another woman of similar age quipped jokingly, "I'm always getting something done. Eyebrows, nails, Botox, and fillers. My plastic surgeon is on speed dial lol! I want to stay looking youthful and in good shape."

These two opinions represent the extremes in approaches to aging. Men and women are availing themselves of all kinds of age-inhibiting processes. I was recently in the office of a successful Dallas plastic surgeon whose reception area featured a display selling age-reducing treatments that began in the twenties and continued through each decade of life thereafter. Some clients will choose to maintain the look they had at a particular point in time, while others will prefer to age naturally. I was often asked by matches how I felt about their approach toward personal maintenance and enhancement.

### "Sex Farts"

Dr. Clif Davis, one of my dating experts, speaks of the uncomfortable but common situations in which an individual finds themselves in a sexual situation and are unable to perform. The physical stimulation is just not there. And it can't be manufactured. In fact, the harder one tries the worse it becomes. Craig had this experience on one of his early dates. The woman was attracted to him, but he was unable to achieve a lasting erection because the attraction was just not there.

This scenario is at best embarrassing for both people. In the worst situations I've seen men and women verbally attacked or accused of being incapable of performing. Dr. Davis calls these situations "Sex Farts." They are embarrassing but not particularly serious, and he encourages clients to stick with their template of attraction: stay with what turns you on and don't apologize for that. That's the way you were wired.

### Event and Environment

One of the principles I've taught my clients through the years is that affection is the environment and sex the event. An environment of caring, affection, touch, consideration, listening, and kindness sets the stage for great sex later on. While the focus may be on the event—how great the sex was last night—it's the environment that makes it possible.

Years ago, I heard a speaker give a lesson titled "Great Sex Begins in the Kitchen." His point was that the atmosphere of the entire relationship sets the stage for wonderful sex. I've found in marital therapy that, when couples are arguing and having problems, sex is usually the first thing that goes out the window. The reason is that sex is basically a form of communication. It is about two people communicating at a deep and profound level, so the experience is enhanced by the overall quality of the relationship. Want a better sex life? The experts would encourage you to up your affection, listening, and caring . . . and then just see what happens.

### "What Happens in Our Bedroom"

I had the privilege of studying Sex Therapy under Dr. Ed Choates, a pioneering sex therapist and professor. His approaches to building intimacy in marriage were profound and practical. He made the statement early on in one class that "What happens in the privacy of a couple's bedroom stays in the bedroom."

This sounds like "What happens in Vegas stays in Vegas," but the point isn't exactly the same. Dr. Choates was teaching us two things. First, couples will experiment and find a range of sexual fulfillment with each other. Whatever they both agree to will probably work for them. Second, there are boundaries around that couple's sex life that should not be violated. I don't need to share the intimate details of my marital life with other people. That would be a recipe for disaster.

### The Long Run

Extended adulthood is a time when we either reap the benefits of a life well lived or pay the price for having abused our bodies with habits that have accelerated the aging process. We cannot stop the aging process, but we can avoid accelerating it by misusing our bodies. By the time men and women hit their fifties and sixties, they will either be reaping the benefits of good diet and exercise or paying the price of a toxic lifestyle. I've had numerous clients tell me as they consider dating at this stage, "I've taken good care of myself, and I have no intention of taking on a spouse who is a medical walking time bomb. I'm not about to become a nurse." The topic of one's overall health will be a major conversation in extended adulthood, as it should be.

### Arm Candy

Grace had been single for a long time. When she went out socially, she had a stable of gay guy friends whom she would prevail upon to be her date for the evening. They were great company, and there was no chance she'd be uncomfortable with any sexual advances. It was a perfect solution.

When she decided to date again, however, she found herself in the confusing position of being comfortable with a non-affectionate, non-sexual partnership. Most of her matches were not looking to be someone's "arm candy" for the evening. After dating briefly Grace abandoned the website and returned to her previous pattern of dating good friends with no expectations of a relationship. From a greater intimacy perspective, Grace was comfortable with a cool and distant parallel partnership that proved difficult for her to find.

This chapter has explored Stage Five: sexuality in dating during extended adulthood. I have presented four possible models of sexuality in dating, along with characteristics of each style, and we've discussed some of the major considerations men and woman face in sexual adjustment during this stage. It may be that the reader has never taken the time to formulate a complete sex history of themselves, looking at the attitudes, behaviors, and events that have shaped their sexual identity. It is not within the scope of this book to suggest how to do so, but this might be an important assignment if it has never been done. Doing this with the assistance of a trained psychotherapist could be a valuable experience at this stage of dating.

In the Sixth Stage I will look at decision-making models that help couples decide whether to move forward in a relationship. How do individuals decide that "this is the person for me"? How do people decide to end a relationship and move on with their lives? What goes into the decision-making process?

Extended adulthood is a time of complexity; extended family, adult children, and changes in work and in one's health, along with many others, can impact a person's life in unforeseen and dramatic ways. There exists no manual or guidebook to help the individual navigate all of these changes as they impact dating and decisions about whether to enter into a committed relationship or get married. In the next chapter I'll present a decision-making model that can help us think through some of the key principles involved in this important process.

STAGE SIX

# DECISION MAKING

# CHAPTER 16

# DECISION-MAKING MODELS

Danni had been in a rollercoaster romance for the past eighteen months. One week she and Darren would be doing great, and the next she'd catch him in lies or failing to follow through with some of the agreements made in couple's therapy. She was a naturally optimistic person, but she was growing increasingly hopeless and tired. Most recently Darren had begged her to give him just one more chance after she'd found out that he'd been talking with a former girlfriend who still had her sights on him.

When I asked her about her internal timeclock, she stated emphatically, "I'm just about done with this. I feel like I'm the only adult in this relationship, and I'm tired of playing cop or detective. I have some things I want out of a relationship, and those things are being completely ignored."

It was clear to me that Danni was running on fumes but not quite ready to pull the plug on Darren and let the old girlfriend have him back! Her internal timeclock had not fully run out, and I never know when that's going to happen with one of my clients. Oftentimes they don't know themselves until it happens.

"I need you to get a three by five notecard and bring it to our next session with you." During the session I explained to her the concept of a "pocket list of non-negotiables." We all have a set of must-haves and "can't stands" that we need out of a relationship. Oftentimes those things are somewhat understood by us but not clearly articulated. Now I went on, "I'd like for you, Danni, to spend the next week thinking about the essential non-negotiables you have to have in any relationship, whether it's with Darren or anyone else. I want you to write them down on the notecard and bring it in next week to share with me."

The next week arrived, and Danni showed up armed with her note-card. She'd written down seven items that were non-negotiables for her in a relationship with any man. I directed her to drop the card into her purse and then, when Darren wanted to have a discussion about getting back together, to explain to him that she had drawn up her go-to list of what she needed to have in order to be happy and committed to work-ing with him and staying together. Danni didn't know how Darren would react, but she did know that she was beginning to gain clarity on her own decision-making processes and needs in a relationship. That clarity would be empowering for her, whether they ending you staying together or breaking up.

When I started dating in extended adulthood, there was a dearth of information on how to approach the complex process of melding two people's lives during their fifties, sixties, or seventies. People have com-plex and challenging lives. They have grown children, extended families, and significant commitments. Deciding with whom and how to fall in love at this point in life, as we have seen in this book, looks dramatically differ-ent from falling in love in one's twenties. I felt that it was essential for my decision making regarding all of my dating to be first and foremost prin-ciple driven. In other words, the partner I would be with externally would have to be a reflection of the selection processes I had gone through internally. And hopefully she would feel the same way.

## Kohlberg's Moral Development

When I was in graduate school to become a marriage and family thera-pist, we studied Lawrence Kohlberg's Stages of Moral Development in my lifespan development course. Kohlberg theorized that moral reasoning passes through three major stages, the final one being Post-Conventional Thought. The Post-Conventional Stage (the one relevant to this discus-sion) consists of a social contract approach in which rules are seen as social agreements between people and may be changed, when necessary, along with a Universal Principles approach wherein moral reasoning is based on universal ethical principles and justice. People at this level make ethical decisions based upon what they internally view as right versus their willingness to follow laws and rules. Those sets of ethical principles can include many considerations, such as the following:

- What is fair in this situation?
- What is just in this situation?
- How might my choice affect others?
- Is this a good decision for everyone?

My first decision was to try to aim for a Post-Conventional Stage in my decision making. I needed a set of internalized principles to which I could commit for guidance in my dating decisions. Without them I would be constantly at the mercy of other people's ethics, morals, values, and opinions.

In psychology we refer to this as an *internal locus of control versus an external locus of control*. An internal locus of control will set the navigation of one's live by an inner set of owned principles, values, and beliefs that characterize that life. An external locus of control requires adherence to an external law or rule in order to be enforced. Danni was functioning from an internal set of values, while her boyfriend was operating from an external set that did not match hers. Their value systems being a mismatch, she was constantly trying to enforce her own internal "rules" onto him. It was a recipe for disaster.

I found that five key principles guided me in my dating decision making and proved to be reliable and applicable across a range of dating situations.

## The Principle of Personal Responsibility

Dr. Richard Stuart wrote in his landmark book *Helping Couples Change* that the first principle of a successful marriage is the Principle of Personal Responsibility. I am responsible for those attitudes and actions that lead to my own personal fulfillment and happiness—not my partner, my parents, or the government. Ultimately, I am responsible for my life. The happiest, most well-adjusted people I encounter have one thing in common: They have taken their lives by the throat and insist, "This life is mine, and I will take ownership of my decisions—good or bad."

The principle of personal responsibility is totally countercultural and always has been. From the time of the Garden of Eden on, people have been projecting blame for their circumstances onto other people. Adam blamed Eve for giving him the fruit. Eve blamed the serpent for beguiling her into temptation. And we've never stopped the process of blaming. It is far easier to blame someone else than to look in the mirror and accept accountability for the things we've said and done.

How does this walk out in dating at this stage of life?

- Am I willing to own what I am looking for in a match, as opposed to what others tell me I need?
- Am I open to looking at my own strengths and areas needing work before becoming a potential match for someone else?
- Have I taken an inventory of my past relationships to look at any repeated problems or patterns?
- Can I identify what I contributed to the failure in my past relationships?
- Do I own and value without apology or justification the things that bring me joy in life?

In the last chapter Craig discovered that he was comfortable on a date with a woman who was contented in her own skin and seemed to know where she was coming from and what she wanted. She had owned the principle of personal responsibility and was able to communicate nonverbally, "This is who I am, and I'm very comfortable with that. I'm not perfect but always trying, and if that's something interesting to you let's see where this might go." The opposite approach is to trade away one's identity and try to morph into someone who will be accepted by the current match, whoever that may be. That person really doesn't know who they are or what they are going to be happy with in a partner.

## The Principle of Commitment

The second principle from which I operated was the Principle of Commitment. My goal in dating was to be in a committed relationship or to get married again at some point in time. I was not interested in dating for dating's sake. I encountered people in the process whose goal seemed to be to date as many people as they possibly could. I, in contrast, had to see some level of potential in the match before being interested in pursuing communication. At the same time, I tried to keep myself open to matches I might not be immediately drawn to but who could possibly carry potential I couldn't see right away. There was definitely a balance there.

Extended adulthood will be a time when daters ask whether they want to get married again. That's both a fair question and an appropriate time to ask it. Some will answer with a resounding yes. They believe firmly in marriage, may hold to strong religious convictions around marriage, and can view themselves only as living within the marriage union. Others will be coming out of marriages that have cost them dearly in terms of financial loss, alimony payments, child support payments, and loss of property and retirement resources. If they have fulfilled those obligations they may insist, "Never again will I risk all of that!" I've found that it is important to give space for all of those conversations as people bounce between perspectives.

I'm a big believer in commitment. I believe that it offers a degree of security when I make a commitment that directs my energies toward a goal. Dr. Frank Pittman, an Atlanta marriage and family therapist, observed, "Marriage is like a submarine. For it to work you've got to get all the way in it." He was talking about the power of commitment, and I believe he was right. Commitment affords both security and the motivation to makes thing work.

At the same time adults at this stage of life are wise not to rush too quickly into a commitment. As we've discussed in this book, there can be many reasons that slowing down the romantic process can actually help build a stronger relationship in the future. In my experience it was not uncommon for dates to ask, "Which do you see as your picture of a relationship—living in a committed relationship long term or getting married?" That's great question and one that opens the door for couples to explore how they view the next stage of their life.

## The Principle of Connection in Complexity

I play a huge double-bass drum set. There are two 24" bass drums, three rack toms that are 10", 12", and 13", and two floor toms that are 14" and 16". There is a brass snare drum, along with about seven or eight cymbals hanging at all angles around my head. Behind me is a large thunder sheet that looks like a square Chinese gong. The setup is massive, and tuning all of those so that they sound like one integrated instrument is a challenge. But I love the complexity.

My more traditional drummer friends think I'm crazy. "Why do you need that big setup? Why do you carry of all that around? Don't you know

I can do everything you can do on a basic four-piece kit?" They roll their eyes and scoff at me for loving my big double-bass set. The answer is simple. After sixty years of playing drums, I play that set because that's how the music moves through my body. The complexity of my drum set is what I need in order to make the music that's in my head.

What does drumming have to do with romance? Just this: We will encounter people in dating who have varying degrees of complexity in their lives. (Note: I see complexity as a positive not to be confused with excessive drama in life).

My parents had a very simple life. They went to work, went to church on Sundays, had their few favorite restaurants, and demonstrated a high level of predictability. They did not want or need complexity in life. When they adopted me, though, they inadvertently discovered high complexity. I do a classic rock drum show, teach graduate school, counsel couples, write books, travel, speak all over the country, and am dad to three police officers. I'm at home in a graduate seminar, speaking in a church, or in the gym lifting weights. I thrive on complexity.

When my dad married my mother, he found a spouse who matched his need for simplicity and predictability. As I began to date, I had to decide whether I was looking for someone who would match up with only a few of my interests or someone who would enthusiastically engage in many areas of my life. I decided after dating matches who were not interested in many areas of my life that I was looking for connection in the complexity of life.

I think it is a mistake to view complexity as a negative. I find people who thrive on variety and creativity to be fascinating because they tend to be constantly growing. As you read profiles and meet potential matches, you will meet individuals who have extremely complex lives. For some of you that will be a turnoff. Like my father, you prefer simplicity and predictability. But others of you may discover that in that complexity is a richness that can't be found in any other way. Your new partner will bring a whole new set of experiences and adventures to your life that you could not have experienced in any other way.

## The Principle of Non-Negotiables

Danni, at the beginning of this chapter, learned that she had slowly been trading away her wants and desires in the relationship to accommodate

Darren's bad behavior. This hadn't happened overnight. There had been a slow ebbing away of respect for a period of months. Now she had to step back in and set clear boundaries, not only for Darren but for her own self-respect. That was the reason I assigned her the Pocket List of Non-Negotiables. This exercise tends to work very well because it is so simple and yet so powerful. "If you want to be in relationship with me, these are the basic things I will have to have from you. Period. No negotiation."

I work with many marriages in which the trust is gone. A spouse has had multiple affairs. Someone can't stop spending money excessively and hiding the credit card bills. A spouse won't stop drinking or refuses to hold down a job consistently. Lying has become such an ingrained part of their nature that a spouse is never sure they are hearing the truth. The list of trust-busters goes on and on. Eventually we hit a point at which there is no gas left in the tank. We are running on fumes. At that point the violator asks for one last chance: "Let me show you I can change and that I'm serious this time." That's when I assign the pocket list of non-negotiables.

But why not back up and assemble the list before we ever get into that situation? Why not sit down and struggle early on with the five or six things I really want out of a relationship? I'm not suggesting a list of thirty items—a catalog so monumental no one could fulfill it. I'm talking about a basic list of five to seven things the person must have in a partner. I suggest that you do this before you start dating.

A word of caution here: Lists like this tend to fly out the window when we meet a cute guy or girl whom we already know violates two or three of our key non-negotiables. We begin to rationalize. *Maybe they aren't really that way. Maybe it isn't really that bad. I'm probably overthinking this and need to chill out.* Perhaps. But I've talked with too many adults who have knowingly blown through every red flag, saying to themselves, *This is probably a mistake, but . . .*

A Pocket List of Non-Negotiables is a highly personal list. Your items will probably look very different from this, but here are some examples of list items I've seen people use:

- Honesty—I need to be told the truth, regardless of the consequences; I need to hear reality.
- Reciprocity—I need my partner to put into this relationship as much as I do.
- Communication—I need to be able to talk through problems with my partner.

- Compassion—I need and will provide a soft place to land.
- Acceptance—I need my partner to accept my children and the key role they play in my life.
- Finances—I need my partner to contribute financial security and responsibility.
- Adventure—I need novelty, variety, beauty, and new experiences in life.
- Respect—I need mutual respect for me and my family.
- Energy—I need a partner who will embrace life with me in a healthy and energetic way.
- Passion—I need a partner with whom I can enjoy chemistry, affection, and sexual expression.

## The Principle of God's Law of Second Best

Some of my clients who come from a conservative Christian background struggle with the concept of divorce. Maybe they are the first person in their family to have been through a divorce. Perhaps they grew up hearing sermons about how "God hates divorce." They may have been through a messy divorce and found that their church friends sided with their spouse and that they lost their church home and friends in the process. I've spent a great deal of my life thinking about marriage, divorce, and remarriage and discussing them with clients, clinicians, and biblical scholars, and I take that conversation very seriously.

One of the most helpful concepts comes from Dr. James Cail, who holds a PhD in the Psychology of Religion. He calls it "God's Law of Second Best." When humankind was in the Garden of Eden and sinned, God's primary plan was thwarted by the introduction of sin into the world. What happened then? He didn't give up on humanity but introduced his plan for a Redeemer to be born into the world—His own Son. God had a second plan, a backup plan, his law of second best.

When Christ was hanging on the cross about to die, he looked at the thief hanging next to him and heard him say, "We deserve to die for what we've done. This man has done nothing wrong." He then told the thief, "This day you will be with me in paradise." Christ extended a plan B to this criminal moments before they both died. When Jesus was presented with a woman caught in the act of adultery, he didn't condemn her or say that she was beyond hope; instead, he told her, "Go your way and sin no more." He offered her hope and warned her not to continue the lifestyle she had been living.

God's Law of Second Best asserts that God extends hope to us when we have made mistakes and life has not worked out for us the way we had planned. He asks us to learn from our mistakes, to not continue them without regard to the people we are hurting—but he also offers a path forward. God and his people are in the business of hope. To extend the hope to someone that tomorrow could be entirely different from yesterday is the greatest gift one can give to another.

Grace, as offered by God through Christ, understands that no matter how "good" I am I will never be good enough to warrant my salvation. Whether I am a "saint" or a "sinner," I still stand before God in need of His grace. I am justified only by my faith in Christ, not by the righteous things I have done. We all are in need of God's grace, of God's law of second best. Many in extended adulthood will long to build a healthy marriage for the first time in their life, to repair relationships with children, and to make contributions to society that far exceed what they have done in their early years. They will not be motivated by guilt but by grace—and by the belief that their story truly can have a happy ending.

By this stage of the relationship couples will have put the past behind them and done their own core work in order to be ready to enter a new relationship. They've explored what they are attracted to; have been involved in dating; either online or traditionally; and have discovered new insights into themselves and their partners. They've built a solid foundation for a new relationship and have decided to move forward with marriage or a committed relationship.

But the dynamics of how to enter another person's family system and build a new couple relationship can be a key challenge. People in their fifties, sixties, and seventies come to dating with long and complex family histories already established. It may be a challenge for a newcomer to make sense of why families operate the way they do. In the coming section we will look at some practical guidelines for successfully entering someone else's extended family and building a new couple's bond.

# FAMILY SYSTEM

# CHAPTER 17

# ENTERING A FAMILY SYSTEM

## Holding Court at the Hospital

The holidays were approaching, and Ann was bracing for another year of unpredictable crises from Andy's mom, Alice. Ann was normally a fairly laid-back individual, but another year of 911 crisis calls were going to make her lose her mind. Ann and Andy had been dating for two years. They had met online, hit it off quickly, and were soon dating each other exclusively. They both enjoyed getting away from their jobs in the tech field by hiking in the mountains on the weekends. Ann had two daughters in college who loved Andy, and he relished teasing and joking with them. The couple's dynamics were fun, easy, and enjoyable for them both.

Then there was Alice. Andy's mom had always been "high maintenance." She loved drama and when life did not offer it naturally was masterful at manufacturing it. She seemed to thrive on chaos, and the calmer her son's life became the more she seemed to throw drama into their lives. The Thanksgiving to Christmas weeks seemed to invite Alice's *tour de force* every year. She would wait for the holidays when everyone was planning parties, travel, and family events to check herself into the hospital for some vague medical condition no one could quite make sense of. Andy would get a call yet again in the middle of the night that his mother was being taken by ambulance to the emergency room and that he needed to rush to the hospital as soon as possible.

Alice had worked as a medical assistant in doctors' offices for many years and knew all the right symptoms and phrases to use to get herself admitted to the hospital for a few days. Once there she would "hold court" by calling all the family relatives in the middle of Thanksgiving dinner or while they were opening presents on Christmas morning, expecting them to drop whatever they were doing to come to her aid. By New Year's Day the mysterious crisis had invariably passed, and she had returned home after having ruined everyone else's holidays once again by faking her need for hospitalization to meet her insatiable desire for attention.

Andy was an only child. His older adopted sister had tired of his mother's ongoing drama and disappeared from the family years earlier. Andy's dad had passed away, so he was left as the medical and legal power of attorney and the only one for his mother to call when she went into 911 mode. Andy would dutifully but begrudgingly go to the hospital, fill out the paperwork, deal with the insurance companies, and pick up an end-less supply of unnecessary medications. Another year, . . . another wasted holiday season. That was just the way Andy's family dynamic worked. His dad had done the same thing for years prior to his death.

When Ann began dating Andy, she had no idea the family drama would revolve around holiday hospitalizations. Her family members had been to the hospital on occasion for routine procedures, but using the hospital system as a way to get one's need for attention met was beyond her comprehension. She and Andy began hiding their travel plans from the family, especially around the holidays. When she would try to talk to Andy about his mom, he would become defensive, insisting, "I'm all she's got. What am I supposed to do?" Ann realized that she had entered a very different family system from her own, one that operated by rules and norms that were totally foreign to her but were having a dramatic impact on her relationship with Andy.

## Our Little Felon

Kirk owned a successful CPA firm and had been divorced from his first wife for about five years when he met Kate through a local dating service. Kate was involved in local politics, and their mutual love of social events and the arts kept them busy while enjoying a wide circle of friends. Kate's son and daughter had gone into the family business with their father and lived several states away, and she loved traveling to visit them and her new granddaughter. Kirk had a great relationship with Kate's kids, and they were thrilled to see their mom dating after her divorce from their father.

The unknown variable in Kirk and Kate's life was Cameron, Kirk's only son. Cameron, now thirty-four, was a mess, an ongoing disaster looking for a place to happen—and it did happen with astonishing regularity. He was picked up for drunk driving and possession of drugs. He had been let go from more jobs than Kate could remember. He was constantly hanging out with individuals who were known criminals and involved in illegal activities. He had wrecked two cars Kate knew of since she and Kirk had been dating.

For years Kirk had tried everything to get his son straightened out. He had sent him to the finest private school in the city, only for him to get kicked out. Cameron had gone to an elite adolescent treatment program . . . from which he ran away. He had been in rehab and to more therapists than Kirk could remember. Kirk had paid for college at a pricey university, only to discover that Cameron was spending more time drinking than going to class. Not surprisingly, Cameron had ended up flunking out of school. Kirk had finally set him up with a job internship through a friend, only to watch Cameron sleeping in and ultimately getting fired.

As Cameron was getting older his offenses were getting more serious, as were the costs to bail him out. The run-ins with the law were mounting up, and his criminal record was getting deeper and more problematic. Kirk seemed intent on "turning his son around," but all he knew to do was write checks. Kirk's bank account was shrinking as his son's criminal record was growing.

Kate loved Kirk and respected his accomplishments as a businessman, but as a father he lacked insight into how to teach his son logical consequences. She had walked into a family system that operated very differently from her own and that might at some point threaten her own financial security. Her question, "At what price love?" was a valid one for her to be asking.

## Milton Bradley Games

I teach my counseling students to view their families as they would a new Milton Bradley board game. When I was growing up, we would go to the Toy Chest store in West Hartford Center to buy board games by Milton Bradley. The Game of Life; Sorry; and my favorite, Stratego, all came in a big cardboard box you opened to find the game board and pieces inside. To learn to play the game I had to flip over the box top and read the rules that were printed on the inside cover. It told me how the game worked and what I had to do to win. The rules weren't clearly written on the front of the box—I had to look underneath to see them.

The same principle applies to understanding family systems. They look a particular way when we view them from the outside: congenial, well-adjusted, or chaotic. But once we get inside and look at the inner workings of the family, we discover how they really operate. It is essential when I am a newcomer to someone else's family system that I learn the powerful but informal rules that control how the game is played. Otherwise, I will feel lost in unfamiliar territory.

## Formal and Informal Rules

When you date someone and are introduced to their family, you will encounter two kinds of family rules. The formal rules are like the box top on the Milton Bradley game. They are the obvious things about the way a family functions. I tell my students that formal rules can be written down and posted on the refrigerator. We can articulate them and describe them. As Ann entered Andy's family system, she might have learned that his family celebrated Christmas on Christmas Eve, not on Christmas morning, and that they had a gift exchange for which they draw names each year. These are examples of formal family rules.

There are other, more powerful family rules, however, that also control how the family functions. Like the rules printed on the bottom of the box top, informal family rules tell us how the family operates, but they are generally not discussed. They exist and run under the table. In fact, if these rules are pointed out the family may deny that they even exist because it would be too embarrassing to admit that they dictate the way people act.

Ann quickly learned an informal rule in Andy's family: that Alice could check into the hospital at any time and hold court there, resulting in Andy's having to drop everything he was doing to come and rescue her. No one in the family confronted Alice on her behavior, so the rule, though destructive, remained active and powerful.

One of my jobs as a family therapist is to observe the unspoken family rules that are at work and present them to the members of the family to

see if they want to keep them operational. Do you want to continue doing this? Is this working for you? Has this rule become outdated, and is
it no longer serving you well? Often in this situation a client will become
defensive because we have touched on a family rule they do not want to
look at, knowing already that it is not working.

When Ann would bring up Andy's running to his mother's side, he
would become defensive and shut down. When Kate tried to talk to Kirk
about his constant rescuing of his son and how that might impact their
marriage, Kirk would take Cameron's side, protesting that his son was a
struggling soul doing the best he could do.

In extended adulthood we come into relationships with a history of
all kinds of rules, both formal and informal, healthy and dysfunctional.
A part of the success of a new couple's relationship is the willingness of
both partners to look at those rules and patterns and decide to throw out
some that are no longer serving them well.

That is why a ReMatch process recommends doing one's core work
before getting into the dating scene. Kirk had some core work to do in his
relationship with Cameron that had nothing to do with Kate, and Andy
had core work to do with his mother over a dynamic going back to his
childhood. Ann could see it and was being affected by it, but the work was
Andy's to do.

## The Primacy of the Couple Relationship

A nuclear family system can include three major groups or *subsystems*.
*The couple subsystem* consists of the husband and wife and is the key to
family health. It is by far the most important and sets the stage for everything else going on in the family. How the husband and wife are doing
reverberates throughout the family system, and when couples are doing
well the chances that the rest of the family will do well go up dramatically.

*The parent-child subsystem* consists of mom, dad, and the kids, as
well as all combinations of those relationships, such as mom and the kids
or dad and the kids. The parent-child subsystem is vital because it trans-
mits the values, attitudes, behaviors, and emotions from the parents to
the next generation. *The sibling subsystem* consists of the relationships
among the children. The oldest may have a different role in the family
than the youngest. Put these three subsystems together and you have the
basis for the dynamics in a family.

When couples marry early in adulthood, they are normally forming their first family system. The couple bond will predate the parent-child and sibling bonds. The new couple generally, but not always, has time to be a young couple and build their relationship before kids come along. Then they are thrown into the complex parenting roles. The key is that the parent-child bonds come after the couple bonds have been formed and established.

In a ReMatch situation the parent-child bonds and sibling bonds predate the new couple relationship. The marriage comes after the kids, which is out of order from a developmental standpoint. What does that mean to a couple getting married later in life? Most importantly, the new couple bond must be of primary importance. There is no way around this. While the relationship between parents and their children is essential, for the new marriage to work the couple bond must be given priority. Otherwise, the children, whether they are adults or still at home, will be operating for the parent at a higher priority level than the new spouse.

Ann discovered that, in order to be in a relationship with Andy, she was going to have to live with Alice's 911 calls and never enjoy a holiday season without the threat of hospitalization. Kate was seeing that Kirk was really "married" to saving his son. The couple's marriage would always play second to bailing Cameron out, and that parent-child bond would be primary. The informal rules in these respective family systems were "I must save my mom" and "I must save my son." These rules had been in place for years and were not amenable to change. In terms of primacy, the couple bond would take a back seat to the mother and son who were driving the car. Ann and Kate would have to decide whether they were willing to sit in the backseat of their own marriage. Many people unwittingly find themselves in this situation.

In my own dating I had very few deal killers when it came to evaluating dating profiles. One standard, however, was a non-negotiable. If a profile made it clear that the woman's top priority was to her children, or grandchildren, or foster care children, etc.—and I would be welcome to sit in the backseat and join their ride—I put on my track shoes and ran the other way.

Don't get me wrong. I am a proud father and take my responsibility of fathering very seriously. However, I am also a firm believer in the primacy of the couple relationship. It has to come first, or we don't have anything solid to build on. There will be matches who want a partner who is really just a "sidecar." Their top priority is their children, their adult children, their mom or dad . . . and the list goes on. They will tend to hook people like Ann and Kate who are good-natured, giving, and hardworking but who wake up one day and ask, "How did I get into this crazy way of living?"

## How to Enter Another Family System

Remember when you were a kid and started spending the night at your friend's house? Their family home just felt different. They watched different programs on TV and ate dinner at a different time. The house smelled different from yours, and the food was cooked in a different way. They had their inside family jokes they all laughed at but you didn't get right away. You came home from that first sleepover having learned that not all families are like yours. In fact, you started to suspect that none of them were.

Fast forward to extended adulthood. People have had years of experience building their own lives. They have had a marriage or marriages and have built customs and patterns they may not even be aware of. They may have older children or grown children and have a history of ten, twenty, or thirty years enmeshed in certain patterns, traditions, and habits. Adults in extended adulthood are definitely not a "blank slate" but a rich tapestry of experiences, traditions, habits, and customs.

To enter someone else's family system can be one of the most challenging and at times exhausting experiences. The old joke "You must love me a lot to put up with all my crazy family" may not be too far from the truth. Like the kid on his first sleepover, we fall in love with someone and then are introduced to their family. How do we navigate that transition in an effective way? What are some things we can do to make that adjustment easier on both partners? Here are some tips for navigating entrance into a new family system:

### Spend more time listening than talking.

When I was first dating my ex-wife, I would stay up late at night talking with my future father-in-law, a retired Air Force Colonel in the Strategic Air Command. Back in the day he had a slide projector set up in the living room, and we would spend hours looking at slides from his travels all over the world in the service. He told me stories he had never shared with anyone else in the family. He was a big talker, and, as he shared his stories, I gained invaluable insight about the family I was marrying into. All I had to do was sit, listen, and ask a few questions. The information was right there to be taken in and understood.

### Get your partner to tell you stories.

When my counseling students ask, "How do I know what the family rules are?" I tell them that they are buried in the stories people tell about themselves and their families. The stories carry the freight of a family's heroes, heroines, victories, and tragedies. They tell us what the values are and what things will spur us to action. If Ann had asked Andy early in their dating, "What are the holidays like in your family?" eventually she would have heard stories about Thanksgiving being interrupted by a mother with an attention deficit. I've also discovered that family rules tend to be repeated from one story to another. Does my partner sound like a victim in this story? Is that a pattern in other stories they tell?

### Reserve judgment.

My behind-the-wheel driving instructor was going crazy correcting me when I was fifteen years old and learning to drive. I was driving two-footed in a car with an automatic transmission; since there was no clutch, why was I using both feet? I had one foot on the accelerator and the other on the brake, prompting his repeated protest, "That's not how you do it. You're going to be riding the brakes and wearing them out." I argued back at him, "Are my brake lights on? Have I mistakenly put on the brakes when I was supposed to accelerate? No—so it's working for me. What's the problem?"

What he didn't understand was that I played drums and was used to having my right foot on the bass drum pedal and my left foot on a high-hat pedal, so the two feet had always operated independently. To drive with only one foot would have been contrary to my twelve years of musical conditioning. When you understood my background and training, my behavior made sense. People are a lot like that. When my clients are doing things that don't seem to be working well for them, I look for the reasons behind their actions. Often there is an identifiable cause for their behavior that has led them to this point in time. My job is not to judge them but to understand them.

When you enter a new family system, your likely response will be "I don't understand that" or "That seems really odd to me." It may be wise to step back and ask why a partner is doing things the way they are. There may be a good explanation underlying the actions, and you may hear an interesting story in the process.

### Build some new traditions.

Couples do well when they enjoy his and her family traditions and, most importantly, build some new traditions of their own. Couples in extended adulthood may have fewer parenting responsibilities, or work requirements may change or they may move to new cities. All of these changes can serve as opportunities for couples to build new lives and new customs around their current wants and needs. One of the keys to success in this stage of life, according to Gratton and Scott, is the ability of the person to stay flexible and adaptable. This will be key to navigating this new era in a successful way.

### Follow the lead partner concept.

For blended families I have long advocated the lead partner concept. In other words, the biological parent takes the lead in dealing with children, adult children, and extended family matters. That just makes sense. The natural parent has the history and relationship, and the biological relative has had much more time in the family system than the new partner starting out. If there are problems to be addressed or boundaries to be set, they ideally need to come from the partner who is already in that family rather than the new spouse. In Ann's and Kate's cases, there were limits to the power they had in both situations to affect any change. The leverage for change had to come from Kirk, dealing directly with Cameron, and Andy, dealing with his mother.

### Practice the One to Ten Rule.

Sometimes, no matter how adaptable we are, there comes a point when we have to say, "I don't care to do that, thank you very much." Telling someone no can be a difficult thing to do. We don't want to disappoint them or appear closed minded. A simple exercise I give my couples I call the One to Ten Rule. When asked about their willingness or desire to do something for their spouse, rather than asking for a simple yes or no I solicit their response on a low to high scale from one to ten.

This is very simple to practice. When there is something I'd like or something I'd like my spouse to do with me, I pose it as a question. She is at liberty to give me her level of interest or agreement based on the one to ten scale. "Would you like to stay in tonight and catch up on a Netflix series?" That would be about a four for me. "Would you like to go out and use the gift card we got at that new restaurant?" That sounds like an eight to me. I know immediately that I would enjoy the new restaurant more than an evening at home watching Netflix, but giving my partner the freedom of expressing without judgment her level of satisfaction is a powerful gift.

## REMATCH REVIEW

We have looked at the seven stages of a ReMatch process. We began exploring ways to process old relationships and moved through the stages of healing, clarification, exploring dating options, and decision making. At the outset I recommended that there is important work to be done at each stage and that to skip any of them will likely mean that the issue will have to be dealt with at some point later in life. By way of review, the Seven Stages we've covered are:

Stage One:     Endings before Beginnings

Stage Two:     Doing the Core Work

Stage Three:  A Strategy for Dating

Stage Four:    ReMatch Red Flags

Stage Five:     Dating and Sexual Styles

Stage Six:      Decision-Making Models

Stage Seven:  Entering a Family System

# ABOUT THE AUTHOR

For four decades Dr. Don Hebbard has been a leader in the field of marriage and family as a speaker, professor, therapist, and consultant. He launched the Family Center of the Metroplex in Dallas, the Genesis Center for Christian Counseling in Atlanta, and the Institute for Marriage and Family in Oklahoma City. He is Professor of Counseling at Amberton University and a Licensed Marriage and Family Therapist and Supervisor working with Restoration Counseling. He teaches courses in Couples' Therapy, Family Therapy, Sex Therapy, and Conflict Resolution.

Dr. Don speaks nationally as a keynote speaker, and thousands have attended his seminars including Couples U, LeaderCare and Leading Through Transitions. He has appeared on Good Morning Texas, the KTVT Morning Show, and numerous podcasts speaking on dating and relationships. He is known for his passionate delivery, common sense wisdom, and memorable stories. His musical talents led him to create Backstage Family Theatre, Marriage Fair, and Die Drumming Classic Rock shows.

He is the author of *Healing Hurting Churches: The Economou Process* and *The Complete Handbook for Family Life Ministry in the Church.* His consulting specializes in healing traumatized organizations and helping leaders navigate difficult transitions. He established "My Learning Style" at Amberton University, identifying adult learning styles in college. His writings have appeared on PBS, in *The London Sunday Times*, and in the *Ladies' Home Journal*.

He has served on the faculties of four universities and holds degrees in Ministry, Communications, Marriage and Family Therapy, and Adult Education. Oklahoma Governor Frank Keating named Don Director of Marriage Education, implementing a statewide marriage initiative, and Dallas Christian Schools selected him as their Alumnus of the Year.

Don and his wife, Lisa, make their home in Houston, Texas. He is the father of three police officers; Jared, Hailey, and Henry.

Visit his website at *donhebbard.com*.

www.ingramcontent.com/pod-product-compliance
Lightning Source LLC
Chambersburg PA
CBHW051416090426
42737CB00014B/2695

* 9 781625 863034 *